Serhiy Kvit

Media, History, and Education
Three Ways to Ukrainian Independence

With a preface by Diane Francis

The publishing of this book is sponsored by BCU Foundation.

BCU Foundation supports cultural projects that promote the rich Ukrainian-Canadian identity and educational initiatives that advance a better understanding of topics related to Ukraine. Most recently, BCU Foundation provides humanitarian aid to Ukraine, including medical supplies and equipment, food, and shelter.

UKRAINIAN VOICES

Collected by Andreas Umland

36 *Olesya Khromeychuk*
A Loss
The Story of a Dead Soldier Told by His Sister
With a foreword by Philippe Sands
ISBN 978-3-8382-1870-0

37 *Taras Kuzio, Stefan Jajecznyk-Kelman*
Fascism and Genocide
Russia's War Against Ukrainians
ISBN 978-3-8382-1791-08

38 *Alina Nychyk*
Ukraine Vis-à-Vis Russia and the EU
Misperceptions of Foreign Challenges in Times of War, 2014–2015
With a foreword by Paul D'Anieri
ISBN 978-3-8382-1767-3

39 *Sasha Dovzhyk (Ed.)*
Ukraine Lab
Global Security, Environment, Disinformation Through the Prism of Ukraine
With a foreword by Rory Finnin
ISBN 978-3-8382-1805-2

The book series "Ukrainian Voices" publishes English- and German-language monographs, edited volumes, document collections, and anthologies of articles authored and composed by Ukrainian politicians, intellectuals, activists, officials, researchers, and diplomats. The series' aim is to introduce Western and other audiences to Ukrainian explorations, deliberations and interpretations of historic and current, domestic, and international affairs. The purpose of these books is to make non-Ukrainian readers familiar with how some prominent Ukrainians approach, view and assess their country's development and position in the world. The series was founded, and the volumes are collected by Andreas Umland, Dr. phil. (FU Berlin), Ph. D. (Cambridge), Associate Professor of Politics at the Kyiv-Mohyla Academy and an Analyst in the Stockholm Centre for Eastern European Studies at the Swedish Institute of International Affairs.

Serhiy Kvit

MEDIA, HISTORY, AND EDUCATION
Three Ways to Ukrainian Independence

With a preface by Diane Francis

Bibliografische Information der Deutschen Nationalbibliothek
Die Deutsche Nationalbibliothek verzeichnet diese Publikation in der Deutschen Nationalbibliografie; detaillierte bibliografische Daten sind im Internet über http://dnb.d-nb.de abrufbar.

Bibliographic information published by the Deutsche Nationalbibliothek
Die Deutsche Nationalbibliothek lists this publication in the Deutsche Nationalbibliografie; detailed bibliographic data are available in the Internet at http://dnb.d-nb.de.

The front cover picture was taken by Oleksandr Kozachenko.

ISBN-13: 978-3-8382-1807-6
© *ibidem*-Verlag, Stuttgart 2023
Alle Rechte vorbehalten

Das Werk einschließlich aller seiner Teile ist urheberrechtlich geschützt. Jede Verwertung außerhalb der engen Grenzen des Urheberrechtsgesetzes ist ohne Zustimmung des Verlages unzulässig und strafbar. Dies gilt insbesondere für Vervielfältigungen, Übersetzungen, Mikroverfilmungen und elektronische Speicherformen sowie die Einspeicherung und Verarbeitung in elektronischen Systemen.

All rights reserved. No part of this publication may be reproduced, stored in or introduced into a retrieval system, or transmitted, in any form, or by any means (electronic, mechanical, photocopying, recording or otherwise) without the prior written permission of the publisher. Any person who does any unauthorized act in relation to this publication may be liable to criminal prosecution and civil claims for damages.

Printed in the EU

Content

Preface by *Diane Francis* 7

Foreword 9

Russia as Evil: False Historical Parallels. Some Peculiarities of
Russian Political Culture 15

Skeleton Key: How to Understand the Changing World during
Ukraine's War for Independence 21

The Battle for History and Building of Identity: Fake News
Confronts Professional News 29

Media, Public Rhetoric, and Culture in the Context of Ukraine's
War for Independence from Russia 41

The Russia-Ukraine War through the Prism of Mass
Communications 49

Towards the Freedom-Seeking Mission of the Ukrainian
University 57

Higher Education in Ukraine in the Time of Independence:
Between Brownian Motion and Revolutionary Reform 65

University Autonomy as a Value Basis and Necessary
Environment for Academic Integrity 91

A Perspective on 'Fake News' 101

Ukraine in the Struggle for Independence in the Age of
Post-Truth 109

Who Writes History? National Memory in the Context of
Network Revolutions and Social Networks 125

One Hundred Years of the Ukrainian Liberation Struggle 133

The Ukrainian Liberation Movement in the Interwar Period (1923–1939) 145

Ukrainian Nationalism, Ustashism, and Fascism: The Matter and Context of the Discussion 155

The Process, Meaning, and Consequences of Ukraine's Revolution 169

A University Degree for Carlos and "Kyiv-Mohyla 2.0": Three Criteria for a High-Quality Education 175

Josyf Zisels: "Yes, I am a Ukrainian Jew" 183

The Ukrainian Challenge by Professor Schlögel 191

Norman Davies on the Objective and Subjective Historian 197

Yaroslav Dashkevych and Subjectivity in Historical Scholarship 201

About the Author 209

Preface

Serhiy Kvit is a well-respected Ukrainian commentator and President of the National University of Kyiv-Mohyla Academy. In his former capacity as Minister of Education and Science in Ukraine, Kvit helped bring about educational reforms that, among other innovations, enabled collaboration between Ukrainian scientists and businesses. His academic research focuses on media and educational reforms, the topics of his several books and the many articles he has published around the world.

Media, History, and Education: Three Ways to Ukrainian Independence, his newest book documents and analyzes the three pillars — media, education, civil society — that have supported Ukraine's liberation from Soviet and Russian influences, a process that extends into our present and has culminated in the current war. A free, unfettered media in Ukraine has proved elusive — due to government control and ownership by oligarchs. However, since Ukraine's departure from the Soviet Union in 1991, and the USSR's dissolution, generations of enterprising and investigative journalists across Ukraine have furthered the cause of true independence even as they have continuously battled the country's systemic Soviet-style corruption.

At the same time, Ukraine's educational pillar has served to correct historical misconceptions. Ukrainian academics have published many textbooks and historical studies that successfully refute and disprove decades of Russian disinformation and historical revisionism. The most poisonous claim of all is that Ukraine is not, and never has been, a nation or an ethnic group with a distinct identity. Professor Kvit and others have dedicated themselves to setting the record straight and their activity has, in turn, informed and emboldened the development of Ukraine's already cohesive and collaborative civil society.

The result has been two street revolutions staged by Ukrainians, who gradually advanced their chosen destiny as a Western-oriented, free-market, and democratic polity. These movements gained in popularity and worked to overthrow Ukraine's rotten oligarchy, its corrupt governments, and Russia's continuing, corrosive influence.

The book addresses all the modern tools that assisted this liberation—from social media to journalism schools and organizations—and also explains who Ukrainians are, why they have struggled relentlessly for a century despite Russian depredations, and why their cause has won the admiration of human rights champions and the world's democracies.

Ukraine is a nation still struggling to be free. The journey has been long, but Ukrainians have been steadfast, as Dr. Serhiy Kvit so adeptly recounts. His book is a must-read for any who want to understand why the world is now at war with Vladimir Putin and his Kremlin. It also reveals why Ukrainians will never give up and why the spirit of the Ukrainian people will never fade. Glory to Ukraine!

Toronto, December 2022
Diane Francis

Foreword

This book focuses on the humanitarian and ideological components of Ukrainians' struggle for independence from Russia in the twenty-first century. As the title suggests, it is about media, history, and education. In the past, Ukrainians, seeking to preserve their own identity during the long period of statelessness, would mostly turn to history. Only after independence was restored, in 1991, did it become possible to talk about domestic educational and media spheres.

The current ongoing Russian-Ukrainian war cannot be viewed as a distant, localized, or peripheral massacre somewhere in the post-Soviet space, no matter how many Western politicians and intellectuals wish it to be seen that way. This war has a crucial impact on global economic and political life, and it is, without exaggeration, changing our world. In particular, its events push us to reconsider many issues previously raised in global discussions which were either thought to have long ago lost their original meaning or, for various reasons, fell out of context.

After the breakdown of the Soviet Union, the end of the Cold War, and the collapse of the bipolar world, Western democracies viewed the processes taking place in Russia and the post-Soviet space as largely irrelevant to their everyday existence. "The world's largest gas station" and, simultaneously, a "fake news factory", Putin's Russia gradually became a cozy partner for many Western experts, business representatives, and political leaders.

When the Soviet bureaucratic dictatorship collapsed, many international champions of social experiments (i.e. "de facto" Russian communist sympathizers) mutated into fans of Putin's regime because they saw the Russian President as advancing a "special path" of social development, or an "alternative" to Western liberal democracy. Both far-right and far-left activists, supported by Russia around the world in order to spread chaos and destroy international law and the global security system, today act as the natural allies of the Putin regime.

Often detached from real-life agendas, their rhetoric continues to thrive despite news of atrocities in Ukraine because it is supported by established stereotypes: the consensus on the need to counter the "rich and powerful", to oppose political corruption. These stereotypes gain strength because of outstanding problems in education, primarily related to the lack of critical thinking.

During the last three decades, Western think tanks, which specialize in Russia and Eastern Europe and ignore Ukraine, have not developed an adequate perspective on the post-Soviet world. Often, they even took a pro-Russian position. However difficult these "experts" find it to explain why Russia attacked Ukraine in 2014 and then launched a full-scale invasion in 2022, I knew from my early childhood that it would eventually happen. It was just a matter of time. All I had to know was the history of my family and the history of my people.

Talk about the current war as the "Ukrainian conflict" looks strange. It would be like presenting World War II as the "Polish conflict". Overlooked in this designation is the chauvinistic sense of the concept of "Russian Orthodox civilization", the fascism of "sovereign democracy", the dramatic consequences of the Russian communists' and the Russian Orthodox Church's political consent, and the natural imperialism of Russian liberals. Also neglected were the elimination of the few remaining independent Russian media outlets and the self-government of national autonomies within Russia.

On the other hand, after the collapse of the Soviet Union, Ukraine was actually labeled by the West as a part of Eurasia, that is, it was seen as falling within Russia's sphere of influence. The penetration of Russian special services, businesses, Russian language and culture into Ukraine was extremely destructive, and included the export of corruption, an oligarchic economy, and tools for suppressing social activity. Remember, for instance, Russia's "temniks"[1] for the media. So, what was there to prevent Vladimir

---

1 Informal political instructions to journalists presenting a list of "desirable" and "undesirable" topics for coverage. The word "topic" in the Ukrainian language, and in the national political context, is consonant with "darkness" and the

Putin from returning Ukraine to his rejuvenated Russian Empire and thus reviving the Soviet Union?

To answer this question, it is necessary to know and understand a lot not only about Russia but also about Ukraine, which is an additional challenge for the West. The explanation lies on the surface: Ukrainians and Russians have dramatically different political cultures. Genuine leadership in Ukrainian political life belongs to the country's strong civil society, which maintains such values as the freedom of speech and freedom of choice in focus. It is important that after the Revolution of Dignity (2014–2015), the Ukrainian nation gained all the characteristics of a political nation.

The unity of Ukrainians and their readiness to defend their independence with arms in hand enable us to talk about the democratic and military traditions of the Ukrainian people. I have tried to consider some political phenomena that are still viewed in a mostly speculative way. These include an armed civil society and the character of political leadership: in Ukraine, it is not professional politicians who are the real leaders leading the people, but, on the contrary, it is society that chooses politicians and pushes them forward, encouraging them to become leaders. Therefore, this provides a good example, not of the role of the individual in history, but about the role of the nation in history.

It is important to understand that Russia's war against Ukraine did not start on February 24, 2022, not even in 2014. The long war aimed at the complete destruction of Ukraine has been waged continuously since 1622, when all copies of Kyrylo Tranqulion-Stavrovetskyi's *Teacher's Gospel*, printed in old Ukrainian in Ukraine, were burned deliberately in Russia. Four hundred years later, Russians still continue to burn Ukrainian books, destroying libraries, educational and cultural institutions.

According to the National Information Bureau, as of May 2023, the Russian army had completely destroyed more than 400 educational institutions in Ukraine, damaging more than 2000.

"obscuring" of the freedom of speech. This extremely successful Russian practice of applying pressure on journalists and the media was rejected by Ukrainian society and turned out to be a complete failure.

Russians killed 480, injured 968, and deported about 20,000 Ukrainian children. Taking these facts into account, along with the entire history of the relations between the two countries, we realize that Russia acts as an "existential enemy of Ukraine".[2]

The reasons for Russia's destruction of the global security system and the reasons for the attack on Ukraine in 2022 are closely related. Having proved unable to effectively manage its own country, Putin's regime chose to pursue the path of appealing to the historical myth of the "greatness" of Russia. For such a path to be possible at all, Ukraine must be taken back under its influence, observing, incidentally, that Ukraine and Kyiv belonged to the genuine lands of historical Rus'. Additionally, there is the desire to get a hold of Ukraine's human resources — required, in particular, to rebuild the Russian army. A particular problem for it is the absence of brave, proactive and competent Ukrainian soldiers and officers who, during the several hundred years of Moscow occupation, made up the backbone of the Russian armed forces. So, there can be no "great Russia" without Ukraine.

For Ukrainians, their own identity naturally intersects with the European one, both from a historical and a value point of view. Life has shown that Ukrainians are ready to idealistically defend these values more than some representatives of Old Europe, who often remember first of all their interests in the circumstances of "real politics", where many things look very relative.[3] Open letter

---

[2] The expression used by Volodymyr Vasylenko, professor of the National University of Kyiv-Mohyla Academy, Ambassador Extraordinary and Plenipotentiary of Ukraine to Great Britain.

[3] Thus, Switzerland maintains neutrality towards the crimes of the Russian army, blocking the delivery of weapons to Ukraine. At the same time, according to the investigations of the Swiss publications SRF and Die Wochenzeitung, since March 2022, the beginning of Russia's full-scale invasion of Ukraine, Swiss factories have received 75 tonnes of gold from Russia for processing, taking advantage of the fact that it is imported through London and does not violate sanctions. "75 tonnes of Russian gold imported into Switzerland since beginning of war", *European Pravda*, June 30, 2023, https://www.pravda.com.ua/eng/news/2023/06/30/7409354/; Olivier Christe, "Goldhandel: Maschine zum Reinwaschen", *Die Wochenzeitung*, June 29, 2023, https://www.woz.ch/2326/goldhandel/maschine-zum-reinwaschen/!EWMS1KXQK499; Marcel Niedermann, "Drehscheibe Schweiz: Auf der Spur von Putins Gold", *SRF*, June 28, 2023, https://www.srf.ch/news/international/drehscheibe-schweiz-auf-der-spur-von-putins-gold.

of Ukrainian writer Oksana Zabuzhko to Dutch writer Arnon Grunberg also about the flaws in European memory and cultural memorialization:

> "I was reminded that the Magdeburg law lasted for almost 600 years in Ukraine: it began being used in the thirteenth century, during the Galicia-Volhynia dynasty, and was liquidated by the Russian Empire in the eighteenth century along with the autonomous Cossack Hetmanate's other institutions.
>
> If you look at the map of this war, a few especially dramatic, multi-episode, already legendary battles stand out: Hostomel, where on 24 February 2022, the Russian paratroopers failed to take control of the airport and retreated, unaware that the only force opposing them was the local territorial defence; Chernihiv — the city of millennia-old churches on the UNESCO list of global cultural heritage, which the Russians razed to the ground from 24 February to 1st of April, as they would later raze Mariupol and Bakhmut, but never managed to take; Nizhyn that held out under siege, as if back in the Middle Ages, for a month, (when food started to run out, the local farmers snuck milk and flour into the city by roundabout routes and distributed them to the residents) but did not allow the invaders in — I cannot fail to mention that these have for centuries been cities of free citizens: Hostomel since 1614, Chernihiv since 1622, Nizhyn since 1625. It's a good thing they had defended their right to be free.
>
> The border of Europe now lies — and not metaphorically at all — here, along the old eastern reach of the Magdeburg law: every Eastern-Ukrainian city (town, village) that faces the enemy is a fortress on the frontier. And the future of Europe depends directly on whether they will stand their ground or fall."[4]

As we can see, the current Russian-Ukrainian war is the result of an irreconcilable confrontation of values. The view that Ukraine must be defended against Russian invaders, that nothing must be forgotten, and ultimately that revenge must be taken against occupiers and criminals pervades Ukrainian society. In this context, any appeals from international experts to the Christian value of forgiveness or to recognize the existence of a separate category of Russians who "suffer" under Putin's regime are seen as irrelevant. This requires more detailed explanation.

---

4   Oksana Zabuzhko, "Dear Arnon, remember: war in my dear Ukraine is Europe's defining moment," *Voxeurop*, June 1, 2023, https://voxeurop.eu/en/oksana-zabuzhko-dont-forget-ongoing-war-ukraine-defining-moment-europe/.

The Biblical injunction to turn the other cheek to the criminal correlates with the metaphor of a "fruitful" hermeneutical conversation, that is, when a criminal internally changes through repentance, or when both sides have the desire, ability, and capacity to listen to and understand each other. In other words, mutual understanding is possible only under the condition of rapprochement by both sides. It is precisely this condition that is lacking given the total support for Putin's regime expressed by Russian society. Polls and surveys show that their society has no shame; instead, it is proud of the crimes committed by the Russian army in Ukraine.

Therefore, entering into the thankless business of political predictions, I must say that Russia has no future within its current borders and the present geopolitical configuration. Its existence will end when feelings of shame, dignity, and the desire to initiate an independent, non-imperial, history awaken in that "prison of nations". Accordingly, Ukraine will move from the status of a frontier of Western civilization to that of a regular civilized state, where the values embodied in the concepts of freedom and justice will be fully secured: it will be a free and effective country for its free citizens.

Kyiv, July 2023

Russia as Evil: False Historical Parallels
Some Peculiarities of Russian Political Culture[1]

Today, many people are trying to compare Putin's Russia with Hitler's Germany. Indeed, the two states have much in common, particularly the human-hating nature of both regimes, their extremely effective propaganda systems, and the presence of persistent political mythologies capable of absorbing even religions. We should not forget that the Nazi concentration camps were a technology learned from the Russian communists who created them earlier, in the times of Vladimir Lenin.

Nazi Germany, Putin's Russia: What Is the Difference?

Despite the obvious similarities, there are significant differences between Nazi Germany and Putin's Russia. The Nazi leader Adolf Hitler exploited the revanchist moods of a Germany humiliated and destroyed by World War I, seizing power before the Germans' mood changed given that their standard of living was already on the rise in 1933. Russia's President Vladimir Putin, on the other hand, began the invasion of Ukraine in 2022 out of hopelessness, because of his inability to successfully manage the country he rules.

Putin, as the self-proclaimed ideological successor of the Soviet Union, saw no other way forward than to impose the extremely stressful conditions of war on his country's population, most of whom live in impoverished conditions. Similarly, in the times of the USSR, Soviet people had to eschew their private interests for the sake of public ones, forget about their daily needs, and accept paper certificates of praise instead of better salaries.

The entire logic of Putin regime's actions has its roots in the Soviet tradition. Technologically, the attack on Ukraine in 2022 can be compared to the absurd Baikal-Amur Mainline railway project,

---

1 *StopFake*, July 19, 2022.

which had a primarily ideological, rather than military or economic, significance. Such a large-scale construction made it again possible to employ the rhetoric of mobilizing "maximum human strength", of "new victories" for the USSR, the "heroism" of the working class, the "wisdom" of the Communist Party, etc. In just this way, Putin needed a short successful war in Ukraine, one that would entrench his image as a "gatherer" of Russian or Soviet lands.

The two regimes, the one led by German Nazis and the other by Russian communists, differ in their attitudes towards corruption. In Nazi Germany, corruption was not as all-encompassing as in the USSR. In particular, Hitler's management system, in contrast to Stalin's model, could offer Germans a certain level of well-being. The Soviet Union, on the other hand, was built on the slave labor of collective farm peasants, GULAG prisoners, and the massive exploitation of other population groups. Russians did not live better in the USSR, but there was a certain psychological compensation in their misguided belief that they lived in a "great" (in reality, a corrupt, criminal and impoverished) state.

There are still debates about how best to identify Hitler's regime: was it authoritarian or totalitarian, like the USSR? To my mind, we can uncover some important typological features by attempting clarification. According to Professor Bohdan Osadchuk,[2] who lived in Berlin during World War II, Hitler could never have had such total control over the editorial boards of Germany's mass media as Stalin had over the Soviet press.

In Germany, the tradition of freedom of speech was so strong that Berlin journalists looked down on the provincial *Parteigenossen* (party comrades) delegated by the Nazis to the editorial offices of the capital's newspapers. After the war ended, German society had aspects on which it could rely during the denazification period and the subsequent modernization of the country's political culture. It

---

2   Bohdan Osadchuk—famous Ukrainian intellectual, journalist, professor at Freie Universität Berlin. During the Second World War, he studied international law, the history of the countries of Eastern Europe and the Balkans at Humboldt-Universität zu Berlin (1941-1944). His intellectual activity took place at the intersection of Ukrainian, Polish and German cultures.

still had certain democratic landmarks associated with the freedom of speech and other political rights and freedoms in place.

Russian society, on the other hand, has never known respect for the individual, has no tradition of individualism, or any respect for human dignity. This is illustrated by many Russian intellectuals, starting with Andrey Kurbsky's letters to Ivan the Terrible, in the sixteenth century, to the diaries of Zinaida Gippius. The small number of independent thinking Soviet-era Russians were completely marginalized by Stalin's regime. They were a minority even in the GULAG, together with Ukrainians, Balts, Jews, and others.

The fact is that Russian political culture has always been autocratic and despotic. It historically sought to subjugate and oppress the initiatives of broader social groups. This sad historical experience can only suggest that political regime change in Russia will not bring results similar to postwar Germany. In the case of Russia, everything looks much worse. The criminals of Putin's regime feel confident in their own impunity.

It was not Putin however, who influenced Russian society; rather, Russians found an idol for themselves and created the political phenomenon that is Vladimir Putin. Now they are proud of him. Destroying the Russian propaganda machine will not alter Russian political culture, because the latter grows out of Russian national culture and is based on the very features that make it unique. The world must also try to understand why the much-touted "great" Russian art somehow raised a demonic society of tyrants, slaves, and sadists.

The Ukrainian philosopher and publicist Volodymyr Yermolenko addresses this very issue in a recent *Foreign Policy* article. He writes: "if you're looking for the roots of Russia's violence against its neighbors, its desire to erase their history, and its rejection of the ideas of liberal democracy, you will find some of the answers on the pages of Pushkin, Lermontov, and Dostoevsky".[3]

---

3 Volodomyr Yermolenko, "From Pushkin to Putin: Russian Literature's Imperial Ideology", *Foreign Policy*, June 26, 2022, https://foreignpolicy.com/2022/06/25/russia-ukraine-war-literature-classics-imperialism-ideology-nationalism-putin-pushkin-tolstoy-dostoevsky-caucasus/.

Ukraine Is Not Russia

Roman Ratushnyi, a prominent and much-respected Ukrainian activist, a Revolution of Dignity participant and volunteer, who died at the age of 24 on the frontline fighting against the Russian invasion near the city of Izium on June 2, 2022, said:

> "Just remember: the more Russians we kill now, the fewer Russians our children will have to kill. This war has been going on for over three hundred years. When we are defeated, we become cannon fodder for Russians. When we win, we get some time to have a rest before the next phase of this war" (Tvoie Misto [*Your City*], June 14, 2022).

These words summarize the entire history of the relations between Ukraine and Russia. It is important to be very clear about certain points when talking about Ukrainians' attitude towards Russians. Firstly, this is not a tribal war. That is, a Russian surname does not indicate an enemy in Ukraine. Ukrainian citizens of Russian origin are defending their state just like ethnic Ukrainians and other Ukrainian citizens.

Secondly, the enemies are not only Russian citizens who came to Ukraine with weapons in their hands, but also all holders of Russian Federation passports who support Putin's regime. That support is extraordinarily high (the Levada Center reports about 83%, according to its March 24–30 survey), high enough that it allows us to generalize about all of Russia: it is a state hostile to Ukraine, a hostile society, and a hostile political culture. Russian opponents of Putin (if there are any) do not stand against his policies. In most cases, they do not like the lack of results, namely Putin's failure to achieve his stated goal: a renovation of the Russian Empire/Soviet Union.

Thirdly, bearing in mind Roman Ratushnyi's words, as well as the totality of previous historical experience, Russia cannot accept the existence of an independent Ukraine, because this would destroy Russia's political mythology, according to which Kyiv is the "mother of Russian cities". Therefore, a war against Ukraine is a holy war for the whole of Russian society, as a result of which Kyiv must become a Russian city.

Fourthly, why is a comparison of Putin's Russia with Nazi Germany not a comparison of equals? Because the Russian problem is much greater. Russia is a problem for the entire Western world. A change in the political regime will not change the Russian political culture, Russian national culture, or Russians themselves. Having no other historical and political experience, they will perceive the loss of "Russism" (totalitarianism, Russian communism, "sovereign democracy", "Orthodox civilization", the "Russian world", etc.) as a loss of their own identity. Therefore, "political Russians" (if such a term can be applied) will immediately start looking for a new Putin, who will play again and again on the "special pride" of the slaves.

What to Do?

There is only one solution to the problem. After all, it is impossible to hope for the modernization, democratization or any kind of civilized integration of Russia into the world community. That's why it is necessary to get rid of the illusion that Russia is a country of indubitable integrity. Also, it should be understood that not everyone with a Russian passport is actually Russian. The time will come when every imprisoned nation in this federated "prison of nations" will declare its right to dignity and self-determination. Then the Russia which we know will cease to exist within its current borders, and we will treat the Buryats not as Putin-armed barbarians (this is exactly how they behaved in the Ukrainian territories temporarily occupied by the Russian army in 2022), but as a not very numerous people whose existence is endangered as a result of Moscow's deliberate criminal policy.

Skeleton Key
How to Understand the Changing World during Ukraine's War for Independence[8]

Despite significant criticism, globalization creates new opportunities for mutual understanding: more and more problems are becoming common issues requiring not only joint solutions, but also a coherent conceptual apparatus. Ukrainians have their own key to comprehending and preserving their independence, and this key can also help to open other doors to more broadly understand the modern world.

Modernization

The theory of modernization (Westernization) has gone through many manifestations. At first, it collapsed in the post-colonial countries of Asia and Africa, having contributed to increased corruption in the newly independent states. Among positive examples one could mention the impact of the "Marshall Plan" on the modernization of Europe, primarily Germany, after World War II. Finally, the countries of the former "socialist camp" and the post-Soviet countries are presently undergoing modernization with more and less successful cases.

The general formula for the post-Soviet environment can be defined as follows: the very first step required is to gain genuine independence from Russia; only after that will it be possible to undertake the real modernization (including democratization) of public life, create an efficient system of state governance and introduce a market economy. Why does the general approach in this specific geographic area require independence first and only after that democracy? It is because the post-Soviet space contains dramatically different political cultures.

The formal presence of democratic institutions or a declaration of fundamental rights and freedoms (e.g. freedom of speech,

---

8   Kyiv Security Forum, June 2022.

freedom of choice, freedom of beliefs, etc.) does not at all mean that these institutions influence important decision-making. Quite often, on the contrary, the informal structures of patriarchal society have much more real political influence: they rely on public consensus rather than on the legally enshrined organizations and ways of governance that we associate with modernity.

Therefore, it is important for the post-Soviet countries to break away from Russia first, gaining the independent ability to make important decisions, and only after that to engage in building democratic institutions. It is at this second stage that one gains understanding that without modernization, i.e. without implementing transparent and socially comprehensible rules of the game, it is impossible to improve standards of living and strengthen the nation-state. It is necessary to protect one's independence from Russia, which, on the contrary, is interested in disseminating corruption across the post-Soviet space.

Today's example of Ukrainian-style modernization is significant not only because Ukrainians are fighting for it with weapon in their hands. Europeanness has become part of the Ukrainian identity. At the same time, Ukrainians often project an idealistic view of the European Union which has little in common with the reality. Nevertheless, after February 24, 2022, it was clear that Russian corruption had become one of the main allies of the Ukrainian army. That is, modernization (Europeanization, Westernization) has already transformed into a way of building strength and growth for Ukraine. This process has been ongoing since the 2014 Revolution of Dignity, but accelerated after Russia's full-fledged invasion in 2022.

Clash of Identities

Our times of deep civilizational crisis are characterized by clashes between new identities. These debates result from a very modernist question: "Who are we?" The postmodern flexibility that attempts to evade this direct question looks extremely destructive.

For Western Europeans, renewing identity means searching for something totally new. It means more than acquiescing to museum exhibits of former glory or turning a blind eye to the unprecedented scale of European political corruption fueled by "the world's largest gas station". Even atonement for the colonial heritage has become part of the usual and convenient penitential rhetoric in Western Europe. At the same time, against the background of the war in Ukraine, well-known European values often look too flexible.

Alla Lazareva, a Ukrainian journalist living in France, expressed it well when she said:

> "A long time ago, when Ukraine's independence was just restored, my friends and I adapted Western journalism standards to the needs of the Ukrainian press to help it get rid of bad Soviet habits. Now, the 'press tours' of the French media to Mariupol, which are made 'with the help' of the Russian army, prompt us to the conclusion that the time has come to pay off debts. Colleagues, why are you cooperating with war criminals? By the simple fact of participating in such press tours you legalize, banalize, and humanize imperial aggression, and present it to your audience as negotiable. What for? A quarter of a century ago, we learned from you how to be impartial and operate with facts. Now it's time for us to switch roles. Learn from Ukrainian journalists how to maintain dignity and sense the limit beyond which journalism ends and collaboration begins".[9]

It should be noted that the above example is general and applies not only to France and the French.

For Russians, their identity has narrowed, and is now defined by their ability to kill Ukrainians. Rhetoric surrounding "great" Russian culture, which might be used to justify Russian crimes against humanity, needs to be analyzed. A rational explanation is needed of how that "great culture" has so strangely influenced Russian society in the twenty-first century that it entirely supports the unprovoked prosecution of a war, permits mass murders of Ukrainians, and takes pride in crimes against humanity committed by the Russian army.

One explanation is that the Russian system of education and research, along with the Russian media, has lost all conception of critical thinking. Russia's political culture is fear-based. Russian

---

9   Alla Lazareva (Facebook, June 16.2022), https://www.facebook.com/1224171833/posts/pfbid0253SJ7K2BYHH9R4fGKZbPRMttNvqoXFzFV1m6hxPeHHxAjDjFVQWZ7rDBcsVdwEAnl

society neither feels the need nor has the ability to use the instruments of democratic institutions to control its government, and its state propaganda machine's effectiveness in brainwashing its own citizens rivals North Korea's.

In this context we could also mention considerable gaps within Western education that sometimes lead to a severe limitation of critical thinking. To fill these gaps, or, in other words, to really comprehend the Russian cultural context and the sources of contemporary Russian political culture, Western experts, university researchers, and independent intellectuals should begin by learning from Ukrainian and Polish intellectual traditions, which have accumulated considerable experience in identifying the distinctive features and understanding the nature of Russian imperialism and chauvinism.

Ghosts of Ideologies

Habitual ideological confrontations within the established triangle, "the Left—the Right—the Liberals", with all their possible differences and nuances, are losing all meaning in the context of contemporary Ukraine. Within this broadly accepted triangle the Ukrainian state has no place. The vast majority of Western intellectuals have traditionally not wanted to notice Ukraine as distinct from the background of "great" Russia, as they had previously always been satisfied to coexist with a "mysterious" or "alternative" system that yet highlighted their own significance. The Ukrainian element seemed no more than an unwanted complication in the perception of the established political landscape (its falsity notwithstanding) of the world.

Historically, in the French tradition, a public intellectual is a person with leftist political views. The context always matters. The Western left, against objective data, generally did not wish to see Russia as a contender for global domination (in a sense analogous to the European colonial tradition). Accordingly, within this paradigm, Ukraine was only reluctantly seen as a suppressed and genocide-stricken colony (Lesia Ostrovska-Liuta). At the very least, after 1991, Ukraine should have received attention and support on the basis of the right of nations to self-determination, but this was inconvenient because it would have meant recognizing Russia as an imperialist power.

Interestingly, the anti-globalization rhetoric of the 1990s (condemning any and all forms of domination) brought together Noam Chomsky, a left-wing U.S. university professor, and Yaroslav Dashkevych, a right-wing Ukrainian intellectual and longtime GULAG prisoner, who also worked in the academic sphere. However, their commonality could only be perceived through close observation and was not related to deep trends.

After all, Ukraine's anti-Soviet (anti-Russian) struggle for independence was usually viewed retrospectively as a manifestation of reactionary "ethnic nationalism", and even fascism, aimed against the Soviet Union as an ally of the West in the anti-fascist coalition. Consequently, Putin's Russia, as the successor of "the first state of workers and peasants", is today seen by many as a kind of alternative to the "unjust" domination of the West.

The world is changing in front of our eyes. The fearlessness of the Ukrainians has highlighted the irrelevance of Noam Chomsky, who, as it turns out, can only sputter with hatred about "this uncivilized, barbaric area of the world that is Europe and the United States".[10] At the same time, he refuses to question the genocidal policies of Russia. In his response to Professor Chomsky, Yuri Gorodnichenko tries to draw him into rational arguments and common sense by emphasizing that: "If you truly value Ukrainian lives as you claim to, we would like to kindly ask you to refrain from adding further fuel to the Russian war machine by spreading views very much akin to Russian propaganda".[11]

The bankruptcy of ideological rhetoric was further revealed by the shift of Jürgen Habermas to the position of a German

---

10 "Noam Chomsky on How to Prevent World War III," *Current Affairs*, April, 13, 2022, https://www.currentaffairs.org/2022/04/noam-chomsky-on-how-to-prevent-world-war-iii

11 Yuri Gorodnichenko. "Open Letter to Noam Chomsky (and other like-minded intellectuals) on the Russia-Ukraine war", Berkeley Blog, May, 19, 2022, https://blogs.berkeley.edu/2022/05/19/open-letter-to-noam-chomsky-and-other-like-minded-intellectuals-on-the-russia-ukraine-war/

burgher in his article "War and Indignation". His vague evocation that Ukraine should not lose this war[12] could not divert the reader's attention from the sincere indignation expressed at the beginning of his publication, which could be restated as follows: "Who are you, Ukrainians, to reproach us with moral arguments?" (Yevhen Bystrytskyi). In other words, since moral arguments have already been privatized by other slick people, Ukraine can no longer claim them.

Anatoliy Yermolenko, a promoter and translator of Habermas since the 1970s, published his answer under the title "Widerstand statt Verhandlung" (Resistance instead of Negotiations), in which he noted:

> "However, there are moments when the endless horizon of communication has its limits: you cannot talk to a killer and rapist, you must resist him. You cannot wait to see what action he will take — you must stop these actions and make them impossible in the future. 'Auschwitz must not happen again', was the new categorical imperative by Theodor Adorno. 'Bucha must not happen again!' — this is how we, Ukrainians, formulate it".[13]

In this case, we must get back to asking modernist questions and giving direct answers to them. Volodymyr Yermolenko claims that the Maidan of 2013–2014 (the Revolution of Dignity) was an ideological cocktail.

> "Emotionally, it was patriotic and nationalistic. Rationally, at the level of reason, it was liberal: the Maidan's slogans — dignity, human rights, rule of law, etc. — were liberal. Yet, organizationally, it was left-wing: it was a space without money, a communal space, a space of mutual assistance. It was rightist at the level of emotions, it was liberal and centrist at the level of reason, and it was leftist at the level of it organization. Its soul was rightist, its mind was centrist, and its body was leftist. This is something that neither

---

12 Jürgen Habermas, "War and Indignation", *Süddeutsche Zeitung*, April 28, 2022, https://www.sueddeutsche.de/projekte/artikel/kultur/the-dilemma-of-the-west-juergen-habermas-on-the-war-in-ukraine-e032431/?reduced=true

13 Anatoliy Yermolenko, "Widerstand statt Verhandlung", *Frankfurter Allgemeine Zeitung*, May, 23, 2022, https://www.faz.net/aktuell/feuilleton/debatten/der-ukrainische-philosoph-yermolenko-antwortet-habermas-18044530.html

the West nor the East has comprehended, trying to pull this or that aspect to the surface".[14]

In other words, we are living in a critical time not easily understood in traditional terms. It is a time when Ukrainians, possessing a strong belief in the righteousness of their cause and the need to protect socially important values, refuse to stand aside and simply observe the great changes and transformations that are going on in their country, their region, and in the world. If we are involved in these processes, we grasp the opportunity to maintain our identity. The decision to take actions goes beyond purely ideological sympathies and becomes an individual's existential choice.

Where the implementation of truly socially important projects is concerned, the idea of "victory" is elevated to an almost a religious level, commensurate with the Christian concept of grace. Representatives of different ideological traditions, even some with openly opposite intentions, associate the accomplishment of important measures with the demands of their political movement. Everyone is satisfied and everyone feels like a winner. It is this effect that Volodymyr Yermolenko describes.

Ukrainian Skeleton Key

Both my grandmothers, who survived two world wars, were convinced that war puts everything in its place. Ukraine must emerge renewed from this war for their independence: a war that in its significance stands close to World War III. If Ukrainians manage to defend their independence and their values, which they identify as European (including freedom and justice), it will give an impetus to the creation of a new global security system and encourage the further development of international law as the basis for inter-state relations.

Ukrainians have established new precedents in the defense of their independence. First of all, our skeleton key includes an armed civil society, which relies on the traditions of Ukrainian individualism. This concept needs some clarification.

---

[14] В. Єрмоленко, "Рідинні ідеології Майдану" [V. Yermolenko, "The Fluid Ideologies of the Maidan"], *Флософська думка*, no. 6 (2014): 9.

Mychailo Wynnyckyi draws attention to the transformation of traditional Western (including Ukrainian) individualism into personalism, which took place during the Revolution of Dignity, and speaks of such distinctive features as vertical and horizontal transcendence, social rootedness in the community, the presence of conscience, the ability and necessity to correlate actions in the public interest. In the context of the philosophy of personalism, a special role is played by the community as a set of individuals united by a common goal and common values.

He writes:

> "This seems to reflect an important tenet of Personalist philosophy, namely that 'community is ontologically prior to the establishment of any political institution', and that political authority is derived from the community — a social union that consists of more than simply an aggregate of individuals."[15]

After 1991, Ukraine did not produce political leaders who led the nation; on the contrary, it gave rise to an active society that forced politicians to become representative leaders. The personal involvement of Ukrainians and their willingness to take responsibility for both their state and the entire public sphere will help them resist the threat of authoritarianism, which often arises in times of martial law.

The faith of Ukrainians in their own strength, in truth and in the possibility of justice is acquiring a special importance. Mutual trust within Ukrainian society is growing and can become an important tool in postwar revitalization. Trust is the key to victory in the war with Russia, and is also a fundamental requirement for the successful implementation of reforms in various spheres of public life after victory has been achieved. Trust should also be seen as a criterion for the successful reform of Ukrainian state institutions.

Like the 2005 Hollywood film *The Skeleton Key*, translated into Ukrainian as "the key to all doors", Ukraine's universal solution, opening all doors, includes personal involvement, belief in justice, and mutual trust. If it is successful, Ukrainians will change this world for the better.

---

15   Mychailo Wynnyckyi. "Unravelling the Ukrainian Revolution: 'Dignity', 'Fairness', 'Heterarchy', and the Challenge to Modernity", *Kyiv-Mohyla Humanities Journal* 7 (2020): 130, https://bit.ly/39Rn7dY.

The Battle for History and Building of Identity
Fake News Confronts Professional News[16]

The "battle for history" thesis (fundamental to the politics of memory) is unacceptable to professional historians because its subjective approach diverges from their prime task of searching for and understanding the truth. At the same time, one cannot deny that the historical agenda has become extremely media-oriented and even news-based. That is, from some point of view, interpretations of history can be seen as matters of concern to society on a par with current domestic problems that directly affect the quality of life.

The interpretation of history can be used as a justification for implementing a particular policy, or for inactivity, which should also be considered a separate policy. Historical mythology is an important factor shaping the national identity of Ukrainians. And Russia, for its part, uses history to construct a counter-narrative of aggression and xenophobia against independent Ukraine, thus denying the sovereign right of Ukrainians to consolidate their own state.

In these settings, the popular-scientific dimension of national history in contemporary Ukraine—an independent state, whose society has been deprived of its own history for centuries, mainly due to the murderous imposition of Russian imperial interpretations—takes on particular importance. It was stressed by Wim Coudenys, a Belgian specialist in Russian history, in his lecture at Stanford University on November 3, 2017.[17]

Throughout its history, the Russian Empire denied the existence of a separate Ukrainian history, a separate Ukrainian nation, and forbade the Ukrainian language. The 54 acts banning the

---

16   *StopFake*, October 23, 2021.
17   Wim Coudenys, "Crimea has always been Russian. Or has it? Historical Arguments in Russian Political Discourse", Stanford Global Issues, https://sgs.stanford.edu/events/crimea-has-always-been-russian-or-has-it-historical-arguments-russian-political-discourse

Ukrainian language from 1622 to 2012 included more than 40 acts of chauvinist Russian policy.[18] Researchers even see the Holodomor as an extension of policies aimed at destroying the Ukrainian language — in this case, through the physical elimination of its speakers.

Sources of the Russian Imperial Narrative Today

In 1991, after the collapse of the Soviet Union, which over time had transformed into a modernized Russian Empire modified by the Bolsheviks, a new non-Soviet Ukrainian historiography developed. Source studies became possible and archives previously kept classified by Russian communists were opened. Simultaneously, a new stage in the development of the Russian propaganda machine started, whose efficacy reached a peak in the Western world during the times of "late Putinism", when the "irreplaceable" Russian political leader, for whom there was no alternative, finally took on the features of a tsar, secretary general of the communist party, and president all in one.

Vladimir Putin improvises and introduces, "when necessary", new historical concepts into the Russian imperial discourse. These include, for example, the thesis of the sacred significance of Crimea for Russian statehood. In fact, this thesis was created to replace the old occupier's myth of Kyiv as the "mother of Russian cities". Because Kyiv turned out to be a hard nut to crack for Putin's Russia.

The "mother of Russian cities", taken from the literature of Rus' (Kyivan Rus'), a state that emerged in the early Middle Ages on the territory of modern Ukraine, is one of the most common statements in Russian chauvinist propaganda. The problem is that this Rus' is simply the old name for Ukraine, and has a Scandinavian origin. It is not synonymous with "Russia", which comes from the Byzantine Greek name of Rus', and was introduced by decree of Peter the Great in the first half of the eighteenth century. Until 1721, his state bore the same name as the capital — Moscow or Moscovia.

---

18 Chronicle of Ukrainian language bans (in Ukrainian): https://zaxid.net/hronika_zaboron_ukrayinskoyi_movi_n1257817

The efforts of Putin's predecessors to trace the history of Moscovia to the early Middle Ages resemble the inclusion into the Eastern European Christian cultural context of wolves and bears that lived in the location of modern Moscow. The same is true of the not very convincing representation of the Vikings, who became the founders of the Rurik dynasty, as Russians.

Another example is the difference between the concepts of "Russkiie" and "Rossiianie", both of which are translated into English and Ukrainian as "Russians". The first word refers to ethnic Russians, the second to all Russian citizens on the way to national depersonalization. The concept "Rossiianie" replaced the concept of the "Soviet people" — a failed 1970s communist experiment.

Putin's historical "discoveries" include the claim that Islam is closer to Russian Orthodoxy than Catholicism. Indeed, the Western public does not often realize that Russia is, first of all, a Muslim country and that membership of the Orthodox Church in Ukraine outnumbers that of the Orthodox Church in Russia. To justify Russia's attack on Ukraine in 2014, the rusty concept of "Novorossia", created by imperial ideologists in the eighteenth century, was revived.

To assess the importance of this historical agenda for the political and global context, the following features of the political culture of contemporary Russian society should be noted.

Firstly, it loves Putin as both person and metaphor. Secondly, it does not require freedom of speech or other political freedoms. Thirdly, it lacks the ability to think critically. Fourthly, it feels comfortable within the fake (totally mythologized) media reality created by the Russian propaganda machine. And finally, fifthly, it has always been what it is now.

Unfortunately, the Western expert community does not seem critical enough of the phenomenon of Russian imperialism. Here, one should mention the strong traditions of Russo/Soviet-philia, often based on dirty Russian money, an interest in the Byzantine tradition, love of Russian ballet, in particular the music of the Ukrainian Petro Tchaikovskyi, Russian literature, in particular the works of the Ukrainian Nikolaj Gogol (in Ukrainian pronunciation — Mykola Hohol), and approval of Putinism as a special civilizational path ("sovereign democracy", "Orthodox civilization", "Russian world", etc.) offering an "alternative" to Western civilization.

Relevant here also is a special category of commentators' Western political storytelling. They might even have been personally acquainted with some Russian dissidents once (who, in practice, turned out to be independent intellectuals of different ethnicities, Ukrainian or Jewish, for example). These science-fiction political analysts are waiting (as in *Waiting for Godot* by Samuel Beckett) for the victory of a democratic Russian government which would finally be ready to communicate common values and integrate Russia into the global community.

The problem is that this will never happen as long as Russia remains, as the Ukrainian poet Taras Shevchenko put it, a "prison of nations", and the majority of independent Russian intellectuals (almost all) remain de facto ordinary Russian chauvinists who see the world through the eyes of the "Russian world" and only sometimes gently condemn either Putin's methods or Putin himself, because, they say, Russia's path is correct overall; it is merely that "the tsar is not altogether right". Only in those cases when he is completely unsuccessful.

The above was noticed by Yuri Afanasiev, a well-known Russian historian and politician, in his open lecture at the Kyiv-Mohyla Academy on January 19, 2012. He stated that "all of Russian history is fully falsified", "traditional Russian consciousness is incomparable with European consciousness", and that "to continue on such a history means the death of Russia". Afanasiev criticized the participants of anti-Putin protests because "they do not understand what they are doing" since "what is necessary today is not to deny Putin, but to demand the demolition of [Russian] autocracy", that is, to change the political culture of Russian society.

Therefore, the main source of today's Russian imperial narrative is not only the "gas money" invested by Putin's government into a propaganda machine of unprecedented power. It is much more important to understand that this narrative relies upon the corresponding demands of Russian society itself. Here we must mention Elihu Katz, a prominent media communications researcher, who pointed out that we need to find out not only what the media do to the audience, but also what the audience does to the media. This view of media impact is related to Uses and Gratifications theory.

In addition, it is not only the Russian public that is ready to accept Russian fake news. Russian "fakes" adapt quite successfully to the social contexts of different states in order to divide, disintegrate, and destroy the unity of the Western world that has declared its intention to defend shared democratic values. One of the sources of the post-truth phenomenon is public demand for untruthful, distorted, but comforting (in different ways for different social groups) world picture that eventually finds its representation in fake news. Since these processes are correlated at a global level technically, Russian influence in the West is growing.[19]

Vladimir Putin's 2021 article "On the Historical Unity of Russians and Ukrainians"[20] is interesting not for its imperial narrative, but as an example of how historical argumentation forms the basis for political decisions. The current political context has been squeezed into the framework of well-known propaganda clichés. In this way, media reality was distorted. Therefore, from a certain point of view, messages such as this can be interpreted as fake news.

Interestingly, in its struggle for Ukrainian identity, the Russian propaganda machine contravened its own principles by publishing this article in Ukrainian on the official website of the Russian president. It strives to be extremely flexible about promoting semi-racist and pseudo-historical claims about the "brotherhood of one blood" of Russians and Ukrainians, something possible in the post-truth era.

For its domestic audience, the goal of the Russian imperial narrative is to provide "proof" that Russia is a "great power" again, just "as it once was". Otherwise, Russian society would notice that

---

19 Serhiy Kvit, "A perspective on 'fake news'", *Kyiv Post*, October 26, 2019, https://www.kyivpost.com/article/opinion/op-ed/serhiy-kvit-a-perspective-on-fake-news.html
20 Vladimir Putin, "On the Historical Unity of Russians and Ukrainians", http://en.kremlin.ru/events/president/news/66181

they live in a beggarly country, would vote for a refrigerator rather than the fake ideology, forget about the TV, and find a new tsar.

Ignorance of History as a Justification for Politics

Germany has a special place in global politics as the main economic power of the European Union and a living example of successful postwar modernization, where restored democratic institutions became the basis for a new political culture and its resultant economic growth. Much more disappointing for Ukraine is the historical ignorance of some German politicians.

Professor Timothy Snyder's address to the Bundestag on June 20, 2017, "Germany's historical responsibility to Ukraine", illustrates this point.[21] Contextually, the German members of parliament looked like neophytes just hearing the facts concerning the history of World War II for the first time. Snyder linked the current triumph of populism, the rise of new challenges and problems in Europe, threats to the constitutional system, and the crisis of democracy in the USA to a lack of historical responsibility.

He reminded German politicians that Hitler had planned to expand Germans' living space, first of all, by using the territory of Ukraine. "The point of World War II from Hitler's point of view, the purpose of World War II from Hitler's point of view was the conquest of Ukraine. It is therefore senseless to commemorate, to remember any part of World War II without beginning from Ukraine. Any commemoration of World War II that involves the Nazi purposes, the ideological, economic, political purposes of the Nazi regime, must begin precisely from Ukraine".

According to Professor Snyder, it is very important not to forget that

> "it is Russian foreign policy to divide the history of Soviet Union into two parts. There is the good part which is the Russian part. And there is the bad part which is the Ukrainian part. I can sum this up: liberation—Russian, collaboration—Ukrainian. That is the line that they follow very consistently

---

21 Timothy Snyder, "Germany's Historical Responsibility for Ukraine" (2017), https://marieluisebeck.de/artikel/20-06-2017/timothy-snyder-germanys-historical-responsibility-ukraine

and in this country [Germany — note, editor] to create a fact. Because Russian foreign policy regards the German sense of responsibility as a resource, precisely as a resource to be manipulated".

A noisy scandal was provoked by German President Frank-Walter Steinmeier's statement that Germans were obliged to complete the construction of Nord Stream-2 as part of their liability to Russia for the crimes of World War II.[22] Not only Ukrainians, but also the former US Ambassador to Ukraine Steven Pifer, the former US Ambassador to Poland Daniel Fried, the German international security and foreign policy expert Marcel Dirsus, the Russian politician Garry Kasparov, and journalists from the *Frankfurter Allgemeine Zeitung* and *Die Welt* reacted negatively.[23]

Since none of the above-mentioned politicians are professional historians, it is clear that in this case the historical agenda conceals the German leader's very specific intention to expand cooperation with Putin's regime. President Steinmeier equates the Soviet Union with Russia, perhaps also Soviet citizens with Russians (or maybe it's not so important to him); he does not know which territories actually suffered most from the Nazi occupation and who most of the victims were.

Quoting Professor Snyder again,

> "In absolute numbers, more inhabitants of Soviet Ukraine died in World War II than inhabitants of Soviet Russia — in absolute terms — and these are calculations of Russian historians — in absolute terms. Which means in relative terms, in proportional terms Ukraine was far, far, far more risked [sic] than Soviet Russia during the war".

Interestingly, in his interview Mr. Steinmeier tries to separate domestic Russian and international issues. He argues that Navalnyi must be released immediately and urges, among other things, "to look for a common ground in foreign policy to turn what is bad today into a better future" in EU-Russia relations.

---

22 President Frank-Walter Steinmeier, interview with *Tageszeitung Rheinische Post*, https://www.bundespraesident.de/SharedDocs/Reden/DE/Frank-Walter-Steinmeier/Interviews/2021/210206-Interview-Rheinische-Post.html
23 Artur Korniyenko. "Does Germany owe Russia 'Nord Stream-2' for the atrocities of the Nazis? Steinmeier's statement and reactions of experts" (in Ukrainian), *Radio Liberty*, February 11, 2021.

It is difficult to understand how overt public cooperation with Putin's regime at the international level (which is exactly what Vladimir Putin needs, as he enjoys the support and even love of Russian society in the domestic arena) can lead to a "better future".

Such an approach may be rational and justified in light of protecting national interests. However, it may lead to the expansion of authoritarian trends currently observable in many Western countries. The idealistically perceived image of the West, as a formation adhering to the principles of human rights and the rule of law with no place for corruption, has seriously tottered over the past two decades.

Frank-Walter Steinmeier has also authored his famous "Steinmeier's formula", which proposes that elections "under Ukrainian legislation" should be arranged in the so-called "Luhansk People's Republic" and "Donetsk People's Republic" — both concocted by Putin's regime. These Eastern Ukrainian territories have been occupied and looted by Russia, filled with Russian military personnel and destroyed by war; their threatened populations, which have been effectively brainwashed by Putin's pseudomedia for seven years, and which have lost over two million internally displaced persons (IDPs) who have fled to the territory controlled by the Ukrainian government, according to Steinmeier, are to arrange "free elections" while still under occupation.

Such paradoxical judgments merit inclusion in postmodern literary fiction. However, they are seriously circulating in international political discourse. Only a lack of basic historical knowledge prevented Mr. Steinmeier from drawing the quite simple analogy with postwar Germany, which needed more than four years, from May 1945 to August 1949, to hold its first democratic elections to the Bundestag.

Although the above examples of historical ignorance indicate that this phenomenon has a very real impact on the shaping of modern international politics, many examples of critical considerations, including media representations of history, also exist. In the German context, I would firstly like to mention Professor Karl Schlögel and his book *The Ukrainian Challenge: The Discovery of a European Country* (to give the Ukrainian version of the title), which was first published in Munich in 2015 and then published by Spirit and Letter Publishing House in Kyiv in 2017.[24]

Prior to 2014, Karl Schlögel had been immersed in the Russian cultural context. However, this responsible intellectual refused to accept the Pushkin Medal from Russian officials and protested against the annexation of Crimea. Having witnessed the events during the Revolution of Dignity in Kyiv and Donetsk, he properly presented them as a historian and sociologist. The question is: why is Mr. Steinmeier employing a Russian imperial narrative, not the high-quality intellectual conclusions offered by Professor Schlögel? Evidently, this is a rhetorical question.

Manipulating Values

> "Where did this Ukraine come from, preventing us from normal cooperation with Putin's Russia? It was not there before. And it would be better if it disappeared again. It is much easier to equate the USSR with Russia, as during the Cold War. So, let's look for reasons why Ukraine does not deserve to be treated as a sovereign European state that has suffered Russian aggression and lost parts of its territory".

The historical component of such rhetoric, quite common in the West, is becoming particularly significant, as it seems to be affecting political decision-making.

Yevhen Fedchenko, director of the Kyiv-Mohyla School of Journalism and editor-in-chief of *StopFake*, in a Facebook post dated September 4, 2021, drew attention to those "who tried to torpedo the visit of Ukrainian President Volodymyr Zelenskyy to the United States. Freedom House was one of them".

According to Michael Abramowitz, the president of this respected international organization, "Online propaganda and malign disinformation campaigns spread false narratives to provoke conflict within society, all of which undermine trust in democratic institutions. As Russia's neighbor, Ukraine is the testing site for

---

24 Karl Schlögel, *Entscheidung in Kiew. Ukrainische Lektionen* (München: Carl Hanser Verlag, 2015; Kyiv: Spirit and Letter Publishing House, 2017). [Karl Schlögel, *Ukraine: A Nation on the Borderland*, trans. Gerrit Jackson (London: Reaktion, 2018).]

Russian disinformation tactics that are then applied elsewhere, including in the United States".[25]

At the same time, Freedom House condemned the closure of pro-Russian TV channels which had been the mouthpiece of Russian propaganda and controlled by Viktor Medvedchuk, a pro-Russian oligarch and Putin's close friend, referring to them just as "three popular Ukrainian TV channels", and recommended that US President Joe Biden demand that the fight against misinformation be exclusively rights-based.

> "So", Yevhen Fedchenko continued, "according to their logic, to have hostile destabilizing broadcasters pursuing an information war inside a country struggling at war is an inalienable right? Most interesting. You can ask: did Freedom House send a similar letter just before the Biden-Putin summit in Geneva, given that the last independent media are really being crushed in Russia? You can guess the answer yourself".

As we can see, according to Freedom House, it is necessary to pressure the victim, not the criminal. Ukraine, which is fighting for its independence, territorial integrity, and democratic values should be ignored. And we know Russia, they say, we know that it will not change; it is a big state with nuclear weapons that we can do profitable business with. That is why we need Russia, not Ukraine. This is just a repetition of the old saw that might makes right.

The examples provided, of values manipulation and the misinterpretation of historical issues, relate to the inability to defend one's civilizational choice. A historical analogy to the helpless behavior of Western democracies endangered by German Nazism and Russian Communism just before World War II can be drawn. Today, Ukraine seems to be "standing in the way" in the view of many Western politicians who do not know which they should fear more: Russia, China, or internal disintegration. As regards the latter, it is again history, including the heritage of colonialism and slavery that is chasing after them.

---

25 Michael Abramowitz, "Advocacy Letter", August 26, 2021: "Ukraine: Freedom House President Sends Letter to Biden Ahead of Zelenskyy Visit", https://bit.ly/3DKK7FL

Modern Ukrainian Identity

The 2013–2014 Revolution of Dignity confirmed that a strong and active civil society exists in Ukraine. A modern Ukrainian identity is taking shape in the framework of growing public trust and a striving for mutual understanding. This identity includes, first of all, a very real Ukrainian component that is grounded in collective memory, the Ukrainian language, a tradition of struggle for independence, and a state policy of memory that supports openness and access to all archival documents.[26]

Secondly, the Ukrainian identity includes the identities of national minorities and indigenous peoples that have no other native territory than that of Ukraine. I am referring in the first place to the Crimean Tatars, who have their own unique national traditions. Crimea, occupied by Russia, is extremely important to them, and they are also part of the Ukrainian political nation. During the Revolution of Dignity, Mustafa Dzhemilev, the leader of the Crimean Tatars, stated that he was proud to be a Ukrainian.

Thirdly, modern Ukrainian political culture, with its ideals of freedom and justice in their broad sense, performs an extremely important integrative function for all citizens of Ukraine. Josef Zissels, one of the leaders of Ukraine's Jewish community, emphasizes the democratic European roots of this culture and sees the main challenge of Ukrainian society as the avoidance of authoritarian revivals of Eurasian (Russian) origin.

Zissels, as one of the leading representatives of Ukrainian civil society, also opposes the attempts by the Russian oligarchs Mikhail Fridman and German Khan, both on the "Putin list",[27] to privatize the Ukrainian historical memory of the Babyn Yar tragedy.[28] Press

---

26 Yohanan Petrovsky-Shtern, "The Only Archive in the World that Fits the Name-metaphor 'Open' is the SBU Archive" (in Russian), https://dostup.memo.ru/story/iohanan-petrovskii-shtern-edinstvenn/?fbclid=IwAR0Ljr8MULyi11AAj NUSGnjEMJR15CMglKoz8tD4auxu62q2VuRv7uF9vhU
27 Daniel Brown, "The 25 Richest Russian Oligarchs on the 'Putin list' that the US Just Released", *Business Insider*, January 31, 2018, https://www.businessinsider.com/richest-russian-oligarchs-putin-list-2018-1
28 "Josef Zissels ponders what the Babyn Yar Museum should be like", *Ukrainian Jewish Encounter*, February 11, 2019, https://ukrainianjewishencounter.org/en/josef-zissels-ponders-what-the-babyn-yar-museum-should-be-like/

outlets, such as *The New York Times*, are paying greater attention to this problem.²⁹

In the context of its war for independence, Ukrainian society may agree to some restrictions on political freedoms, such as suspending the right to broadcast of the three above-mentioned TV channels that represented the interests of the aggressor country in Ukraine. For Ukrainians, their own state is not an abstraction, but a collective value that must now be protected against the aggression of the "Russian world" since the latter deliberately destroys any sprouts of democratic political culture. The Ukrainian state, with all its legal systems and institutions, should be allowed and empowered to protect the previously mentioned ideals of freedom and justice.

With these considerations in mind, it is important for Ukrainian society not to perceive the behavior of Ukraine's international allies, aimed at protecting their own national interests, as a kind of "hybrid partnership" whose actors are heedless of their own declared values and principles. On the contrary, it is important for Ukraine itself, while the situation of undeclared war with Russia persists, to act in accordance with its instincts for self-preservation and survival, relying, first and foremost, on its own forces, army, economy, and robust society.

Even before the need to fight corruption and ensure economic growth, the very first question that Ukrainians must answer is the question: who are we? And this question is directly related to collective dignity and national identity.

---

29 Maria Varenikova and Andrew E. Kramer, "A Tech-Savvy Holocaust Memorial in Ukraine Draws Critics and Crowds", *The New York Times*, October 5–8, 2021: https://www.nytimes.com/2021/10/05/world/europe/ukraine-holocaust-babyn-yar.html

Media, Public Rhetoric, and Culture in the Context of Ukraine's War for Independence from Russia[30]

Just before this latest Russian attack on Ukraine, I published an article entitled "The Battle for History and Building of Identity: Fake News confronts Professional News".[31] Now that hostilities are going full blast, it is clear that this conversation needs to continue in order to analyze its three main actors: Russia, Ukraine, and the so-called "Collective West". This conversation is about the world in which we live, a world which is facing enormous problems related to honesty and dignity.

Russia Is an International Terrorist And Russian Society Is Putin's Accomplice in Crime

Russia's attack on Ukraine has revealed many problems in mutual understanding, and the search for common ground in a globalized world. If we do not find a way to understand each other, we will simply destroy our planet. We should start with the definition of the "Ukrainian crisis". It is not a crisis; it is a war. And it did not start in 2022, and not even in 2014. In fact, it has been going on for centuries, ever since it became possible to talk about the history of Ukraine and the history of Russia.

It is very problematic to find common ground even among professional historians as to when these two histories began and what the actual difference is between Ukrainian and Russian cultural products. This is because Russia has never had any qualms about using a stolen name, acting as no more than a marginal product of Mongol slavery.

That is why Putin is now trying to seize Kyiv, a city which is the capital of both modern Ukraine and of the state called Rus' in

---

30 *StopFake*, April 9, 2022.
31 Serhiy Kvit, "The Battle for History and Building of Identity: Fake News confronts Professional News", *StopFake*, October 23, 2021, https://bit.ly/3iZ2Mo4

the early Middle Ages—at a time when neither Moscow nor Russia, which dates back to the beginning of the eighteenth century, even existed. The history of relations between Ukraine and Russia is not simply the history of the Ukrainian struggle for independence. Russian society deems it necessary to destroy Ukraine because that society perceives Ukraine as a mirror that it finds frightening to look into. That is why Russia is the existential enemy of Ukraine. This really is a question of life and death.

In addition to this irrational background of Russian imperialism (today, Putinism), there is another quite rational reason for Russia's barbarous behavior towards Ukraine. Two days before Russia invaded Ukraine, Professor Robert Person and Ambassador Michael McFaul wrote that "Putin is threatened by a successful democracy in Ukraine. He cannot tolerate a successful, flourishing, and democratic Ukraine on his borders, especially if the Ukrainian people also begin to prosper economically".[32] In other words, this is about two different political cultures and the two different geopolitical choices made by Ukrainians and Russians.

Thanks to the inverted Russian public consciousness that inspired Vladimir Putin to create the world's largest fake news factory, the names of many criminal regimes along with their practices, such as 'Nazism', 'fascism', and 'genocide' have been depreciated. And now we are documenting actual genocide—the deliberate and systematic destruction of Ukrainians, Ukrainian cities, Ukrainian statehood, Ukrainian language, and Ukrainian history.

We are seeing numerous bodies of tortured and murdered civilians strewn on the streets of Ukrainian cities and villages liberated from the Russians, we keep hearing survivors' recounting the terror, harassment and rapes during the Russian occupation. In the temporarily occupied territories we see attempts to replace Ukrainian street names with Soviet names, to remove and destroy Ukrainian books and impose Russian as the language of instruction in Ukrainian schools.

---

32 Robert Person and Michael McFaul, "What Putin Fears Most", *Journal of Democracy*, February 22, 2022, https://bit.ly/3jiFtG0

Intercepted conversations between Russian military personnel in Ukraine and their wives and parents (published on social media) are unprecedented evidence of base and brutal family relations and a frightening insight into the degradation and depravity of Russian society. Russian mothers use profanity even more freely than their sons (such brutal communication is impossible in Ukrainian families and Ukrainians regard such speech as proof of Russians' extreme barbarity). Wives tell their husbands what household items and clothing they should steal from Ukrainian shops or loot from living or dead Ukrainians.

Russians send looted televisions, washing machines, air conditioners, electric scooters, video cards, batteries, children's toys, women's products, shampoos, shower gels, frying pans, etc. by post; other looted items, including stolen cars, are being sold at a special bazaar in Narovlia, a town in Belarus. This market was specifically opened for buying and selling possessions looted in Ukraine.

This shameful behavior has global consequences. In London, for example, an initiative was launched to take old items and furniture, rags, used household appliances, and other rubbish to the Russian embassy[33] — this is what the Russian army and its citizens really need today.

At the beginning of the twenty-first century, we must face a nation of looters, and this must serve as a warning to others: human regression is possible and you can observe it in Russian society. This society loves Putin[34] and supports a "final solution of the Ukrainian question", i.e. the complete destruction of Ukraine as a state and the physical annihilation of Ukrainians.

Special plans and ideological justifications were prepared for this purpose. The most eloquent was the Russian political strategist

---

33   https://bit.ly/3fUK4jy
34   According to a survey conducted by the Levada Center on March 24–30, 2022, support for Vladimir Putin's actions by Russians rose to 83% (more than 10% compared to similar polls in January and February of that year); 15% of Russians "disapprove" of Putin's actions. Interestingly, 51% of respondents said that the actions of the Russian armed forces in Ukraine have intensified feelings of pride in Russia, https://bit.ly/3DBGQJp

Timofey Sergeytsev's article explaining the need for a systematic destruction of Ukrainians and the Ukrainian state based on Putin's policy goals.[35] It's a matter of fact that Russian society is unable to look at itself ironically from the outside and be horrified by the depth of its own degradation.

The Russians are afraid of us because they understand that we know everything about them. For centuries, Ukrainians have been witnessing Russian crimes. After the liberation of the suburban settlements near Kyiv, one liberal Ukrainian humanitarian, horrified by the mass killings, which the fleeing Russian military did not have time to hide, wrote on social media: "Your language is inhuman. Your literature is inhuman. Your whole 'culture' is inhuman. Burn in hell, beasts. We will kill you all here. And after our victory, we will not leave you alone anywhere in the world, don't doubt this even for a moment".

It should be noted that fact-checking technologies will shortly allow the creation of a comprehensive evidence database of the crimes committed by Russia and Russians in Ukraine. For example, according to information gathered by InformNapalm, a volunteer intelligence gathering NGO, the soldiers of the 64th separate motorized infantry brigade of the Russian Defense Ministry's combined army executed the genocide of Ukrainians in Bucha, near Kyiv (photos and videos of their atrocities have been published in the world's media).

This military brigade is stationed in Kniaze-Volkonskoje, a village of the Eastern Military District in the Khabarovsk area. The brigade commander is Lieutenant Colonel Azatbek Omurbekov (patronymic: Asanbekovich), his email: mnac1981@gmail.com, tel. (4212) 397103. Anyone who wants to can even find lists of all the looted items sent by the Russian military to their families, as well as the names of their relatives who are now using items that once belonged to murdered Ukrainians, as well as their addresses and telephone numbers in Russia.

---

35 Timofey Sergeytsev. "What Should Russia do with Ukraine?" (in Russian), *Ria Novosti*, April 3, 2022; *The Ukrainian Post* (in English), April 5, 2022, https://bit.ly/3LN2yg8

Ukraine and the Collective West: The Need to Know Each Other

This war has demonstrated not only Ukrainians' amazing resilience and their determination to resist. This war has also given a new articulation to old stereotypes of Russians, who throughout their history have been unable to create anything of their own, but have always tried to steal what they liked from others. Such judgments are only now beginning to sound pertinent in the global media context of a suddenly "awakened" collective West. It is also quite possible that the Bolsheviks' desire "to grab (something from somebody) and divide" does not come from Marxism as such, but has its roots in Russian tradition.

The Russian army wanted to plant fear in Ukraine and it wanted a blitzkrieg. Instead, it was met with the contempt of a free people for slaves who don't have their own will or their own understanding of events. Russians were shocked and awed by the iron discipline, the highly competent response of Ukraine's Armed Forces, the country's nationwide mass volunteer movement, and the fantastic self-organization of Ukrainian society. A nation of looters against a nation of volunteers—this is all you need to know about the Russian-Ukrainian war, a battle which still threatens to escalate into World War III.

The Ukrainian media discussion is developing in step with the evolving war. In a disrespectful and disparaging way, Ukrainians call the Russian military "moskals" and "katsaps" (pejorative Ukrainian terms for Russians originating in the eighteenth century), "orcs" (the evil forces serving darkness in *The Lord of the Rings* by J. R. R. Tolkien), as well as looters, rapists, murderers (this corresponds to the established behavior of the Russian army), and Rushists (from the famous neologism coined by Chechen leader Dzhokhar Dudaiev, who combined two meanings in one word: Russian and fascist).

The collective West can no longer hide behind pretended historical ignorance and "convenient" legends about the USSR as a "great ally" in the World War II struggle against German Nazism. Elementary common sense helps one to understand that Stalin started the war as a natural ally of Hitler and only later, under certain circumstances, escaped punishment for the crimes of communism, including the "invention" of the GULAG concentration camps and crimes of the Holodomor (Great Famine). Today, we understand better than anyone that unpunished evil continues to push Russia into committing new crimes against humanity.

The collective West has itself created the image of its clumsy counterpart in the form of tsarist Russia/the Soviet Union/Putin's Russia, which also played a certain positive role as it emphasized the propriety of the Western way of life, even as it allowed it to admire the "mystery of the Russian soul", its achievements in opera, literature, figure skating, and ballet. The problem is that all Russian culture is imperial and chauvinistic, permeated with hatred of other cultures and traditions.

A whole caste of admirers of "great Russian culture" was formed in Western think tanks, mostly funded by the Russians themselves. Until 2022, this caste persistently justified the "special path" of Putin's regime. Its supporters, Western journalists with similar views, were long ago given the informal name of "the Duranty club"[36] in Ukraine.

They were busy spreading Russian fakes and narratives, promoting the myth about the existence of independent journalism and a free press in Russia, creating the modern pro-Russian discourse. According to Ukrainian political analyst Olexiy Haran, even now, during the war, international journalism was largely captive to Russian propaganda; it could improve by being more professional and presenting better materials with a real understanding of Ukraine.[37]

Here we are talking about a deeper crisis of the collective West, which includes the impotence of the UN, the corrosion of the moral compass of the Red Cross, which is helping to gain "international approval" for the forced deportation of Ukrainians to the

---

36 Walter Duranty (1884–1957) was an American journalist who headed the Moscow bureau of *The New York Times*, interviewed Stalin, and won the Pulitzer Prize in 1932. He claimed that there was no Holodomor.
37 Olexiy Haran, "Exactly according to Goebbels: how Russian propaganda penetrates world TV channels", *Local History* (in Ukrainian), April 1, 2022, https://bit.ly/38e6w2S

Russian Federation[38] during the current war, the openly pro-Putin position of Hungary, which is a member of the EU, and other similar examples.

And what is happening beyond the borders of good and evil? Today there is a fair number of viewpoints that, in fact, it was not Vladimir Putin who intimidated Russians when creating his totalitarian regime, but rather that Russian society found in Putin the much desired "strong leader" embodying the entire spectrum of Russian imperial stereotypes and complexes. Such social mechanisms support the phenomenon of post-truth, in which large segments of the national audience, without any pressure or coercion from the authorities, do not want to see a holistic and true picture of the world. Instead, they demand convenient and comfortable news only. In other words, they choose fake news.

Conclusions

If we compare Ukrainian and Russian social values, we will see that they differ dramatically. It is not just about different political interests, but about two completely different ways of thinking and living, and, as mentioned above, two different political cultures. The demand for freedom of speech and the ability to think critically on the Ukrainian side is being attacked by the fake media reality and deep moral degradation on the Russian side.

Hence, the slogan "Kyiv versus Moscow", coined by the Ukrainian liberation movement in the twentieth century, is superimposed on the clash of older, early modern metaphors: "Second Jerusalem" (Kyiv as a symbol of justice) standing against the "Third Rome" (another name Moscow chose for itself, to symbolize its imperial Russian despotism). In an interview with the Polish journalist and literary critic Sławomir Sierakowski, Timothy Snyder said that "If Ukrainians were not fighting, the world would be a darker

---

38 EuroMaidan SOS Statement on inadmissibility of international "approval" of the forced deportation of Ukrainians to the Russian Federation: https://www.facebook.com/531592303/posts/10158568141847304/?d=n

place"; "Putin's ideology and propaganda got exhausted"; "Ukraine is acting bravely and wisely".[39]

These days, looking at Ukraine as it defends its independence, dignity, and justice, many politicians in various countries around the world are asking themselves: "How would my country and I myself behave in such a situation?"

[1] Serhiy Kvit. The Battle for History and Building of Identity: Fake News confronts Professional News // Stop Fake, Oct 23, 2021: https://bit.ly/3iZ2Mo4
[2] Robert Person and Michael McFaul. What Putin Fears Most // Journal of Democracy; February 22, 2022: https://bit.ly/3jiFtG0
[3] According to a survey conducted by the Levada Center on March 24–30, 2022, support for Vladimir Putin's actions by Russians rose to 83% (more than 10% compared to similar polls in January and February of that year); 15% of Russians "disapprove" of Putin's actions. Interestingly, 51% of respondents said that the actions of the Russian armed forces in Ukraine have intensified feelings of pride in Russia: https://bit.ly/3DBGQJp
[4] Timofey Sergeytsev. What should Russia do with Ukraine? // Ria Novosti, Apr. 3; The Ukrainian Post, Apr. 5 (in English): https://bit.ly/3LN2yg8
[5] Walter Duranty (1884–1957) — An American journalist who headed the Moscow bureau of the New York Times, interviewed Stalin, a 1932 Pulitzer Prize winner. He claimed that there was no Holodomor.
[6] Olexiy Haran. Exactly according to Goebbels: how Russian propaganda penetrates world TV channels // Local History, April 1, 2022: https://bit.ly/38e6w2S
[7] EuroMaidan SOS Statement on inadmissibility of international "approval" of the forced deportation of Ukrainians to the Russian Federation: https://www.facebook.com/531592303/posts/10158568141847304/?d=n
[8] Tymothy Snyder: If Ukrainian were not Fighting, the World would be Much Darker // Texty.org.ua, 10 March 2022: https://bit.ly/3x58rBg

---

39   Timothy Snyder, "If Ukrainian were not Fighting, the World would be Much Darker", *Texty.org.ua* (in Ukrainian), March 10, 2022, https://bit.ly/3x58rBg

The Russia-Ukraine War through the Prism of Mass Communications[40]

Ukraine's struggle for independence from Russia has become truly global from the perspective of mass communications. This war is universally covered in the world media. It is extremely visible. It is a war that demands the expression of public judgment, thus becoming a point of political identification. The current confrontation between Russian and Ukrainian media discourses is not an ordinary clash of warring parties' propaganda rhetoric. In this war, Western civilization is searching for an answer to a question of utmost importance: can it stand in its own value framework — or is it no longer able to do so?

The idealistic self-image of the Western world and the system of international security which was shaped after World War II have gradually receded into the past. After the collapse of the Soviet Union, a wave of corruption that was no longer held back by the Iron Curtain and by Russia's aggressive politics fully destroyed both the image and the system. At the beginning of the twenty-first century, the "Ukrainian question" created a new global context in which political time has accelerated with vertiginous speed: many political leaders do not have the time to orient themselves and change their rhetoric to adapt to new circumstances that are often unsustainable.

"Convenient" Russia and Unusual Ukraine

In fact, before it could begin to understand the causes of the current Russian-Ukrainian war (which started with the Revolution of Dignity in 2014) as the result of many centuries of confrontation between the two countries (their political cultures and civilizational choices), the convenient and supposedly comprehensible Russian context, which was fully shaped in the Cold War, began to fall apart in the mindset of the Western world. Michael McFaul outlined the

---

40 *StopFake*, May 13, 2022.

emergence of this new global confrontation, connected with Putin's regime, as a transition from Cold War to Hot Peace.[41]

In its reset confrontation with Russia, the Western world, in 2014, was surprised to see Ukraine on its side as a player guided by idealism. That seemed strange to practice-oriented and materialist-minded Western politicians. Moreover, they had not seemed to ask Ukrainians for anything. In time it became clear that nobody would be able to remain silent or hide from the new realities.

It should be noted that not everyone understood this at once. For instance, in 2017 Council of Europe Parliamentary Assembly President Pedro Agramunt did not realize that the days of such high-profile pro-Putin politicians and well-paid managers as Gerhard Schroeder were over. After his trip to Syria with a delegation of Russian parliamentarians and meeting with the Syrian president Bashar al-Assad, Agramunt was stripped of his powers after the Council passed a vote of no confidence against him. A benign image of Russia and Russian institutions is still psychologically held by many Western leaders, who see them as part of the global order and a necessary element for international stability.

Even the Vatican sometimes has difficulty distinguishing between good and evil, what is black and what is white, who is the victim and who is the criminal. The Vatican's symbolic decision to have a Russian woman and a Ukrainian woman carry a cross together[42] during a Good Friday procession presided over by Pope Francis, in the face of numerous crimes against humanity being committed by the Russian army in Ukraine, and despite the uproar of many Ukrainians, could only stem from the fear of calling things by their right names.

The non-contextuality of the Vatican was evidenced by the Pope's dubious allusions to and vague retellings of Russian-Leftist conspiracy narratives about NATO's "guilt", "other states" that provoked the war, and the possible "harm" of arms aid to

---

41 Michael McFaul, *From Cold War to Hot Peace: An American Ambassador in Putin's Russia* (New York: HarperCollins, 2018).
42 Inés San Martin, "As pope extols peace, Ukrainian and Russian women carry the cross together", *Crux*, April 16, 2022, https://bit.ly/3KyyS5p

Ukraine.[43] It was also unclear how the 5 million Ukrainian refugees forced out of their homes by Russia's war should react to the Pope's remarks that they are better received in the countries where they've sought refuge because they are white.[44] Such an inability to express or unwillingness to understand the true causes of the tragedy lie at the root of the crisis of the contemporary West, a crisis characterised by an almost complete lack of responsibility and the absence of genuine leadership.

One of the most disturbing and cartoonish examples of the West's crisis of values was the letter from a "group of German intellectuals" to German Chancellor Olaf Scholz demanding that Ukraine capitulate.[45] It is necessary to understand that such logic, or rather its absence, is common not only in Germany, with its complicated guilt over the crimes of Nazism, the legacy of the omnipresent East German Stasi (*Ministerium für Staatssicherheit*) political police, and their habitual policy of loyalty to Russia, a policy that has already passed into the realm of tradition. It should be noted that under the impact of the Russian-Ukrainian war, dramatic ideological changes are taking place within German society and the Germans are reconsidering their business-as-usual views of the world.

The eighteen authors of the above-mentioned letter to Chancellor Scholz demanded that the chancellor stop supplying weapons to Ukraine as Ukraine would likely lose the war anyway. Likewise, Russia is demanding that Ukraine stop resisting the Russian military offensive and its occupation atrocities. According to these politicians, diplomats, singers, and writers, a recognition of the occupation of Crimea, the "independence" of Ukraine's eastern regions, and addressing Russia's "legitimate security interests" would reduce the number of victims and limit the destruction of

---

43 Francis X. Rocca and Evan Gershkovich, "Pope Says NATO Might Have Provoked Russian Invasion of Ukraine", *The Wall Street Journal*, May, 3, 2022, https://on.wsj.com/3w7DMBd
44 "Refugees treated according to their skin colour, Pope says", *Brussels News*, April 16, 2022, https://bit.ly/3MUDzli
45 Tomas Kurianowicz, "Offener Brief fordert von Scholz Stopp der Waffenlieferungen an die Ukraine", *Berliner Zeitung*, April 22, 2022, https://bit.ly/3F1cdxs

Ukrainian cities. It is important to note that Olaf Scholz did not agree to the demands of this letter.

Crisis of International Organizations

In this context, it becomes clear that whatever their viewpoints — professional, conceptual, or moral and ethical — the policy of many international organizations regarding Ukraine and Russia is completely irrelevant. Perhaps, the most striking example is the OSCE's lack of understanding of the fact that Russia has no freedom of speech, no independent media, no professional journalism, and that today one can only distinguish this or that Russian media as either still authoritarian or already totalitarian.

At the time of the Revolution of Dignity, Russian media was completely dismantled and became part of the state propaganda system, which was described in detail in the classic work *Four Theories of the Press*.[46] Putin's Russia saw a return to the Soviet totalitarian models of control over public information, but in much uglier forms.

In particular, the phenomenon of the so-called "Aesopian language" disappeared, along with the extremely small intellectual layer of society able to "read between the lines" of the Soviet propaganda press (no other press existed in the USSR), searching for true messages. Also, the Russian public mind saw the discrediting and burial of the memory of Gorbachev's short-lived "glasnost" (transparency) — the first, small ray of freedom permitted from the top in the entire history of Russia. Instead, since the beginning of the current Russian-Ukrainian war, the OSCE has gone to great lengths to organize cooperation between Russian and Ukrainian journalist organizations in order for them to understand and collaborate with each other.

Since 2014, representatives of Ukraine's Independent Media Trade Union, the Ukrainian National Union of Journalists, and the

---

46 Fred Siebert, Theodore Peterson and Wilbur Schramm, *Four Theories of the Press: The Authoritarian, Libertarian, Social Responsibility, and Soviet Communist Concepts of What the Press Should Be and Do* (Champaign, IL: University of Illinois Press, 1963).

Union of Journalists of Russia held regular meetings to "raise professional standards and improve the safety of journalists in and around the crisis in Ukraine", particularly expressing "their belief that common sense and professional solidarity will be able to overcome the stereotypes and attempts of politicians and propagandists to divide journalists of both countries and turn them into an instrument of manipulation".[47]

Interestingly, the manipulating agent in this project was not only the OSCE, as the organizer, but also the well-known organization Reporters without Borders. These respected media professionals criticized Ukraine for trying to defend its independence from the propaganda impact of the aggressor state: "Information warfare with Russia has had negative consequences that include bans on Russian media and social media, cyber-harassment and treason trials". It also put the blame for the state of affairs in the Russian-occupied Eastern Ukrainian territories on Ukraine, presenting the situation as an internal problem: "The separatist-controlled east of the country is still a no-go area without critical journalists or foreign observers".[48]

In other words, both above-mentioned international organizations worked mostly within the framework of the Russian propaganda discourse, promoting the interests of the aggressor state in the Ukrainian journalistic community. On the other hand, the irresponsible behavior of the leadership of Ukraine's National Union of Journalists turned into open lobbying for Russian interests in the Ukrainian media sphere. Thus, Union chairman Serhiy Tomilenko condemned Ukrainian sanctions against TV channels NewsOne, ZIK I, and 112, which were controlled by Viktor Medvedchuk, a pro-Russian politician close to Putin.[49]

---

47 Maria Kuchma, ed., *Two Countries – One Profession: The proceedings of the meetings of representatives of journalistic organizations from Russia and Ukraine under the auspices of the OSCE Representative on Freedom of the Media* (in Russian) (OSCE: Vienna, 2016), https://bit.ly/3LBh2QO
48 "Ukraine" (2021), Reporters without Borders, https://rsf.org/en/country/ukraine
49 "Serhiy Tomilenko on Zelenskyy's sanctions against Kozak, Newsone, ZIK, and 112", NRUS.info, February 3, 2021, https://bit.ly/38H8wRH

Transparency International took the same road, constantly representing Ukraine as a country more corrupt than Russia. According to the Corruption Perception Index 2021, Ukraine was three points ahead of Russia.[50] This was convincingly refuted by the very course of hostilities in late February 2022. The Ukrainian Army, unlike the Russian army, has proved itself to be competent, motivated, and better provisioned. It is quite obvious that Russian corruption is one of Ukraine's main allies. It was this corruption that turned the Russian army into a gang of killers, rapists, and looters.

The lack of professionalism that international organizations have shown in their attitude towards Ukraine is rooted in their lack of understanding of the role of a strong civil society in all spheres of Ukrainian public life, from the high level of public demands made to the authorities, to the public's impact on the progress of necessary reforms, to the fight against corruption—and to the huge mobilization potential of the volunteer movement. According to a survey conducted by the *Rating* sociological group on April 6, 2022, about 80% of Ukrainians support their country financially or by volunteering.[51]

Armed Civil Society

If the West wants to understand Ukraine better, it should start with Ukrainians themselves, because today it is Ukrainian society that acts as the real leader of the country, forcing the politicians to meet its demands. In recent years, this society has been restructuring itself.

Today local communities and their leaders have demonstrated extraordinary endurance and resilience, even under Russian occupation. These are the fruits of Ukraine's successful decentralization reform. Impressive Ukrainian self-organization, mutual assistance, confidence in society, and the ability to deploy a decentralized

---

50 Corruption Perceptions Index—2021 (Ukraine: 32 points; Russia: 29 points), Transparency International Ukraine, https://cpi.ti-ukraine.org/
51 Ukrainian Ministry of Finance, April 6, 2022, https://minfin.com.ua/ua/2022/04/08/83414797/

armed movement to resist Russian aggression—these are the phenomena that should primarily interest Western experts.

The military volunteer movement deserves special attention. It even has a separate term in the Ukrainian language—"dobrovoltsi", meaning good-willed. During this war in particular, Ukrainian territorial defense units and other volunteer formations often proved more effective than the so-called elite Russian troops. These are not mercenaries or paramilitary formations. In modern terms, we are talking about an armed civil society.

To understand the origins of this movement, we have to look at the roots of the deeply respected traditional Ukrainian values of personal rights and freedoms, the history of the democratic political culture of the early medieval Kyivan Rus, the military culture of the frontier, which was the basis for the early modern formation of the Ukrainian nation in the sixteenth and seventeenth centuries, the national liberation movement of modern and contemporary history, and finally the Ukrainian revolutions of the twenty-first century: the Orange Revolution (2004) and the Revolution of Dignity (2013–2014).

Conclusions

As we can see, in order to truly understand, one needs to know a fair amount. The post-truth phenomenon has forced us to rethink in what way postmodernism differs from lies, to what degree the return of history with its accompanying wars is a modernist project, and whether the global conflict of interpretations over the nature of justice can ever be truly resolved. Finally, the lethal considerations over which is more important, law or justice, helplessly sketch out the skepticism of the world's largest states about the prospects of democracy.

China and the Russian Federation, the two largest states on our planet, question the effectiveness of democracy. (Russian president Vladimir Putin long ago made it clear that democracy needs to be "managed" and he has been doing exactly that since he came to power.) China and Russia want the era of "Western domination" to end and to replace it with their own domination. There is, of course, considerable shame in the history of Western civilization. However, the West has the capacity to look at itself from the outside, to criticize itself and consider an array of opinions, to reconsider its actions and, eventually, to renew itself. China and Russia would never dream of giving in to such dangerous self-analysis.

Some say that democracy and international law are nothing more than a means of domination invented by the West to the detriment of other countries that also want to dominate. A new global critique of modernization and Westernization as a kind of evil design, but now opposed by a different, undisguised malevolent intention. And, again, because there is no place for an idealistic Ukrainian society seeking truth and justice, Ukrainians are expressing their views on the battlefield.

From the perspective of the clash of concepts and public rhetoric, Ukrainians' courage and the responsible leadership and actions demonstrated at the national level first of all by Poland, the Baltic States, the United States, the United Kingdom, and Canada require a deeper analysis to find a new common political language and global understanding. Civilized nations do not impose their "brotherhood" or supremacy on others. They should rather respect each other and agree on rules for cooperation and conflict resolution. They should help each other in difficult circumstances. These simple truths must be embodied in a new public discourse that would be understandable by and acceptable to everyone.

Towards the Freedom-Seeking Mission of the Ukrainian University[52]

What do we know about the challenges faced by universities and intellectuals in a country with a long history of statelessness? In this essay, I address this question by looking at the development of the Ukrainian university. In the post-Soviet environment, institutions that are regarded as higher education entities very often have nothing to do with genuine university traditions. For example, the ability to issue higher education diplomas is not a sufficient condition for being an institution of higher education. However, that is not always obvious in the post-Soviet circumstances. Instead of adhering to global organizational standards of purpose and values, some post-Soviet politicians and academics show a tendency to take pride in the international competitiveness and scientific achievements of the Soviet period, when the totalitarian state spent considerable resources to meet the needs of the military-industrial complex and communist propaganda. In this way, university communities are tempted to remain in the shadow of the narratives created by the colonizer. In this essay, I will explore the implications of this from the viewpoint of decolonization, increased social significance, and, as a matter of fact, the (re)establishment of Ukrainian academia.

Farewell to the Soviet University

My disagreements with the Soviet university began back in 1987, when, as a student, I was defending my right to wear a homemade blue-and-yellow badge (the colors of the Ukrainian national flag). At the time of Perestroika, Soviet power still labeled the Ukrainian national flag "fascist". In addition, I was not allowed by the university library to borrow books by Mykhailo Hrushevskyi, who was a prominent Ukrainian historian and head of the first Ukrainian parliament (1917–1918), as he was labeled a kind of "fascist" as well.

---

52 *Universities & Intellectuals* (2021) 1, no. 1: 30–35.

The Soviet ideologues did not actually care that Hrushevskyi was a socialist. He was a Ukrainian—and that was a problem.

My final farewell to the Soviet university took place in 1989. The Associate Dean of my Faculty of Journalism, a Communist party member who was born and raised in the USSR, but who had hated the Russian and Communist occupation regime all his life, asked me to help him carry a huge bust of Lenin out of the university room, as if we were planning to wash it. This was our explanation to those who asked us: "Where are you taking Lenin?" However, as soon as we stepped into the dark basement, the Associate Dean suddenly said: "Now, Serhiy, just throw it as far as you can!" That was the first, but not the last, destroyed monument of Lenin that I witnessed. At about the same period, optional attendance of university lectures was initiated at the Faculty of Journalism, which allowed students to give up many communist (or so-called "Marxist-Leninist") subjects, which had previously been mandatory.

Thus, the first precondition for the creation of a non-Soviet university was that it be Ukrainian. Lenin was perceived as the leader of the colonizing and repressive power, and his presence had to be removed from the national academy, symbolically as well as ideologically. The opposition forces aimed at breaking Ukraine free of the USSR were gaining in strength. In the history of the pro-independence movement, it is deeply representative that the first open public meeting in Kyiv was organized in 1988 by "Hromada" (literally, "community" or "the whole society"), an informal, illegal, but no longer underground student organization. Among other political claims, the rally demanded the restoration of the Kyiv-Mohyla Academy.

The memory of the Kyiv-Mohyla Academy, founded in 1615 and closed in the first years of Soviet rule in the mid-1920s, was so strong that it was absolutely obvious to the Ukrainian intellectuals that this higher education institution had to be restored. In 1992, the National University of Kyiv-Mohyla Academy was re-established and enrolled its first students. In symbolic terms, this was the first time in modern history that the new Ukrainian discourse defeated the (post-)Soviet discourse. It became a Ukrainian university, one where Ukrainian was not a declarative or tokenistic term anymore.

After the collapse of the Soviet Union, the Kyiv-Mohyla Academy became the experimental platform for practically all innovations implemented in Ukrainian higher education, including the first Bachelor's, Master's, and PhD programs; two languages of instruction (Ukrainian and English); a unique system of entrance exams, which later served as the basic model for the creation of external independent exams at the national level; the cross-disciplinary terms of admission to master's programs; as well as a range of university policies (e.g., on academic integrity, internationalization, comprehensive university autonomy, anti-corruption, etc.), which served as new benchmarks for reforming Ukrainian academia.

The Challenges of Comprehensive University Autonomy

After the Orange Revolution (2004), the concept of comprehensive university autonomy was shaped by a Consortium on University Autonomy, which included reform-oriented representatives of eight universities in different regions of Ukraine, committed to embracing academic, financial, and administrative self-sufficiency. The idea was promoted through the Law of Ukraine "On Higher Education", which was drafted by the intellectual community with the support of Ukrainian civil society. This law represented opposition to Viktor Yanukovych's authoritarian regime, which was advocating stronger business relations with Russia; it also counteracted the legislative revisions enacted by the Russian chauvinist Dmytro Tabachnyk, Minister of Education and Science in 2012–2013. The process of adopting the new law, as designed by grassroots academics, was a tiring battle. The law was promulgated by the Verkhovna Rada (Parliament) of Ukraine only after the victory of the Revolution of Dignity in 2014.

At present, every step in developing the higher education system in Ukraine is directly and indirectly viewed through the lens of implementing comprehensive university autonomy. This movement is widely supported. It is seen as a safeguard against corruption, since the importance of reputation comes first. Comprehensive university autonomy is also used as a means of internationalization, quality improvement, and fundraising at Ukrainian higher educational institutions (HEIs) (Konrad-Adenauer-Stiftung Ukraine Office, 2017).

However, university transformations take place in a market-oriented economy, and in the context of global neoliberalism. Notably, in Ukraine there is no clear understanding of the peculiarities of the neoliberal approach. Opponents of university autonomy include politicians and bureaucrats who are supporters of the Soviet-style power of "hands-on control" over HEIs by the Government. Indeed, the implementation of comprehensive university autonomy, with all its market rhetoric of competition, self-regulation, and institutional responsibility, undoubtedly represents a challenge to such politicians — they do not understand the importance of education for the future of society.

In seeking liberalization of the university, which in the past promoted strict ministerial control over social and economic discourses and professional development requirements, Ukrainian intellectuals had to identify a way to create a new mission for the contemporary Ukrainian university, enabling it to exist in the new reality, where the national economy, in deep and permanent crises of transformation, was unable to support a "free-floating" system of as many as 1,200 higher education institutions. To succeed, the Ukrainian university needed a thoroughly sophisticated concept of "comprehensive university autonomy", as I have argued earlier.[53]

Clash of Ideologies and Political Context

It has been very interesting to observe the return of a left-wing discourse to the Ukrainian political agenda. This time, the discourse claims to be modeled after the Frankfurt School traditions.[54] Yet it is rather aggressive in its opposition to the national liberation discourse, despite the seemingly obvious fact that decolonization is

---

53 Serhiy Kvit, "Higher education in Ukraine in the Time of Independence: Between Brownian Motion and Revolutionary Reform", *Kyiv-Mohyla Humanities Journal*, 7: 141–159, http://kmhj.ukma.edu.ua/article/view/219666
54 A. D. Livtochenko, "Critical Sociology of the Frankfurt School: Between Science and Ideology" (in Russian), *Sociological Studios* (2014) 1, no. 4: 24–29.

extremely vital in Ukraine's struggle against Russian aggression since 2014. The neo-Marxist rhetorical criticism used by modern authoritarian regimes does not remove its historical affinity with various "progressive" and alternative conceptions of the past, including the traditions of the 1917 Russian revolution and the "Marxist and Leninist" infringements of "just order".[55] Also, the neo-Marxists uncritically shy away from the fact that Soviet communism was nothing if not a reincarnation of ordinary Russian imperialism. The post-Soviet versions of neo-Marxism, which are typically extremely intolerant of other opinions, ignore the postcolonial nature of the Ukrainian liberation tradition. The neo-Marxists reactivate their habitual rhetorical clichés, including accusing members of the Ukrainian liberation movement of "fascism" (welcome back to the USSR!).

At the same time, even supporters of market-based approaches to educational reforms tend to perceive "leftist" demands as justified, because of "academic freedom", which gives equal consideration to ideological discourses—presumably the only way to create high-quality education in Ukraine. I venture to suggest that such an approach to the marketplace of ideas, although customary in the Western context, is very problematic in "embattled Ukraine".[56] Unfortunately, the anti-Ukrainian rhetoric promoted by Russian propaganda and pro-Russian forces presents a challenge to the concept and practice of the modern research university, as it is understood in the discourse of international higher education.[57] To implement a freedom-oriented project of higher learning, the vulnerable Ukrainian state needs a powerful strategy for ideological and organizational capacity-building, and economic

---

55 Serhiy Kvit, "Ukraine in the struggle for independence in the age of post-truth", *Kyiv Post*, June 13, 2019, https://bit.ly/3m8MJ7Z
56 Serhiy Kvit, *The Battlefront of Civilizations: Education in Ukraine* (Kyiv: Kyiv Mohyla Academy Publishing House, 2015); Anatoly Oleksiyenko, Serhii Terepyshchyi, Olga Gomilko and Denys Svyrydenko, "'What Do You Mean, You Are a Refugee in Your Own Country?': Displaced Scholars and Identities in Embattled Ukraine", European Journal of Higher Education 11, no. 2 (2021): 1–18, https://doi.org/10.1080/21568235.2020.1777446
57 Philip G. Altbatch and Jamil Sami, eds., *The Road to Academic Excellence: The Making of World-Class Research Universities* (Washington, DC: The World Bank, 2011).

resources to mobilize this strategy. However, the state lacks a strategic vision.

Talk of neoliberal reforms in Ukraine continues to sustain the rhetoric of the "transition period". The perpetuation of this rhetoric is advantageous to many political forces, above all, to Ukraine's oligarchs. Thirty years after the collapse of the Soviet economy and higher education system, we still have not developed a new model of the Ukrainian university. Ukrainian state power is still weak—postcolonial. At the same time, the Ukrainian nation is fighting against a powerful aggressor, that is, authoritarian chauvinist Russia. Ukraine must mobilize its society and implement reforms in extremely difficult circumstances. In this environment, enabling indiscriminate freedom means empowering the adherents of the "Russian World" to support Putin's efforts in occupying and destroying Ukraine.

The creation of an independent Ukrainian state and university does not, and should not, imply defiance of modernization efforts, simply because of problems with neoliberal interpretations of the global competition of ideas. The rejection of the neoliberal discourse of competition tends, indeed, to underpin the rejection of the modernization of Ukrainian society. This is revealed, on the one hand, in careless implementation of the best international models of quality assurance in higher education. It also seen in the neglect or depreciation of the diversity of institutional models: e.g., teaching universities, polytechnics, community and vocational colleges. On the other hand, the rejection can be traced to unwillingness or inability to establish a modern research university in Ukraine that would be internationally competitive.

The modern Ukrainian university should be based on the priorities facing the independent state of Ukraine today. It should serve the purposes of intellectual mobilization in defense of the values underpinning the traditions of Western democracy, for which millions of Ukrainians died in the last century and are still dying today in Crimea and Donbas. Only then could the freedom-seeking values of a Ukrainian university be considered holistic and universal. Only then would it address the most fundamental needs of contemporary Ukrainian society.

However, the first priority must be Ukrainian independence. If Ukraine does not withstand Russian attacks, it will become part of the "Russian World" with its characteristic authoritarian models of political culture.[58] In other words, an up-to-date Ukrainian political model, including a new Ukrainian university, is incompatible with any extreme right-wing (authoritarian rejection of pluralism) or extreme left-wing (authoritarian "politically correct") intolerance. In the context of the war with an imperial revanchist power, it is essential to ensure the pluralism that primes society for decolonization, prevents the questioning of the status of the Ukrainian language, strengthens public institutions, and guarantees the rule of law, thus protecting the national security of an independent Ukraine.

What Kind of University Mission Does Ukraine Need?

It should be a simple matter for Ukrainian universities to combine such concepts as nurturing national leadership with the ability to interact globally, to embrace radical modernization (Westernization and internationalization), to *implement* the university's social mission, as well as shape an ambitious agenda for the development of a national state, one which would be capable of ensuring the effective realization of democratic rights and freedoms, economic prosperity and sustainability.

Most importantly, Ukraine must abandon (post-)Soviet traditions of self-isolation, and Ukrainian intellectual discourse must become global and contextual.

---

58 Serhiy Kvit, "A perspective on 'fake news'", *Kyiv Post*, October 26, 2019, https://bit.ly/3digpvk

Higher Education in Ukraine in the Time of Independence
Between Brownian Motion and Revolutionary Reform[59]

The goal of this chapter is to identify major milestones and set out the relationships between the main tasks involved in reforming Ukrainian higher education. This goal can be met on the condition that one understands the nature and process of reforms. On the one hand, I am called upon as a scholar to maintain an "objective" position. However, I have frequently been a participant in events, so my view is somewhat biased by my position in the process, and is not that of an outside observer. This determines my research methodology: case studies. Each case belongs to a certain time period, political situation, with its available opportunities and, therefore, involves differences in the way tasks were set and the degree to which achieving successful results was realistic.

Since the collapse of the Soviet Union in 1991, higher education in Ukraine has constantly undergone significant change. Two main time periods can be identified: before and after 2005. Prior to the Orange Revolution (2004), changes were chaotic and mainly aimed at the survival of higher education institutions during the transitional period, which was characterized by a severe economic crisis. This period was more reminiscent of Brownian motion than a defined reform agenda. Starting in 2005, the concept of university autonomy gradually became dominant in Ukraine's higher education discourse, and so today, changes, one way or another, are viewed in terms of whether they further this paradigm.

A global agenda-related rhetoric prevails in today's Ukraine, with both the state and the development of many (if not most) sectors being compared, in the first place, to their counterparts in the European Union. After the Revolution of Dignity (2013–2014), Ukrainian society became increasingly integrated into international

---

59 *Kyiv-Mohyla Humanities Journal* (2020) 7: 141–159.

contexts, and as a result, academic integrity, numerous violations of which were a constant reminder of the slow pace of reform in higher education, has received increasing discussion. In this chapter, we will examine the course higher education reform in Ukraine has taken in the period of state independence, with the aim of identifying its main achievements and failures, as well as the reasons desired progress has stalled.

Shaping the Concept of University Autonomy

From the very beginning of Ukrainian independence, it was unclear what exactly should be done to reform the higher education system. Although isolated from global trends, Ukrainian universities still felt part of the competitive Soviet system, which had, however, suddenly ceased to exist with the collapse of the Soviet Union. An illusory notion gained popularity, and it was believed that if the "best achievements" of the Soviet heritage (i.e. centralized, state-led management of the higher education sector) could be maintained and modernized, they could be harnessed to serve the newly-established Ukrainian state. In such a context, the conceptualization of university autonomy in Ukraine was delayed by at least 14 years. The following factors influenced the process:

1. The collapse of the Soviet system of higher education and scientific research in the late 1980s.
2. The chaotic nature of the changes implemented in the Ukrainian higher education system during the 1990s and early 2000s.
3. Globalization, in particular the need to shift from Soviet to modern Western concepts, which was accompanied by a lack of agreement as to reform priorities, typified by endless discussions as to relevant "models" of higher education systems in other countries that Ukraine should follow.
4. The Orange Revolution (2004), which led to the creation of the Consortium for University Autonomy in 2005.
5. The negative reaction of the Ukrainian academic community to the attempts by Dmytro Tabachnyk, Minister of Education and Science (2010–2014), to establish an

authoritarian "Russian-style" management system for higher education in Ukraine.
6. The Revolution of Dignity (2013–2014), enabling the adoption of the Law "On Higher Education" in 2014, based on the concept of university autonomy.

The Soviet system of higher education and academic research had certain advantages, which could be attributed to borrowings from the pre-Soviet Russian and Austro-Hungarian empires, and to the total militarization of the country. The latter demanded a certain level of development of engineering skills and knowledge, and advances in the natural sciences. The humanities, sociology, and political science were completely subordinated to the imperatives of communist propaganda. The system was inflexible and unsustainable. As one would expect, it actually ceased to exist during Gorbachev's perestroika, when targeted central funding was cut.

However, Soviet-era practices, which fostered educational superficiality, self-isolation, corruption, the tolerance of plagiarism, and underestimated the importance of integrating higher education with academic research, proved intransigent. Nevertheless, systemically, Ukrainian higher education changed in the 1990s. During this period "reforms" reflected two distinct priorities. First, higher education institutions needed to survive after being abandoned to their fate by the state. Second, the discourse of the "market" meant that society's understanding of the goals and tasks of higher education was transformed. If it was a business like any other, then education had surely to yield money.

Ukraine witnessed the rise of a huge number of new "universities". This process was engendered both by the opening of new private institutions with numerous branches, and in the changing status of former Soviet institutions. Former Soviet-era technical schools, having changed their titles to "colleges", though without proper systemic reform, reincarnated themselves as higher education institutions. Considering also the conservatism of most state officials involved in education and university administration, their limited experience of life beyond the Soviet bloc and ignorance of

English, one can understand the total misconception[60] that plagued discussions at the time regarding the agenda of necessary reform.

Ongoing terminological confusion still plagues discussions among university leaders in Ukraine and is a cause of various misunderstandings. The fact is that a "philological" translation from one language to another is not enough when we are dealing with different political languages, often based on different civilizational realities. Ukraine joined the Bologna Convention in 2005. However, for a long period thereafter the country made few real attempts to change post-Soviet higher education practices, focusing instead on non-essential formal and bureaucratic aspects. Nevertheless, regular reports to the international community on its quasi-involvement in the Bologna process were produced.

This fact outlines an important feature of post-Soviet society, in which laws and official regulations are not as important as their practical application. For reformers, therefore, it is always important to seek a balance between a formal change and the actual possibilities for its realization. For example, the English word "implementation" in the context of a new law means both approval by parliament and enforcement by the relevant authorities. That is, both meanings are synonymous. In Ukraine, however, the adoption of a law is one political task, and its further implementation is a completely different one. We have a number of laws and policy acts that were originally approved but never actually implemented.

The signing of the Bologna Declaration proved to be of exceptional significance for Ukraine, as it marked the start of two parallel

---

60 I have already tried to describe this phenomenon using the examples of the concept of "public" in the Ukrainian language (translated into Ukrainian with terms that reflect a contrast between the state and the public sphere per se, whereas in English it stresses the affinity between both); the concept of "leadership" (in Ukrainian universities, the rector is a charismatic leader, whereas in the Western English-speaking tradition leadership is a team notion to be realized at all levels of management); and also through the difference between the words "state" and "society" (unlike English, Ukrainian does not use these words as synonyms, as the post-totalitarian Ukrainian reality assumes that the state has its own specific interests, which are different from those of society). See Serhiy Kvit, "Reform in a Time of Cholera", in *Battlefront of Civilizations: Education in Ukraine* (Kyiv: Kyiv: Kyiv Mohyla Academy Publishing House, 2015, 2015), 150–152.

processes: formal harmonization of regulations and eventual integration with European institutions, and, simultaneously, discussions and disputes over the agenda of higher education reform aimed at realizing a Western vector. At the same time, these processes did not immediately result in a closer approximation to Western standards in the daily life of Ukrainian universities. Appeals to take pride in Ukrainian traditions of higher education were common during this period. Implied were the Soviet totalitarian traditions that had, in fact, collapsed together with their system. Most importantly, such traditions did not view universities as integral parts of civil society—i.e. as platforms for freedom of speech and free thought.

Post-Soviet "language games" turned into a bad joke during the Yanukovych regime (2010–2013) when the humanities policy became the responsibility of Dmytro Tabachnyk, then Minister of Education and Science of Ukraine. Tabachnyk vulgarized discussions around the concept of university autonomy: in some cases broadening it to include everything that it was not, and in others, narrowing the idea of autonomy to include only the possibility for higher education institutions to issue their own (non-state) diplomas. Tabachnyk deliberately evaded discussions about the substance of comprehensive university autonomy—an idea that received significant dissemination in Ukraine thanks to the efforts of the Consortium for University Autonomy.

Case No. 1—Agent of Change: The National University of Kyiv-Mohyla Academy

The experience of the National University of Kyiv-Mohyla Academy (NaUKMA) as an agent of change in higher education is of particular significance given the general lack of such agents in Ukraine. For various reasons, neither students, nor their parents, nor academic community members, nor employers, nor universities themselves as institutions, not even university rectors, have traditionally played the role of agents of change in Ukraine.[61] Grounded in 400 years of history, yet lacking a Soviet heritage, Kyiv-Mohyla Academy was reincarnated in 1991 as if from scratch.

Virtually all innovative changes in Ukrainian higher education during the period of Ukrainian independence were first implemented at NaUKMA and spread from there, more or less successfully, across the whole system. These include the first Bachelor's, Master's, and PhD programs, freedom to choose academic courses as well as groups of courses (program minors), cross-discipline Master's programs, regular anonymous student surveys of the quality of teaching and learning, and perhaps most significantly, entrance exams, whose success fostered the establishment of external independent exams throughout the country. Finally, one should mention the significance of English having been adopted as the second working language at NaUKMA, and the university's corruption-free environment.

The activism of Kyiv-Mohyla Academy in the struggle for university autonomy was motivated in large part by the institution's need to survive under extreme conditions, rather than by some unique agglomeration of progressive views within its walls. Since the early 2000s, the state bureaucracy launched a drive to unify higher education institutions, in reaction to its own chaotic practice of issuing licenses to newly-created institutions of higher education in the 1990s, which had resulted in the declining quality of higher education. This threatened NaUKMA with dissolution. Some of the innovations instituted by NaUKMA, such as two-year Master's programs, were declared financial violations;[62] others, such as

---

61   This is not to impute conspiracy or evil intent. Existential reality leads Ukrainian rectors to understand their task as maintaining the survival of their institutions. From the perspective of the state, rectors bear full and virtually sole responsibility for the institutions they lead, and therefore they have exclusive authority, including informal power. As a result, rectors rarely delegate. The currently frequently-used term "rector feudalism" arose during discussions of the working group that drafted the new law "On Higher Education" (2012–2014), to denote one of the main risks to the implementation of university autonomy in practice.

62   The state periodically reminded the Kyiv-Mohyla Academy administration of its accountability for "excessive" spending of public funds (which amounted to an accusation that could lead to criminal charges of "non-targeted"

entrance exams, were largely vulgarized.⁶³ Repeated attempts were made to disavow English as the second working language and to deny university status to NaUKMA because of its "insufficient" number of students. Thus, by promoting the project of university autonomy, Kyiv-Mohyla Academy was in fact defending its achievements in the hope that these could be preserved and eventually disseminated across the entire Ukrainian system of higher education.

Yet the main contribution of NaUKMA to the overall improvement in the Ukrainian higher education system was its example of university spirit, and its unique internal culture of mutual respect, honesty, transparency, tolerance, and a respect for independent thought coupled with universally enforced strict quality requirements. Kyiv-Mohyla Academy served as an independent tribune sheltering various civic movements with different opposition agendas, in particular those opposing political censorship, negation of the Holodomor, or oppression of the Ukrainian language. In 2004, the university community actively supported the Orange Revolution and in 2013–2014 the protests that came to be known as the Revolution of Dignity. These mass events eventually also contributed to the promotion of autonomy as a higher education reform project.

The Kyiv-Mohyla Academy case is important for demonstrating institutional capacity as key to implementing self-regulation

---

expenditures, i.e. why should Master's students be taught for so long, instead of just one year?).

63 When nationwide External Independent Testing (EIT) was introduced by the Decree of President Viktor Yushchenko on July 4, 2005, its rationale mentioned the successful example of the admission exams at NaUKMA. Paradoxically, NaUKMA's experience was aggressively rejected at the same time. The EIT project was seen as an instrument for combating corruption, a conceptually insufficient and even erroneous view to some extent. The main reason for Kyiv-Mohyla admission exams was not to overcome corruption (a derivative effect), but to develop autonomy (by creating one's own contingent of students motivated to study at that particular university). The undoubtedly positive effects of EIT in combating admission-related corruption should not overshadow the temporary nature of this benefit in the context of implementing university autonomy and creating a pool of high-quality universities. In terms of Kyiv-Mohyla Academy, EIT has meant the elimination of its own admission exams and a dramatic drop in the admission requirements for its applicants.

and the power of critical thinking. It illustrates that a small but active university community that fosters free thought, initiative, and leadership can achieve great success in fulfilling its public mission. This case helps to shape a "boutique" vision of a university in which a unique brand becomes the basis of reputational capital.

Case No. 2. — Consortium for University Autonomy (2005–2010)

Even before the Orange Revolution (2004), the President of Kyiv-Mohyla Academy, Viacheslav Briukhovetskyi, submitted a formal proposition to Leonid Kuchma, then President of Ukraine, to introduce university autonomy as a national policy. However, that proposition never received a response. Later, in 2005, NaUKMA's president presented this idea to a meeting of university rectors. The newly-elected President of Ukraine, Victor Yushchenko (2004–2010), attended that event and asked that a draft Resolution be prepared for his approval in a couple of days. The relevant document was submitted to the President's Secretariat in time, yet a Decree was never issued.

In the same year, 2005, a meeting between Viktor Yushchenko, Ivan Vakarchuk, Rector of Ivan Franko National University of Lviv, and Borys Gudziak, Rector of the Ukrainian Catholic University, was held to discuss the ideological and organizational development of the university autonomy project. The President of Ukraine verbally supported this project, and afterwards it received financial support from the International Renaissance Foundation, funding that lasted for 5 years. A Consortium of Ukrainian Universities was established for its implementation.

Eight universities with various forms of ownership from different regions of Ukraine joined the Consortium. Listed geographically from west to east, they were the private Ukrainian Catholic University (Lviv), Ivan Franko National University of Lviv, Yurii Fedkovych Chernivtsi National University, the National University of Kyiv-Mohyla Academy, the private University of Economics and Law "KROK" (Kyiv), Oles Honchar Dnipro National University,

V. N. Karazin Kharkiv National University, and Donetsk National University.[64]

The reaction of Ukraine's state bureaucracy to the activities of the Consortium was not helpful. Instead of rallying around the question of how university autonomy could be implemented, representatives of virtually all branches of government sought arguments to show the impossibility of implementing this reform. Thus, one of the then deputy Ministers of Justice stated: "According to the legislation, Ukrainian universities are already autonomous and self-governing, so I do not understand at all what is being talked about".

Another example of intransigence: during a seminar at the University of Cambridge (UK), devoted to university autonomy issues, Cambridge's Vice Rector said to the members of the Ukrainian delegation: "In order to implement any important project, three things are necessary — the right people, traditions, and trust". An official from the President of Ukraine's Secretariat, the person who was formally curating the project of university autonomy, responded by saying: "Trust? Such a concept does not exist in Ukrainian legislation".

Still, the Consortium revealed sufficient flexibility and initiative. The concept of comprehensive university autonomy was developed to include academic, administrative, and financial autonomy. The experience of the United States, Great Britain, the countries of continental Western Europe, and Canada was studied. The Consortium contributed to implementing sociological research, publishing and expert activities, preparing the legal background, lobbying the government, and promoting university autonomy in the media.

For Ukraine, those steps were largely in line with the adaptation of the norms of the Bologna process. The consortium proposed two models for university autonomy implementation. The first was to be experimental: Consortium members would take responsibility for activities in an autonomous environment for a five-year

---

64 From time to time, new members hoping for additional budget funding would appear in the Consortium only to disappear as their illusions faded away.

period so that later, based on the results, necessary amendments to legislation would be made and relevant practices be disseminated to all Ukrainian universities. The second model was based on a special agreement on autonomy to be signed between an individual higher education institution and the Ministry of Education and Science, involving a commitment by the institution to ensure transparency and accountability for all its activities and making all of its reporting openly available on the Internet. Since both proposals were finally rejected because of the alleged impossibility of implementing them under the existing legal framework, the need for a new Law "On Higher Education" became clear.

The Consortium for University Autonomy ceased it activities in 2010, the same year that Viktor Yanukovych came to power (2010–2014). However, thanks to the Consortium, the idea of university autonomy was disseminated and became extremely popular in society. The idea was discussed in the press, in terms used by various political forces, in expert circles, in student environments, and, what was extremely important, in Ukrainian universities themselves.

Case No. 3—The Struggle for a New Law "On Higher Education" (2010–2014)

After Viktor Yanukovych came to power, an interesting situation developed. Control over humanities policy was transferred to Dmytro Tabachnyk,[65] the odious Ukrainophobic "intellectual", who was selected to head the Ministry of Education and Science. On the other hand, the Committee for Economic Reforms under the President of Ukraine developed the "Program of Economic Reform for 2010–2014" entitled "A Prosperous Society, a Competitive Economy, and an Efficient State"—a document that was authored with the help of Western experts.[66] The section dedicated to higher

---

65 Dmytro Tabachnyk acted as a thinly disguised Kremlin agent, denying not only university autonomy, but also the sovereignty of the Ukrainian language, Ukrainian history, and the existence of a separate Ukrainian people.
66 Committee for Economic Reforms under the President of Ukraine, *Zamozhne suspilstvo, konkurentnospromozhna ekonomika, efektyvna derzhava: prohrama ekonomichnykh reform na 2010–2014 roky* [*A Prosperous Society, a Competitive*

education reform was progressive in its rhetoric. After all, no alternatives to university autonomy exist in the West.

The political regime of the Party of Regions had no intention of implementing the published reform program, using it instead to divert attention from its actual kleptocratic intentions. Yet, for a period of time, this document allowed supporters of university autonomy to pressure representatives of the political forces in power, gaining temporary advantage in anticipation of a new mobilization of society. Later, an intense struggle was engaged for a new Law "On Higher Education" based on the concept of comprehensive university autonomy — precisely the concept that had been previously developed by the Consortium for University Autonomy.

As Minister, Dmytro Tabachnyk liked the idea of adopting a new Law "On Higher Education". His draft law was presented to the Council of Rectors of the Kyiv region in November 2010. It is interesting that almost all of the rectors who attended this meeting spoke against that bill, but when it came time to vote, only Kyiv-Mohyla Academy declared its position "against", while the other participants supported the idea of "taking the document as a basis for further development". A representative from the Ministry of Education assured the gathered leaders that this draft would be adopted by the Verkhovna Rada of Ukraine before the start of 2011.

That draft law rejected university autonomy and strengthened the rights and powers of the Ministry itself through more than 100 provisions. Critics started to call the text a draft law "on the Ministry of Education", not on higher education. Its intent was to implement the so-called "Russian style" of administration in Ukraine's higher education sector, with its rigid centralized system concentrated around the presidential power vertical. However, Ukrainian social realities dramatically differed from the Russian context. Although in March 2010 only the Ukrainian Catholic University supported Kyiv-Mohyla Academy's call for a protest against the appointment of Tabachnyk, by the end of the year mass protests

---

Economy, and an Efficient State: The Program of Economic Reforms for 2010–2014], accessed June 2, 2010, http://www.president.gov.ua/docs/Programa_reform_FINAL_1.pdf.

termed the "Anti-Tabachna campaign"[67] and "Against the degradation of education" spread across Ukraine.

In 2011 the Ukrainian academic community lobby was able to stop Dmytro Tabachnyk's draft law, blocking its submission to the Verkhovna Rada four times and, on one occasion, even managing to have it removed from the agenda of the Parliamentary session. Public protests against the provocative activities of the Minister of Education had a damaging effect on the government's reputation. As a result, in early 2012, Prime Minister Mykola Azarov created a working group to formally prepare a compromise draft law to be based on three documents that had already been submitted to the Parliament. In addition to the "ministerial" one, these included a draft law from Yurii Miroshnychenko, MP and Representative of the President in Parliament, and a draft law from MPs Arsenii Yatseniuk and Lesia Orobets — both from the opposition.

The newly created working group was headed by academician Mykhailo Zhurovskyi, Rector of the National Technical University of Ukraine "Kyiv Polytechnic Institute". It worked very productively during 2012 with meetings held primarily at Kyiv Polytechnic — a fact that resulted in the institutional awakening of one of Ukraine's largest universities. This awakening had far-reaching consequences beyond the framework of developing the Law "On Higher Education": the 2014 Revolution of Dignity in Kyiv was institutionally supported not only by Kyiv-Mohyla Academy, as had been the case in the protests during the Orange Revolution, but also by Kyiv Polytechnic Institute and Kyiv Borys Hrinchenko University.

It was within the framework of the working group that representatives of the academic environment, experts, leaders of student and various non-governmental organizations, including international ones, trade union representatives, and employers — altogether about 100 institutions and organizations — united their efforts for the first time. Anyone could contribute using the Internet

---

67 The name of this protest campaign contained a dual meaning, fusing the name of Dmytro Tabachnyk and a word corresponding to "tobacco". Tabachnyk himself was an avid smoker.

or regular mail.⁶⁸ More than 4,000 proposals were seriously discussed. Controversial provisions were adjusted under a consensus-based principle,⁶⁹ so as to avoid losing a stakeholder and prevent splits within the working group.

In the second half of 2012, the Cabinet of Ministers of Ukraine approved the concept of the future Law "On Higher Education" developed by the working group and later, in December, the draft law itself. However, the October 2012 parliamentary elections resulted in the formation of a new government in which Dmytro Tabachnyk remained in office, while more opponents of university autonomy entered the new government. Oleksandr Lavrynovych, a former deputy leader of Narodnyi Rukh (the People's Movement of Ukraine) and a close associate of Viacheslav Chornovil, who then betrayed the national-democratic cause to become the newly-appointed Minister of Justice after 2012, even accused the working group of "reanimating Stalin's norms" (regarding the creation of an independent National Agency for Higher Education Quality Assurance).

By the beginning of 2013, new draft laws "On Higher Education" were (conventionally) registered in Parliament "by the majority" and "by the opposition". The draft law by the working group was registered separately. It should be noted that, conceptually, the opposition and working group bills were similar. The same experts often worked on the basic principles of the two documents.

Later, as a result of negotiations between representatives of the working group and the authors of the opposition document, the (now former) opposition's draft was withdrawn, and a single document by the working group was promoted. It was adopted by the

---

68   "Zakonoproekt 'Pro vyshchu osvitu' [The Draft Law 'On Higher Education']", National Technical University of Ukraine "Igor Sikorsky Kyiv Polytechnic Institute", August 28, 2012, http://kpi.ua/12-03-07.
69   The principle of consensus was the only possible solution, but not the best way out of the situation. In particular, it preserved some Soviet norms: the degree of Doctor of Sciences in addition to the PhD degree (as insisted by the National Academy of Sciences of Ukraine). Also, some populist statements were included: a student scholarship at the subsistence level (at the insistence of student activists).

Verkhovna Rada of Ukraine on July 1, 2014 after the victory of the Revolution of Dignity.[70]

Case No. 4 — Implementation of the Law of Ukraine "On Higher Education"[71]

In order to have an idea of the main obstacles to the implementation of this law, one must understand the context of the decision-making process in the Ukrainian government in early 2014.

The Soviet planned system had not been completely demolished in 1991. It continued to exist in the rhetoric of politicians and the behavior of Ukrainian public administrators. After the collapse of the Soviet Union, the Ukrainian state failed to define its priorities, and so did not have an independent strategy for its further development. As a result, the political elites, as in all former Soviet republics, continued to copy the Soviet style of governance. Yet it was Russia that was the true heir to the communist system: it had the necessary resources to implement authoritarian policies. Against that background, Ukraine and other post-Soviet countries for a long time simulated a kind of "mini-USSR" or "mini-Russia". This was felt especially sharply in the financing of education and research.

Although initially, after 1991, the Ministry of Economic Development (the heir to the Soviet State Planning Committee) was most influential in assessing the financial priorities of the Ukrainian government in the education sector, the Ministry of Finance later took the lead. This transfer was precipitated by a catastrophic lack of funds: education and science were funded under a residual principle, receiving whatever was left after other priorities had been met. Since the very beginning of Ukrainian independence, education and research were traditionally not seen as attractive targets for

---

70 Law of Ukraine "On Higher Education", No. 1556-VII, July 1, 2014, https://cis-legislation.com/document.fwx?rgn=72719.

71 For more detail, see Serhiy Kvit, "Implementing Ukrainian Law in Higher Education: Successes and Challenges", in *The Research Initiative on Democratic Reforms in Ukraine*, comp. Olenka Bilash (Edmonton: University of Alberta, 2020), 3-16, https://www.ualberta.ca/canadian-institute-of-ukrainian-studies/centres-and-programs/ulec/ulec-news/ridru_publication.pdf.

investment in the future of the nation, but rather as necessary expenditures that the state budget had to bear.

The situation changed in 2015, a year after the Revolution of Dignity. The then Minister of Finance Natalia Jaresko dismissed one of her deputies who over the years had skillfully opposed reforms and had continuously looked for opportunities to "optimize" (cut) educational expenditures. Following this measure, the long-term rift between the Ministry of Education and Science and the Ministry of Finance was overcome. This episode illustrates not only the importance of staff issues, but the need to resolve the problem of a systematic lack of communication, to introduce dialogue and interaction, and to change decision-making methods.

Still, many obstacles—both subjective and objective—remained on the path to implementing the 2014 Law "On Higher Education". The following were among the most significant:

1. Post-Soviet values that were prevalent among a large number of Ukrainian politicians who did not understand the importance of education and research for the future of the country.
2. A fragmentary approach to educational reforms that ignored the context of other changes and processes taking place in Ukrainian society and the national economy.
3. The established post-Soviet practice followed by a considerable number of public officials who believed that the state must "control" universities.
4. The conservatism of university communities—a large part of university rectors in particular.
5. The extreme conservatism of the leadership of the National Academy of Sciences of Ukraine, who resisted any changes.[72]

---

72 Such conservatism, in particular rejecting the integration of scientific research and higher education, was the main threat to the development of the Ukrainian research sphere, as it fed the desire in political circles to eliminate the system of research institutes at the National Academy of Sciences of Ukraine allowing the available property and land plots to be commercially used (without any relation to science).

6. A fundamental lack of funds due to the economic crisis and circumstances of Russian armed aggression and the protracted war.

In the process of implementing various provisions of the Law "On Higher Education", Ukrainian universities gradually obtained real academic autonomy. The regulatory burden was significantly reduced. Institutions of higher education gained the ability to establish their own uniqueness and to manifest this in appropriate organizational forms related to their educational processes (by creating educational programs, by special methods of learning and teaching); they could now institute their own academic quality assurance systems and deepen international cooperation.

More than 30 so-called "mandatory academic subjects" — Soviet-era relics that contradicted the principles of autonomy — were canceled in 2015; the rules for awarding academic degrees were changed; opportunities for academic mobility and student self-governance were expanded; work began to develop new standards of higher education; and important steps were taken to ensure the openness and transparency of university activities. The first legislative initiatives were introduced to change the funding system for higher education, so as to move away from the Stalinist system of "state order"[73] and to introduce the concept of block (basic) funding.

However, the movement towards the financial autonomy of Ukrainian universities remains blocked. The relevant amendments in education-related legislation were not extended to the legislative norms and regulatory framework governing financial relations with the state. For example, universities still have to gain approval for their staff lists from the Ministry of Education and Science. Also, in practice, the use of banking services was made artificially complex in a way that favors the State Treasury. In other words, the autonomy of Ukrainian institutions of higher education remains

---

73 Serhiy Kvit, "An Illogical Way of Funding Universities", *University World News*, May 27, 2012, http://www.universityworldnews.com/article.php?story=2012052314121089&query=kvit.

incomplete: the state continues to interfere in their operational processes and blocks attempts to improve self-regulation.

Most importantly, higher education institutions cannot capitalize on their academic uniqueness. Therefore, the heads of many universities often view academic autonomy as a problem: if once they could simply follow the Ministry of Education's instructions and those received from political leaders, now they must increasingly take on responsibility for "free navigation". Accordingly, the implementation of some important norms of academic autonomy, for example, the creation of structured PhD programs,[74] or the introduction of genuine choice of academic subjects, is mostly formal, and accompanied by deep conservative inertia.

New Tasks— "The Roadmap of Higher Education Reforms" (2018–2019)

Gradually, higher education reform was de-emphasized on the Ukrainian political agenda. The following are proposed as explanations for this trend:

1. Retaining focus on multiple important reform projects simultaneously is problematic for the Ministry of Education — after 2016, the emphasis switched from higher education reform to the transformation of Ukraine's primary and secondary school sectors. As proved by the experience of neighboring countries from the former so-called socialist camp, and which have now become EU members, it is best to have two ministries of education: one (tentatively) responsible for higher education and science, and the other for public education.
2. Ukrainian politicians lack the skills and traditions necessary to make important decisions based on scientific research and professional expertise.

---

[74] Considerable progress in implementing such reforms by regional universities should be noted. In particular, Zaporizhzhia National University provides a good example of developing contemporary PhD programs.

3. A large number of higher education institutions that offer a low quality of learning and teaching are able to mount effective lobbying to preserve the status quo.
4. Changing attitudes to higher education as a social project in times of economic crisis. When it is difficult for young people to find good jobs, the number of HEI is huge and their quality, on the contrary, is low. Such a situation does not promote an agenda of quality assurance and the fostering of academic integrity.

Reforming universities means building their capacity to assure their own quality, but unfortunately, not all universities are capable of accomplishing this task.[75] And so again we return to the vicious circle: why has little qualitative improvement taken place in Ukrainian universities? Because most are incapable of reforming themselves. Why are Ukrainian higher education institutions still uncompetitive internationally? Because they have not undertaken qualitative improvement.

The key to exiting this vicious circle is the implementation of real financial autonomy. Its blockage perpetuates the notion that the state continues to bear formal responsibility (in fact, it bears no responsibility at all) for the quality of universities. In reality, the state continues to control universities by interfering in their operational processes.

Universities will be able to take responsibility for their own quality, including what concerns academic integrity, and improve their own reputations, only once they have the full set of instruments to do so. First of all, they require the financial and economic tools necessary for their own development. The Ukrainian state does not trust universities and continues to control them, which in fact contradicts national interests. If these interests include the creation of high-quality (autonomous and responsible) universities, important for the development of an innovative economy, human capital, and civil society, then higher education institutions must be allowed to pursue their own path.

---

75 The progress of Sumy State University in developing its internal system of education quality assurance deserves praise.

In order to draw attention to the goals of higher education reforms, the "Roadmap to Higher Education Reform in Ukraine"[76] was elaborated with the support of the International Renaissance Foundation. This document demonstrates that if comprehensive university autonomy is implemented, first, the system by which higher education is funded will change. Second, the number of Ukrainian universities will decrease and their quality will grow. Third, they will establish close relationships with national industries and the labor market. Fourth, their financial state will be strengthened: salaries and material and technical facilities will be improved. Fifth, and very importantly, a generational change of rectors and other educational managers will take place. Sixth, the role of the Ministry of Education and Science will become that of an intermediary rather than a controlling or directive body — i.e. the Ukrainian Ministry would approximate its EU counterparts.

In sum, the importance of reputational capital for the success of higher education institutions will increase, in the first place as a result of decentralization, self-regulation, and self-governance. This will also contribute to internationalization and the development of concentrated research priorities in Ukrainian universities, particularly through the integration of higher education and research. The logic of this movement towards autonomous and responsible university activities will form the basis for genuine quality assurance and academic integrity.

It should be noted that this case considers only the main tasks of reforming higher education, and does not cover the Vocational Education and Training (VET) sector. Unfortunately, the expansion of discussions of systemic reform priorities has been overshadowed by secondary arguments as to whether scholars should be required to be proficient in English at a B2 level and whether their research

---

76 Serhiy Kvit, "Dorozhnia karta reformuvannia vyshchoi osvity Ukrainy [The Roadmap to Higher Education Reform in Ukraine]", *Osvitnia polityka*, March 23, 2018, http://education-ua.org/ua/articles/1159-dorozhnya-karta-reformuvannya-vishchoji-osviti-ukrajini. Also in English: Serhiy Kvit, "A Roadmap to Higher Education Reform via Autonomy", *University World News*, March 16, 2018, http://www.universityworldnews.com/article.php?story=20180316092127837.

should be published in peer-reviewed journals; similar peripheral debates turn on whether plagiarism should be fought when many Ukrainian HEIs consider adherence to principles of academic integrity as an additional burden rather than as a means of developing their own unique culture and competitive reputation.

Case No. 5 — National Agency of Higher Education Quality Assurance (2019–2020)

The idea of creating a National Agency for Higher Education Quality Assurance (NAQA) provoked heated discussions during the preparation of the draft Law "On Higher Education" by the Zhurovskyi working group in 2012. The main problem was the status of this new institution. The legal system of post-Soviet Ukraine did not envision the creation of a non-political public authority; therefore, no alternative to NAQA members being state officials was anticipated.

However, such politicization is unacceptable from the point of view of the Standards and Guidelines for Quality Assurance in the European Higher Education Area (ESG-2015) — an EU regulation that became part of Ukrainian legislation after the signing of the Ukraine-EU Association Agreement. If NAQA were to become a state institution that formally conformed to Ukrainian law, it would no longer be an independent organization according to ESG-2015.

NAQA is responsible for the accreditation of educational programs, institutional accreditation of HEIs, accreditation of dissertation defense committees, accreditation of independent quality assurance institutions, academic integrity issues, internal university quality assurance requirements, academic degree requirements, national university rankings, etc.

The first attempts to create NAQA took place in 2015 and 2016. Several members of the Agency, elected in conformity with the original selection procedure, were in fact deemed ineligible according to the provisions of the Law "On Government Cleansing" (Lustration Law) of 2014; others were accused of violating academic integrity and corruption, as well as involvement in political games that became an obstacle to the real launch of NAQA.

In 2017, changes to the Law "On Higher Education" were adopted, requiring selection of NAQA members through an international selection committee rather than through elections by congresses of university leaders (in reality—university rectors). The new membership (21 persons) was selected and approved in December 2018, and the first NAQA meeting was held in late January 2019.

During the first year and a half of its activity in 2019–2020, NAQA successfully implemented the provisions of the Law "On Higher Education" (2014) and ESG-2015, built mutual trust in the academic environment, completely abandoned the previous paperwork-heavy system of accreditation, transferred all procedures online, and overall made all processes open to the general public. NAQA also selected and trained 2,528 experts, 329 members of Sectoral Expert Councils (for 29 SECs), 35 trainers, and 62 Secretariat staff.

During the 2019–2020 academic year, NAQA completed the accreditation process for 909 study programs. The breakdown of quality grading was as follows:

- about 1%—exceptional 5-year accreditation (level A);
- about 62%—5-year accreditation (level B);
- about 35%—conditional one-year accreditation (level E);
- about 2%—denials of accreditation (level F).

In this short time, NAQA became a full member of the International Network for Quality Assurance Agencies in Higher Education (INQAAHE), the Network of Central and Eastern European Quality Assurance Agencies in Higher Education (CEENQA), the International Center for Academic Integrity (ICAI), and gained affiliate status in the European Association for the Quality Assurance of Higher Education (ENQA).

During the COVID-19 lockdown, from March to September 2020, NAQA organized more than 540 site visits using videoconferencing technology[77] in order to continue its educational program quality assurance activities. Progressive approaches to building online accreditation procedures have aroused the interest of relevant agencies in the United Kingdom, Saudi Arabia, and other international partners.

For the first time, NAQA has posed important questions to the Ukrainian higher education community regarding quality assurance. During this short period of time, Ukraine's external quality assurance system became fully correlated with the approaches of the European Higher Education Area, and internal quality assurance in higher education institutions is quickly following this reform example.

On the initiative of NAQA, starting from 2019, accreditation decisions by agencies that are part of the European Quality Assurance Register for Higher Education (EQAR) are recognized in Ukraine. This creates international competition in the accreditation of educational programs, and the possibilities for institutional accreditation of Ukrainian universities — an area in which NAQA has not yet become involved due to undercapacity.

Unfortunately, NAQA's activities are gradually losing the support of the Ukrainian government, which treats education reform as an unnecessary problem. The fashion for political populism seems to threaten to turn higher education policy back from the revolutionary reform agenda, adopted after 2014, to the Brownian motion of the previous period.

The implementation of the concept of comprehensive university autonomy is also under threat due to the authoritarian style of management of the current leadership of the Ministry of Education and Science of Ukraine. The introduction of financial autonomy for Ukrainian universities (radically transforming the post-Soviet economics of higher education) is now off the table. Furthermore, the latest policy steps of the Ministry of Education and Science threaten the very principle of academic autonomy of Ukrainian universities.

---

77 Mychailo Wynnyckyj, "Crisis Has Shown Virtual Quality Assurance Can Work Well", *University World News*, July 6, 2020, https://www.universityworldnews.com/post.php?story=20200706101702976.

Not only can it be said that the Ministry of Education and Science does not want to continue the reform launched after the Revolution of Dignity; the current team is nothing less than incompetent and unable to understand the content and purpose of educational reforms. According to the monitoring of the implementation of the Association Agreement with the EU, Ukraine fulfills only one of the obligations (the third of eight) set out in this document. This point concerns quality assurance in higher education. The achievements of NAQA were recognized as "advanced" compared to all others that received a failing grade.[78]

In today's Ukraine talk of strengthening comprehensive university autonomy and instituting independent external quality assurance has become unpopular in state circles. Instead, there are attempts by the government to displace reformers from influential positions, discredit the higher education reform agenda, and restore personal political loyalty as the arbiter of career and institutional advancement.

In these circumstances, NAQA continues to fight for its institutional independence. After the identification of academic plagiarism in publications by the acting Minister of Education and Science of Ukraine Serhiy Shkarlet, attacks on NAQA, using such methods as manipulative press releases, the use of official power to pressure rectors, and pressure by court decisions, intensified. However, all efforts to control NAQA's activities have been unsuccessful. NAQA has established itself as an exemplar of a strong, well-intentioned, effective, professionally independent institution.

Interestingly, at the end of September 2020, two public documents appeared almost simultaneously: "A Collective Appeal by Members of the Academic Council of 'Chernihiv Polytechnic' National University" (September 28), prepared in the Soviet style of an

---

78 "The Agreement is Five Years Old. What Has Ukraine Done? Ukraine and the Association Agreement with the EU. Monitoring of the Implementation, 2014–2019", *Ukrainian Center for European Politics*, July 16, 2020, https://cutt.ly/QgW1Prj. In 2020, during the preparation of this Monitoring for 2014–2019 for publication, the success of NAQA in ensuring the quality of higher education in 2019–2020 was noted. At the time of writing, the full text of the Monitoring has not appeared on the website of the Ukrainian Center for European Politics.

"appeal by workers", and ENQA President Christoph Grolimund's letter to the Speaker of the Ukrainian Parliament and the Prime Minister of Ukraine (September 29).

The first document denied even the possibility of academic plagiarism in the publications of Serhiy Shkarlet (formerly rector of that university) and appealed to the government to investigate the legality of NAQA's activities. The second supported NAQA's policy of the implementation of ESG-2015 in Ukraine, the convergence of Ukrainian higher education with the EHEA, the independence of NAQA, and cited Ukraine's commitments under the Association Agreement with the EU.

On October 1, EQAR President Karl Dittrich addressed a similar letter of support for NAQA's independence to acting Minister of Education and Science of Ukraine Serhiy Shkarlet. Finally, on November 5 the European Students' Union adopted a "Resolution on the Acting Minister of Education and Science of Ukraine Serhii Shkarlet"[79] emphasizing, in particular, the importance of NAQA's independence, academic integrity issues, and the involvement of students in higher education decision-making.

The ESU also denounced the growing authoritarianism of the Ministry of Education and Science of Ukraine. As can be seen, NAQA received substantial international support. However, we understand that education reform is the sole responsibility of Ukrainian society itself.

Conclusion

The task of advancing Ukrainian higher education reforms in the direction of ensuring comprehensive university autonomy is of a political nature, and must be returned to the political agenda of contemporary Ukraine. This idea was developed over the long term and became fundamental to the success of reform efforts when the opportunity to implement them arose. It must not be allowed to die.

---

79 "BM79: Resolution on the Acting Minister of Education and Science of Ukraine Serhii Shkarlet", European Students' Union, https://www.esu-online.org/?policy=bm79-resolution-on-the-acting-minister-of-education-and-science-of-ukraine-serhii-shkarlet.

The concept of comprehensive university autonomy requires the existence of a professionally independent NAQA. Only autonomous universities can be universities of high quality and integrity. Continuing the practice of state patronage, interference, and control has proven to be extremely harmful. The successful decentralization policy pursued by the Ukrainian government after the Revolution of Dignity has proven the viability of the comprehensive university autonomy agenda.

The Ukrainian political class and civil society must reconcile a shared vision of Ukraine's future with all the political rights and freedoms of a democratic society, good governance, and a strong economy. It is necessary to start by joining forces to create a modern system of education and research, where the formation of national leaders capable of changing the country and taking responsibility for important decisions comes to the fore.

Ukraine needs a decisive break with Soviet political culture and its practices of social interaction. This is possible only if the approach to national education change: from the ideal of a competent task performer to a leader who is able to develop the culture of an organization, field, nation-state, and play a part globally. One last note: the success of educational reform is directly related to the ability of Ukrainians to defend their own independence in times of uncertainty and anxiety.

University Autonomy as a Value Basis and Necessary Environment for Academic Integrity[80]

The Overcoming of the Soviet / Russian Legacy

The realization of any declared social values, including political rights and freedoms, is only possible together with the existential choice of a particular society living in its own national state. For example, if a society wants to have freedom of speech, it will obtain it by demanding it from its government and, as a result of this public demand, by creating favourable national legislation and economic opportunities. Likewise, academic integrity is based on the traditions of academic life, as well as the formal and informal rules that are prevalent in the academic culture and legislation of various countries and societies that adhere to them.

Along with the development of modern Ukrainian political culture, the legacy of the so-called "Soviet legal consciousness" is becoming history. But it still has an impact. What kind of a phenomenon is this? To explain briefly, legislation in a post-Soviet country is important but not as important as the practice of its application, which, in turn, is influenced by such phenomenon as "notions" (Rus.: "poniatija"). These "notions" are related to the criminal legacy of GULAG. They mean the obligation or, on the contrary, impossibility to perform a certain action, according to the factual, most often informal, status of a certain person or institution, since a formal status encourages actions stipulated by the current legislation.

It is important for Ukrainian society to overcome the Soviet legacy and strengthen its own cultural principles. Thus, the political culture of modern Ukraine is based on the priorities of the discourse of freedom, primarily freedom of speech and freedom of

---

80 Speech held at the European Conference on Ethics and Integrity in Academia 2023 (ENAI Annual Conference) on Jul. 12-14, University of Derby, UK: https://academicintegrity.eu/conference/

choice, which were preserved by historical memory and put on the modern agenda in the course of the Ukrainian revolutions and the armed struggle for independence from Russia. At the same time, the case of academic integrity has appeared to be more complicated.

The Communist Party of the Soviet Union created sufficient conditions for the creative work of intellectual labour people (researchers, also, to a large extent, people of art and journalists) in exchange for political loyalty and proper quality of their intellectual product. Plagiarism would mean destroying such a conspiracy, which is why it was not a trend in the academic sphere during the totalitarian times. It would undermine the "persuasiveness" of communist propaganda inside the country and counter-propaganda in the international arena. An imitation of scientific research would also immediately affect the competitiveness of the Soviet military-industrial complex. After all, military equipment was supposed to fly, drive, and shoot.

That is why, in Soviet times, plagiarism was not a way of building an academic career. Instead, in independent Ukraine, in the 1990s and early 2000s, plagiarism became total and pervasive. However, that did not mean that the Soviet authorities were honest. Many young researchers were forced to work first on dissertations for their bureaucratic bosses, and only after that could they defend their own theses. That is, we can define ghost writing as the most common form of academic integrity violation in Soviet times. At least, if we do not consider international industrial espionage as part of the economic development policy of the USSR.

The Soviets practically turned a blind eye to any thefts from behind the "iron curtain", as well as thefts carried out from Ukrainian culture and the heritage of other peoples enslaved by the Russian Empire, for the benefit of Russian culture (Alla Yevtushenko, 2022). To illustrate, we can mention the world-famous Soviet "Kalashnikov machine gun", immodestly "borrowed" by Russian Mikhail Kalashnikov from Sturmgewehr 44 designed by German designer Hugo Schmeisser (BBC, 2017) without mentioning the actual author, and "March of the Aviators", extremely popular in the Soviet Union, which was actually plagiarised from "Herbei Zum Kampf", the anthem of Nazi's assault troops (ISTV, 2021).

One of the main questions that need to be answered in the context of adherence to the principles of academic integrity in Ukraine is the following: who is directly responsible for such principles?

Academic Integrity: Who is Responsible?

It is common knowledge, it is universities that had to be most interested in observing these principles since the development of their reputational capital depends on it. Unfortunately, this isn't so in Ukraine yet. After the adoption of the Law "On Higher Education" in 2014, Ukrainian higher education institutions have gained academic autonomy, but still do not have financial autonomy, provided for in the law. That's why they cannot capitalize on their academic achievements, and their place in the market and access to the resources necessary for development are not yet dependent on their reputation (Serhiy Kvit, 2017).

That is, we have not yet completely overcome one of the basic principles of the Soviet economy of higher education, which means that the state controls the financial life of higher education institutions and is therefore responsible for the quality of each of them. So far, there are only some precedents for the emergence of universities having an internal culture of autonomy and responsibility. Among them is the National University of Kyiv-Mohyla Academy. The revival of the Kyiv-Mohyla Academy, the oldest Ukrainian institution of higher education, founded in 1615, but closed down by the Soviet authorities in the 1920s, to the status of a national university led to the emergence of a unique institutional agent of education and social change.

In the field of academic integrity, in particular it meant the adoption of the Provisions on the Institutional Policy for Observance of Academic Integrity, the first regulation of this kind in Ukraine (1998, KMA). It resulted in zero tolerance for plagiarism as the most common form of academic integrity violation in Ukraine. The public activity of Kyiv-Mohyla Academy proves that the reputational factor comes to the forefront in the task of ensuring the quality of higher education and academic integrity.

The next obstacle that needs to still be overcome is related to the translation and understanding of key concepts. For example, the term "academic integrity" has a slightly different meaning in the Ukrainian language, which has more to do with "correct", well-doing behaviour rather than with a violation of the integrity (as wholeness) of academic life as such. There is also a conceptual clash of approaches between the National Agency for Higher Education Quality Assurance of Ukraine (NAQA), which uses the concept of "common sense" in its normative documents, and the position of the Ministry of Justice of Ukraine, which denies the possibility of using such a norm in national legislation.

One more example. Although we can translate the word 'excellence' into Ukrainian as "perfection", it is hard to render the corresponding concept since it has no relevant cultural tradition and is only now being established in Ukrainian social realities. The concept of excellence is phenomenological by its nature. It allows us to see the horizon of academic quality to which we aspire and at the same time leaves space for continuous improvement. That is, it is both a direction and a goal. The content of excellence can also be transformed over time without affecting its significance.

The experience of the development of Ukrainian higher education after the collapse of the Soviet Union has also led to the following interesting conclusion: bureaucratic institutions and autonomous universities have a clash of concepts implemented in Ukraine within the European Higher Education Area (ESG 2015). This applies not only to the terms and concepts mentioned above. In particular, the status of NAQA as professionally independent, primarily from Government institutions, was defended in 2020-2022 in heated public debates, even though at the beginning many saw NAQA as a so-called central public authority that should be positioned within the government hierarchy according to the established post-Soviet tradition.

The Case of NAQA

The establishment of NAQA, stipulated by the above-mentioned Law "On Higher Education" (2014), led to the emergence of one more institution that defined its mission as working on the basis of trust, initiative, and mutual values (NAQA, 2019). The Agency identifies itself as a partner of universities, not their controller, which, in addition, offers practices of supportive communication (Serhiy Kvit, Nataliia Stukalo, 2021). In particular, NAQA is responsible for the accreditation of Ukrainian universities and the development of their systems of internal quality assurance.

It is also important that NAQA has set an effective international Advisory Board (NAQA, 2020), which provides extremely valuable assistance in taking principled decisions, forming a regulatory framework, and participating in court cases. The openness of NAQA's accreditation procedures is unprecedented. Anyone using the public interface has access to its online system, which contains complete information on all educational programs at all stages of accreditation, including all necessary documents: https://public.naqa.gov.ua/

NAQA has implemented the practice of independent international assessment of its own draft regulatory documents (Leah Wortham, 2019), public self-assessment (Self-Assessment Report, 2021), conducting regular research on how Ukrainian universities feel about NAQA's implementation of new forms of quality assurance from ESG 2015, how much they trust NAQA experts, how the experts evaluate the quality of training, the effectiveness of the process of study programs assessments, etc. It was found that the Agency tried not only to spread trust in the Ukrainian academic environment but also relied on counter-trust from it.

The history of NAQA's defending the appropriateness of its decisions in the courts deserves special attention. Thus, in 2021 alone, the NAQA was involved in 16 court cases simultaneously. Those were mostly lawsuits from individuals who had disagreed with NAQA's identification of plagiarism in their publications. It is interesting that they mainly challenged not their violation of the principles of academic integrity, but only the procedural right of NAQA to take decisions on such cases, although it has been provided for by the national legislation.

The list of authors whose plagiarism in publications was detected included the previous minister of education, a politician who had been actively involved in making the Ukrainian legal system corrupt and who is now under US sanctions outside Ukraine (they both had a common lawyer), the dean of a university law school, and a doctor who had stolen the original information from the practitioners who provided medical care to police-injured participants during the Revolution of Dignity (2013-2014) on the Maidan. Studying such publications, the NAQA Ethics Committee sometimes made real "discoveries." For example, in one of the dissertations, they found a "technology" to increase the size of the text by randomly repeating pieces in different parts of the paper.

A number of obstacles prevent improving the situation in the field of academic integrity in Ukraine, including the widespread use of plagiarism and other forms of dishonesty in the 1990s and 2000s, selective accusations of integrity violations, lack of awareness of the rules of academic writing, public settling of private scores, the use of such accusations in political campaigns, and attempts to present the problem as if it were inevitably unsolvable.

This approach makes it possible to fight against violations of the principles of academic integrity by focusing on the process rather than the end result. While it is crucial, first of all, to eliminate the social preconditions that give rise to such violations, other questions arise for which there are currently no answers, such as: does this entail an intention to forgive or, conversely, to catch and punish all those who committed violations of academic integrity in the past?

Judicial casuistry became the main tool in the fight against NAQA activities. In particular, a new member co-opted into NAQA in 2022 managed to halt the Agency's activities through the courts, claiming that students should not only have their own representatives there but also represent all fields of knowledge, like academicians. He was not the only one to imitate a public activist. The Agency's operations were restored by the Government given the obvious absurdity of the situation. In the end, the Supreme Court of Ukraine recognized all NAQA's efforts to uphold the principles of academic integrity appropriate and legal (The Supreme Court of Ukraine, 2023).

In Ukraine, fruitful and often emotional discussions are going on concerning the importance of adherence to the principles of academic integrity and ways to protect them. Let us recall the debate between Maksym Strikha and Ihor Anisimov, on the one hand, and Maksym Matsala, on the other (Ihor Anisimov, Maksym Strikha, Maksym Matsala, 2023). Despite the heated debate, in both cases, the authors agree on the importance of the role of civil society activists and that instances of violations of academic integrity deserving attention goes far beyond plagiarism and other examples of manipulation with academic texts. In fact, any kind of dishonesty in the academic field can be classified as a certain type of such violation.

The Case of the Bill "On Academic Integrity"

Natalia Kuznetsova, Ivan Nazarov, and Leonid Yefimenko believe that HEIs lack a critical attitude towards themselves and they also tend to hide the facts of violations of academic integrity. The authors draw the conclusion that

> "well-known international principles of academic integrity in the field of higher education and scientific activities are recognized, but mostly not observed. In most cases, this is not connected with conscious, systematic activities that are incompatible with the concept of academic integrity, but most frequently indicates a desire to prevent the disclosure and dissemination of information about violations detected and resolve conflicts 'peacefully'."

Understanding the temporary nature of such measures, they recognize that

> "an effective scenario of solving a considerable part of the problems of compliance with academic integrity can be the adoption of the Law of Ukraine "On Academic Integrity", which would ensure not only recognition of the importance of this phenomenon for the future of Ukrainian higher education and its presentation in the European Space, but also clearly define that not only the National Agency, the Ministry of Education and Science of Ukraine, or other state body, but also all higher education institutions and scientific institutions are responsible for the quality of higher education and research results, and, accordingly, for compliance with the principles of academic integrity" (Natalia Kuznetsova, Ivan Nazarov, Leonid Yefimenko, 2021).

Considering all the above-mentioned issues, the NAQA decided to draft a special bill "On Academic Integrity" in 2020, which means that the main responsibility in the current environment is transferred to the national level. This law will also establish the key concepts and procedures, which will make it impossible for violators to use casuistic approaches for their defence in court. The first version of this draft law was published in the Agency's Annual Report (NAQA. Report, 2020).

That was a highly unconventional step which however opens up significant prospects for finding effective solutions. Intriguing was the discussion involving the members of the International Advisory Board. Eventually, the idea was supported as the most relevant to the current Ukrainian social circumstances. Unfortunately, debates between the members of parliament and experts are still ongoing regarding the form and aim that the law should pursue: to establish a system of punishment or, on the opposite, incentives.

I would like to emphasize that the draft law "On Academic Integrity" cannot encourage initiative; it can only distribute responsibility and create tools to counter legal casuistry. There is no other way to promote initiative within higher education institutions and university communities than by establishing comprehensive university autonomy, which in Ukraine has so far stopped when facing the issue of financial autonomy. And the argument that it is not the right time to address the issue with the full-scale Russian war against Ukraine does not work. Without comprehensive university autonomy, Ukraine will not have world-class universities.

Academic achievements should correlate with increased opportunities to find more resources for the development of higher education institutions. It is not only about money, but it is also about values. It is also a path to intellectual independence, freedom of speech, and freedom to carry out research. From a certain perspective, we can view the university as a mass medium, an independent tribune for expressing socially important ideas. That is, we will eventually see the growth of the social value of Ukrainian universities through financial autonomy.

Conclusions

Fortunately, in Ukraine, an active civil society represents a critical mass of activists and volunteers ready to drive reforms in every professional field. It should be added that this broad volunteer movement transformed very easily and quickly into an armed civil society. The academic sphere deserves not only reformation as a certain stress resulting from a transition from one quality to another but also attention and support from the government.

The implementation of comprehensive university autonomy will lead to the creation of a group of responsible and independent HEIs that will become centres of innovative ecosystems. They will transform into influential social players, contributing to the dissemination of critical thinking values, the growth of up-to-date political culture, and the strengthening of the cultural identity of Ukrainian society. The issues of academic integrity are among the most sensitive indicators of such reforms.

All the efforts aimed at developing the academic sphere in independent Ukraine in the context of achieving appropriate standards of academic integrity will continue to focus on the implementation of comprehensive university autonomy and the development of a unique internal culture in each HEI. Only the real self-governing status of Ukrainian universities will enable to activate the importance of reputational factors to ensure their quality and academic integrity. Accordingly, the role of responsible university communities and their ethical choices will be growing.

References

Alla Yevtushenko. Collection of music stolen by Russia: proven facts (Ukr.) // Espresso TV channel, June, 1, 2022: https://espreso.tv/kolektsiya-kradenoi-rosieyu-muziki-dovedeni-fakti-plagiatu

Ihor Anisimov, Maksym Strikha. Academic (dis)honesty: what's wrong with it?; Maksym Matsala. There are no shades of gray when it comes to plagiarism (Ukr.) // Svit (World) Newspaper, 2023: https://cutt.us/pYc0O

Kalashnikov statue changed because of German weapon // BBC, 22 September, 2017: https://www.bbc.com/news/world-europe-41367394

Leah Wortham. ENHANCING ACADEMIC INTEGRITY IN UKRAINIAN HIGHER EDUCATION COMMENTS ON PROPOSED PROCEDURE FOR THE ANNULMENT OF DECISIOINS OF SPECIALIZED ACADEMIC COUNCILS TO CONFER A RESEARCH DEGREE, November 2019: https://en.naqa.gov.ua/wp-content/uploads/2019/12/NJ_Leah-Wortham_Report-with-Recs_on_Academic-Integrity_Dec-11_2019_ENG.pdf

NAQA. Mission Statement and Strategy of The National Agency for Higher Education Quality Assurance (2019): https://en.naqa.gov.ua/?page_id=642

NAQA. Advisory Board (2020): https://en.naqa.gov.ua/?page_id=1035

NAQA. Report on the Activities of the National Agency for Higher Education Quality Assurance (2020), pp. 210-229 (Ukr.): https://cutt.us/NkPWw

NAQA. Report on the Activities of the National Agency for Higher Education Quality Assurance (2022), pp. 123-127: https://en.naqa.gov.ua/wp-content/uploads/2022/12/REPORT-ON-THE-ACTIVITIES-OF-THE-NATIONAL-AGENCY.pdf

Natalia Kuznetsova, Ivan Nazarov, Leonid Yefimenko (2021). Areas of reforming the statutory regulation of academic integrity in Ukraine. Journal of the National Academy of Legal Sciences of Ukraine, 28(3), 176-185: https://www.researchgate.net/publication/355072519_Areas_of_reforming_the_statutory_regulation_of_academic_integrity_in_Ukraine

Self-Assessment Report of the National Agency for Higher Education Quality Assurance, 2021: https://en.naqa.gov.ua/wp-content/uploads/2021/02/Self-Assessment-Report.pdf

Serhiy Kvit. A roadmap to higher education reform via autonomy // University World News, 2018: https://www.universityworldnews.com/post.php?story=20180316092127837

Serhiy Kvit, Nataliia Stukalo. FIDES FACIT FIDEM: Building Trust-Based QA through Supportive Communication and Transparency // Quality Assurance Review for Higher Education, Vol. 11, No. 1−2, 2021, pp. 39–47: https://www.aracis.ro/wp-content/uploads/2022/03/4-Kvit-Stukalo.pdf

Standards and Guidelines for Quality Assurance in the European Higher Education Area (ESG), 2015 // https://www.enqa.eu/wp-content/uploads/2015/11/ESG_2015.pdf

The Supreme Court of Ukraine. RESOLUTION ON BEHALF OF UKRAINE dated March 17, 2023, Kyiv. Case No. 640/835/20, administrative proceeding No. 9901/8729/21 (Ukr.): https://reyestr.court.gov.ua/Review/109635836

The USSR stole anthems from the Nazis (Ukr.) // ICTV Channel, 2021: https://ranok.ictv.ua/ua/videos/srsr-krav-gimni-u-natsistiv/

A Perspective on 'Fake News'[81]

In order to understand current social processes in the global and national (local) dimensions related to the post-truth era, we need to understand their recurrence in history. That is, it is important for us to take space and time into consideration. Then, according to Wilhelm Dilthey, a classic of romantic hermeneutics, if we understand general patterns, it will be easier for us to understand their unique nature in each new historical period.

The phenomenon of fake news has a long history. After all, it is human to tell a lie sometimes. Deliberate misleading has always been part of the political life of any society. In other words, there is nothing new when a person or a corporation is trying to mislead another person or even the whole society. Authoritarian and totalitarian regimes, such as German Nazism and Russian Communism, offered nothing but fake news.

Leftist intellectuals have repeatedly claimed that the Western news industry is not truthful enough. The classic work *Manufacturing Consent: The Political Economy of the Mass Media* (1988) by Edward S. Herman and Noam Chomsky can be mentioned here. Although these authors did not use the term "fake news", they perceived American media critically, thus protecting the public interest against the explicit or implicit media representation of the interests of various power groups through the so-called "news filters".

The ideological legacy of postmodernism, based on the ideas of the contextuality, relativity and multiplicity of meanings, has substantially contributed to the justification of fake news. It seems that all depends on one's point of view: credibility is relative, and no genuine truth exists. We only play with words and meanings. You can really consider some news as fake news. And that's OK. However, it may look quite true to another consumer. If one news

---

81 *Kyiv Post*, October 26, 2019. This is the text of a speech given at a Swedish conference that took place on October 10–12, 2019, called "Fake News Cultures: The Context of Viral Disinformation Across East and West".

producer has their own view of events, then another is said to have a right to a different interpretation of the same events.

In fact, such "applied postmodernism", as Timothy Snyder says, is a kind of manifestation of authoritarian power in new social circumstances. We find it directly connected to the liberal rhetoric of free choice. The word "interpretation" loses its fruitful hermeneutical meaning here, breaking away from critical thinking and shifting into propaganda.

Postmodernism has also chosen tradition in its general meaning as an object for deconstruction, treating it as a potentially dangerous phantasm. According to the founder of philosophical hermeneutics, Hans-Georg Gadamer, a tradition means the ground on which the participant of a conversation stands. It forms a prior judgment in a fruitful conversation in which all the participants are striving to discover the truth. Thus, the hermeneutical position is of a modernist nature. It can clearly distinguish truth from lies, or fake news.

We are also facing a phenomenon pointed out by Neil Postman when he explained the difference between two dangers: a prohibition on reading books and no need to read them. His follower in Ukraine, professor Boris Potiatynnyk, speaks not only about media literacy, but also about media philosophy, media criticism, and media ecology: identification and resistance to dangerous "pathogenic" texts, which are brought up by critical thinking.

Coming back to the issue of modern fake news, we see the main problem not in the attempt of a certain political force to mislead a mass audience (such attempts have always taken place), but in the reaction of that audience. According to the Uses and Gratifications theory, we need to find out not only what the media do to the audience, but also what the audience does to the media (Elihu Katz). That is, what the audience wants to see in the media.

The post-truth era is characterized by the reluctance of the mass audience to see a truly holistic picture of events, ignoring reliable sources of information and wishing to select only cozy and comfortable, yet invariably fake, news. From a certain point of view, the general public has itself created a demand for such news. I remember very well that in the Soviet Union we had another problem, namely, the lack of reliable sources of truthful information. That is why "Aesopian language" became so widespread there: people tried to "read between the lines", searching for a hidden truth.

Today's global triumph of post-truth indicates that not only in post-totalitarian countries like Ukraine but also in bastions of the free press such as the United Kingdom and the United States of America, mass audiences fall prey to special informational operations during election campaigns or referenda. Anyone who wants to mislead addresses information to consumers with messages they want to hear. Contradictory promises are thrown altogether — promises that are impossible to realize. Experts are talking about a crisis of critical thinking: this skill is not now generally considered a social value.

In Ukraine television remains the most influential of all media, counting for 74% of impact versus the 24% of social media (Detector Media, 2019). However, the role of social media is much bigger since it executes a selective function by ranking media news through different interpretive lenses. In this way, freedom of speech is losing its professional grounds by producing different sets of fake news instead. Various consumer groups select the kind of news which they like. Such news is misleading and produces parallel media realities.

A new category of politicians is emerging: populists. They are those who offer easy solutions to hard problems. This phenomenon is not new either, as any politician has at all times tried to promise more than he or she could deliver. However, populism appears to be the only way to real power in media discourse because of the parallel media reality created.

According to the research done by the Kantar TNS company, which was commissioned by the Center for Economic Strategy in August 2019, 84% of Ukrainians support populist politics, while 59% of the population find it a realistic option. This is exactly the dimension of a media reality in which the majority of society is literally thinking with the help of fantastic categories.

It means that social changes have taken place on a global scale. No less dramatically have the mass media changed. Earlier, such transformation was impossible due to a lack of technological capacity. The explosion of social media brought the opportunity to get inside every home, as cheaply and efficiently as radio once did. Vladimir Lenin, the father of modern political marketing, could not even dream of such a possibility to convey his arguments, which were propagandistic fake news back then, to everyone, the largest and the smallest social groups.

In parallel with emerging internet and citizen journalism, Edward S. Herman, the co-author of the *Manufacturing Consent*, expressed hope for the technological strengthening of truly independent news. Now every citizen journalist can create their own content and compete with professional media. However, very quickly everything changed into its opposite: the new media undermined the economy of professional media, declaring that there was "no need" for professional (responsible) journalism; accompanying the talk about the political indifference of social media platforms, there grew "high technologies" for manipulating mass consciousness.

Propaganda opportunities, unheard of even by Joseph Goebbels, have been created. Public tastes have declined and a new atomization of mass audiences has taken place. At least it can be called new if we link the first atomization to the Magic Bullet theory and Hypodermic Needle theory, which were developed in the last century on the basis of the Great Depression in the United States and in response to the fear of Western democracies of Nazism's propaganda possibilities. Of course, it is easiest to manipulate poor people who have no job, nor property, but also a society most concerned with the hedonistic whims of its members, who are not deeply connected to common cultural values.

In this regard, Zbigniew Brzezinski complained about the ignorance of the public at large and a lack of traditional values among the elite, and, as a consequence, the spreading of a garrison-state mentality or else a wallowing in self-righteous cultural hedonism. The atomization of society is not a new phenomenon, either. Even the ancient Greeks knew that it led to ochlocracy (the rule of the mob). Problems of education and culture, as well as the exceptional impact of fake news, are common to both the first and the second waves of atomization.

What is the difference between today's post-truth and fake news and the manipulations of mass consciousness in ancient Rome?

First of all, the presence of the internet and social media. Ancient Oriental despotisms were not yet totalitarian states. It was only in the twentieth century that it became technologically possible to control all the information people received during their lifetime, as well as their education and behavior.

So today, the press, and first of all, but not exclusively, social media are largely shaping the political agenda. Mediatization theory says that politicians are increasingly trying to tailor their messages to the demands of mass media, and so perhaps the press is not just a tool for informing, mediating and interacting. Mass media are acquiring an important systematic weight of their own and independently affecting public life. Therefore, in order to better understand society, it is important to understand modern media. Coming back to our topic, we would like to add that it is important to understand not only mass media but particularly the nature of fake news.

The theories of mass communication which deal with globalization processes tend to over-generalize. Thus, Glocalization theory talks about a certain marketing interaction between the global and the local, in which global ideas and patterns of behavior are mostly adapted to local rhetoric and national peculiarities. In fact, in order to understand the impact of fake news, in each case, we need a deeper understanding of the situation at the national state level. After all, freedom of speech can only be realized in the framework of specific national legislation created in response to demands from society. That is, the ideal of the freedom of speech can be successfully fulfilled only when the society needs it and treats it as a value.

The impact of fake news is not just a global trend. The largest state by territory, which can be seen simultaneously as a global gas station and as the biggest propaganda media corporation, plays a special role in disseminating fake news. As an authoritarian state, Russia has been most successful in creating and spreading fake news, including for domestic use. Putin's efforts have actually created a parallel fake media reality there. Considering the fact that Russia is a global investor in fake news, we can talk about a global informational war, or rather, a hybrid war started by Russia against the Western world.

Ukrainian political reality also deserves strong criticism, yet from the opposite perspective. Ukrainian society can be characterized as extremely naive, as it thinks within the categories of an impossible "ideal state". What does this mean? — If the political party in power does not meet public expectations, Ukrainian society immediately launches into a process to completely reload power. This is probably grounded in valuing political rights and freedoms as such, rather than in the comprehension of the value of having an independent state: not yet perfect, but already one's own.

On the other hand, public institutions are weak. Due to naive public attitudes to the liberal rules of the game, understanding the reasons for their creation is often absent. For example, openly pro-Russian media can function legally in Ukraine, which obviously cannot be accepted as normal. A powerful and demanding civil society was a major positive achievement of the Revolution of Dignity, also known as the EuroMaidan Revolution, in particular the volunteer movement and the new traditions of direct-action democracy.

Today civil society is facing new challenges related to the overwhelming majority ("mono-majority") of pro-presidential political parties in the Parliament and the accompanying temptation to authoritarianism. The unwillingness to ask real questions and take on responsibility also result in the degradation of the journalist's profession. This was evident in the rudimentary questions that Ukrainian journalists asked Oleg Sentsov and Oleksandr Kolchenko during their first press conference after Russian imprisonment.

So, fake news does have influence in Ukraine and Russia, but the reasons for that are different. In Russia, there is a kind of public agreement to an authoritarian state. In general, imperial "greatness" appears to Russians as a higher value than democratic rights and freedoms. In Ukraine, on the contrary, excessive democratic turbulence and the absence of traditions of effective state institutions are intensifying the influence of mass consciousness manipulation. The tough critical media discourse in Ukraine very much resembles an informational war of all against all. What is more, none of the parties take into account the participation of the external Russian factor.

We can conclude that fake news does influence and win under all kinds of political circumstances and systems—including liberal democratic countries and societies that prefer authoritarian rule. Modern technologies can also contribute to post-truth. Under such hybrid circumstances, various philosophical, economic, and political theories and ideologies are losing their meaning because liberals and conservatives, right and left, Christians and agnostics are unable to stand against fake news by offering a truly genuine agenda for society.

The title of a book by the Ukrainian intellectual and diplomat Dmytro Kuleba sounds precisely the right note: *The Struggle for Reality: How to Win in a World of Fakes, Truths, and Communities* (2019). People should hear and learn to understand each other by meeting one another in real life, not through social media. Politicians should be held accountable for the real matters in which they are involved. This is possible with the help of critical thinking, which can be enabled by true education and relevant social circumstances, including the opportunity to enjoy political rights and freedoms.

How to Fight Fake News?

So, let us try to summarize. How can we fight fake news? In order to answer this question, we need to consider the following points.

Firstly, for an open and serious conversation in society, critical thinking initiators of such a talk (intellectuals and politicians) must be present, as well as the technological ability to extract this discourse from the ambient informational noise and fabricated manipulative messages.

Secondly, the response of the audience matters. Public energies should be directed to support educational institutions and academic research—only they can motivate people to start thinking in a really critical way. It is important to preserve what makes us human, stressed Martin Heidegger, one of the founders of hermeneutic tradition in philosophy, meaning the ability to think deeply. He spoke of philosophy as "the benefit of the useless", as the denial of a superficial, consumerist, and selfish approach.

Thirdly, tradition can no longer be opposed to critical discourse. It is important to keep your attention, as was urged by Paul Ricœur, a distinguished representative of philosophical hermeneutics and honorary professor of Kyiv-Mohyla Academy: Europeans should not forget anything, but they should not be kept hostage by their own memory. At the same time, according to the founder of philosophical hermeneutics, Hans-Georg Gadamer, tradition is part of our identity and shapes the necessary pre-judgments for our critical thinking.

Fourthly, a victory of professional media, professional journalism, and professional news (value-oriented news) over fake news is possible at the level of the independent state. It is not the global, but the national level that is fundamental: every society must resolve this challenge for itself.

Ukraine in the Struggle for Independence in the Age of Post-Truth[82]

Rhetoric is important. It can be formed not only on the basis of independent research but also on established stereotypes, depending on the political intent. In this way, very often the actual essence of some social phenomena or events slips away from our understanding. Rhetoric will make you wise or stupid, a hero or a criminal. It all depends on what type of discourse you fall into. Especially when it comes to Ukraine's struggle for its independence from Russia and finding its place in the modern geopolitical space. This means primarily fighting battles for the formation of rhetorical frameworks for understanding and interpretation.

In Ukraine, the word "patriotism" is connected with the rhetoric of the Soviet period. In its place, the most common term in use throughout the country is "nationalism", which expresses the fight against aggressive imperialism and chauvinism—in the present context, Russia. In Ukraine, "nationalism" and "patriotism" are also often used interchangeably. However, such nuances do not affect the global hybrid confrontation, in which Ukraine is forced to endure numerous planned attacks and provocations.

On April 23, 2018, over 50 members of the U.S. Congress signed a letter to U.S. Deputy Secretary of State John Sullivan requesting diplomatic pressure be applied on Poland and Ukraine for their alleged tolerance and even funding of Holocaust denial, xenophobia, and anti-Semitism.[83] Representatives of the Ukrainian government and civil society immediately denied the allegations. The Association of Jewish Organizations and Communities of Ukraine considered the "letter to be a piece of anti-Ukrainian defamation which is already in use by the propaganda sector of Russian Federation's hybrid war on Ukraine".[84]

---

82 *Kyiv Post*, June 13, 2019.
83 https://khanna.house.gov/sites/khanna.house.gov/files/Combat%20Anti-Semitism%20Letter.pdf
84 "Statement of the Presidium of the Vaad of Ukraine in Response to the Letter of US Congressmen Concerning Anti-Semitism in Poland and Ukraine",

At its core, the letter displays a total lack of awareness of Ukraine, its history, and current policies. For many Americans, Ukraine is a little-known land, located somewhere between Poland and Russia, relentlessly causing petty problems that prevent US officials from engaging in important business.

However, the letter also suggests that deeply ingrained stereotypes may be responsible. Incessant and coordinated defamation, insufficiently challenged, in time becomes fact. Hence, the stereotype that virulent anti-Semitism is inherent to Ukraine is a part of popular culture, academic discourse, and journalism in the West.

The recent election of a Jewish President in Ukraine and, simultaneously, the presence of a sitting Jewish Prime Minister seriously undermines some of the accusations in the letter, but not all. Many reporters and analysts have tried to resist the lifting of the cloud of anti-Semitism that has been put over Ukraine. In their articles and studies, they routinely note Ukrainians' inability to condemn their anti-Semitic past, especially during the liberation struggle of the twentieth century. Hence, the story goes, despite Ukraine being one of the most tolerant countries in the world toward its Jewish minority, the specter of persecution and pogroms lies just below the surface.

This narrative is pervasive in the West. One of many examples of such rhetoric is an article by Melinda Haring in *The Washington Post*.[85] Ms. Haring's article is worthy of note because she is part of a program at the Atlantic Council think thank that is focused on contemporary Ukraine. For this reason, it is important to look at these issues from a perspective that takes into account the origins of political rhetoric, especially at this time, a seeming turning point for Ukraine in its quest for mature nation-statehood.

---

https://www.vaadua.org/statement-presidium-vaad-ukraine-response-letter-us-congressmen-concerning-anti-semitism-poland-and

85 Melinda Haring, "Putin calls Ukrainians 'fascists.' They're about to swear in a Jewish president", *The Washington Post*, May 13, 2019, https://www.washingtonpost.com/opinions/2019/05/13/putin-calls-ukrainians-fascists-theyre-about-swear-jewish-president/

Whence Came Ukraine?

How to understand Ukraine, this strange nation, which seemed to appear on the map of Eastern Europe after the collapse of the Soviet Union in 1991, exactly where the Western world was accustomed to seeing Russia? What is even more baffling to many is that the political culture of Ukrainian society dramatically differs from that of Russian society. For some reason, Ukrainians, unlike Russians, need freedom of speech and freedom of political choice. Moreover, they are ready to die for their freedom. Ukrainians are desperately fighting for their country against Russia, invoking Western values, and refusing, at the cost of their blood and lives, to join Putin's *Rusky Mir* (Russian world).

Usually, we regard national interests that lead to conflict and military confrontation as manifestations of "nationalism". Many views on Ukrainian nationalism involve much misunderstanding and manipulation, something akin to equating (Kyivan) Rus' with Russia. If Rus' (tenth to thirteenth centuries) is the medieval name of the first great state on the territory of modern Ukraine, the concept of Russia doesn't even appear until 1721, and then as a consequence of a political decision by Peter the Great. Until then Russia was known as "Moscow" or "Muscovy", according to the tradition that a sovereign territory bore the name of its capital.

Russian imperialist dogma claims Kyiv (the capital of Ukraine) as its own. Kyiv is a crucial component of the Russian imperial myth, without which that state construct implodes. Hence, we are saddled with the fake political thesis of Kyiv as "the mother of Russian cities", deliberately misrepresented from medieval chronicles, deliberately misidentifying or equating "Rus'" and "Russia". To be clear, this "misunderstanding" is not an esoteric exercise. On the contrary, it has a very specific and immediate real-world purpose: to validate the invasion, occupation and territorial absorption of Ukraine by Russia.

Ukrainian political leaders have always been portrayed by Russia in demonic terms. Ukraine's eighteenth-century Hetman Ivan Mazepa was even officially anathematized by the Russian Orthodox Church. From the eighteenth to the twenty-first centuries, political and intellectual leaders who dared to insist on the separateness of the Ukrainian people, language, history, and political culture were persecuted. Depending on the period, they were labeled as "traitors", "Mazepintsy", "separatists", "Petliurivtsy", "fascists", "Ukrainian-German bourgeois nationalists", "Banderivtsy", or simply "bourgeois nationalists"; today, again, they are "Banderivtsy" and "fascists".

Different Shades of Nationalism

The word "nationalism" has many connotations. Merriam-Webster provides positive and negative meanings. Nationalism is "loyalty and devotion to a nation; especially: a sense of national consciousness". It is also "exalting one nation above all others and placing primary emphasis on promotion of its culture and interests as opposed to those of other nations or supranational groups; intense nationalism was one of the causes of the war".

The use of the word in modern media is indiscriminate and occurs in very different, unrelated settings and senses, and without appropriate context and clarification. This term can be used to refer to the liberation of Ukrainians,[86] one of the main internal factors leading to the collapse of the Soviet Union as an empire, one that was itself based on Russian "nationalism", the Cold War operating as the external factor. It can also be maintained that Ukrainian state-building "nationalism" resists the imperial "nationalism" of the Putin regime. The media also uses "nationalism" to denote various current marginal xenophobic movements in Western Europe.

Hence, the same word—depending on its use by an author, and/or understanding by a reader—can cast political phenomena in a positive or negative light. In this regard, the Ukrainian liberation movement of the twentieth century continues to be perceived through the lens of Russian imperialism and communism, as it relates to Nazism and fascism (terms also used as synonyms of

---

86 The term "nationalists" was gradually applied not only to representatives of the Ukrainian resistance movement fighting against Soviet power and Russian imperialism, but also to all Ukrainians who, as a matter of principle, did not switch to speaking in Russian even under total Russification.

nationalism). Some Western researchers who adhere to this Russian interpretation are from what could be called the neo-Soviet historical school.

The pejorative term "fascism" is so often used in the post-Soviet space interchangeably with "nationalism" that its true meaning has become obscured. In his classic treatment of this topic, historian Alexander Motyl of Rutgers University notes an important precondition of fascism: an already existing state. The key distinction between nationalisms and nationalists, professor Motyl contends, concerns not the goal, but the means.

> "Whereas legally, democratically, and constitutionally inclined nationalists will employ legal, democratic, and constitutional means, illegally, undemocratically, and unconstitutionally inclined nationalists will employ illegal, undemocratic, and unconstitutional means. That is to say, they will break laws, be conspiratorial, regimented, disciplined, hierarchical, and use violence. This is why sloppy scholars believe that nationalists 'look like' fascists".[87]

In Putin's interpretation of history, the most important concept is the "Great Patriotic War" — a term coined specifically to divert attention from the USSR's cooperation with Nazi Germany at the beginning of World War II. That is to say, the period between September 1939 and June 1941 is simply ignored. Yet it is this very period which really reveals the kinship of the two totalitarian regimes in terms of imperialism and crimes against humanity.

However, "historical discourse" takes place not only (conditionally) from pro-Russian and pro-Ukrainian standpoints. A group of Western intellectuals, including professional historians, issued an open letter against the decommunization laws adopted by the Verkhovna Rada of Ukraine on April 9, 2015.[88] They opposed

---

87 Alexander Motyl, "On Nationalism and Fascism, Part 2", *World Affairs*, June 14, 2013, http://web.archive.org/web/20130620101216/ http://www.worldaffairsjournal.org/blog/alexander-j-motyl/nationalism-and-fascism-part-2; also in: Alexander J. Motyl, *Ukraine vs. Russia: Revolution, Democracy, and War. Selected Articles and Blogs* (Washington, DC: Westphalia Press, 2017), p. 527

88 David R. Marples, "Open Letter from Scholars and Experts on Ukraine Re. the So-Called 'Anti-Communist Law'", Krytika, March 2015, https://krytyka.com/en/articles/open-letter-scholars-and-experts-ukraine-re-so-called-anti-communist-law

alleged state interference in the field of academic historical scientific discourse, since, according to them, the law falsifies "real" history, denies freedom of speech, and even criminalizes a "wrong" interpretation of history.

The latter statement is not true. According to the research conducted by the Institute for Development of Freedom of Information, thanks to these laws, Ukraine has provided the most openness and given the greatest access to all archival materials from the totalitarian period in the post-Communist space.[89] The Ukrainian Institute of National Remembrance is working to remove all ideological stereotypes associated with the most difficult periods of Ukraine's past: to omit nothing and to speak of everything, to prevent populist and demagogic abuses, and to move toward substantive and document-based open discussions of the past.

The decommunization laws aim to free Ukraine from the consequences of communist ideological indoctrination conducted on a massive scale. They also prohibit the symbols of totalitarian regimes, equating the criminality of communism and Nazism. The decommunization of Ukraine should be compared with the de-Nazification of postwar Germany. Without these measures, deep social transformations and a decisive break with the political culture of the post-Soviet world, dominated by Putin's Russia, are impossible.

Take a single illustrative example. After the EuroMaidan Revolution that ended President Viktor Yanukovych's presidency in 2014, all Lenin monuments were removed in Ukraine. Similarly, in Kharkiv, the areas around the monuments to Lenin and to the Ukrainian poet Taras Shevchenko in the city center were symbolic spaces where pro-Putin and pro-Ukrainian forces rallied, this resulting in clashes between them. After the removal of the Lenin monument on September 28, 2014, the communist and Russian chauvinists lost their symbolic space in Kharkiv, became demoralized, and ceased organizing regular street protests and violence.

---

89   Open Archives, 2018 Rating, http://www.open-archives.org/en/rating/index/?year=2018

Neo-Soviet Historiography

The roots of neo-Soviet historiography in the American academic tradition lie in the protests against the Vietnam War and in similar processes that took place in Western European universities in the 1960s. During those years, there was a "leftward" transformation of American universities. This shift involved a progressive critique of capitalist discourse, including imperialism, militarism, and the remnants of McCarthyism.

Importantly, it also heralded the democratization of university life with a special progressive focus on human rights, in the spirit of the coryphaei of the Frankfurt School. However, along with criticism of various Western reactionary circles and their political practices, this shift in academic life, openly or otherwise, also brought with it a corresponding positive stance toward the Soviet Union and international "communist experiments".

As a result of the academic leftward shift of American universities in the 1960s, some scholars regard the Ukrainian liberation movement as a deeply reactionary phenomenon. The problem was that such interpretive traditions did not make a clear distinction between critical theory (neo-Marxism) and Russian communism as an imperial project. Both have common sources. However, they pursue different goals.

Such academic discourse is rather reminiscent of media trolling, including cherry picking historical facts and events, imposing current political correctness without regard for objectivity and verification, and avoiding the creation of a complete picture. Today, in particular, this discourse is characterized by a denial of the postcolonial status of Ukraine; democratic values are advocated without an acceptance of the restoration of the Ukrainian state as an expression of these values, even depicting Russia's military invasion in 2014 as an internecine civil war.

For illustration, one need only look at the group of scholars surrounding the American-Canadian professor John-Paul Himka. This group mostly consists of his former graduate students. Its activities are more akin to a political mission than to historiography.

Taras Kuzio, the British-Canadian academic and expert, described a situation at a seminar in Columbia University in April 2013.[90] After Himka's presentation, titled "The Lontsky Street Prison Memorial Museum as an Example of Postcommunist Holocaust Negationism", a Swedish researcher Per Anders Rudling, moderating the meeting, interrupted Volodymyr Viatrovych (one of the founders and a member of the Supervisory Board of the Lontsky Museum) and refused him the right to speak. The seminar moderator prevented Viatrovych from stating that Himka had not only never been to the Museum, but was not even familiar with the Museum's website. Taras Kuzio considered this unacceptable in an academic environment, as it showed the biased approach of the event organizers and contradicted the principle of freedom of speech.

Perhaps a few more examples of the neo-Soviet approach to understanding contemporary political reality, resulting from ideological intrusions into historiography, are warranted. Of course, we are talking about the erroneous understanding of the tectonic changes in Ukrainian society related to the value-based and geopolitical shift of Ukraine towards the West. Volodymyr Ishchenko, an activist and researcher, consistently promoted the notion that the ongoing war in Donbas was a "civil war".[91] That is, he regards the hostilities in the Donbas region as an internal Ukrainian conflict.

In September 2015 in San Francisco, Ivan Katchanovski, a Canadian academic, presented his "study" on how the Maidan activists themselves shot the "Heavenly Hundred".[92] This study became a part of Viktor Yanukovych's judicial defense. In March 2017, a

---

90   Taras Kuzio, "This Is Not How Ukrainian History Should Be Debated (at Columbia or Elsewhere)", *The Ukrainian Weekly*, May 19, 2013.
91   Volodymyr Ishchenko, "Ukraine's Fractures", *New Left Review* 87, May-June 2014, https://newleftreview.org/II/87/volodymyr-ishchenko-ukraine-s-fractures; "Ukraine has ignored the far right for too long—it must wake up to the danger", *The Guardian*, November 13, 2014, https://www.theguardian.com/commentisfree/2014/nov/13/ukraine-far-right-fascism-mps
92   Ivan Katchanovski, "The 'Snipers' Massacre' on the Maidan in Ukraine", Paper prepared for presentation at the Annual Meeting of the American Political Science Association in San Francisco, September 3-6, 2015, https://yadi.sk/i/4u4vSXi4jLDEF. Interestingly, this researcher was never previously associated with criminology. He positioned himself as an economist, historian, and political scientist.

German expert, Andreas Umland, sought to dissuade Ukrainians, on live TV (Channel 5), from regarding members of the Ukrainian Insurgent Army as fighters for Ukraine's independence (or at least advised Ukrainians to somehow hide this fact), arguing that the difficult circumstances of Ukraine's international position required this.[93] At the same time, in his opinion, the Poles, Lithuanians, and Belarusians did not need to take similar steps regarding their liberation movements, as their present political situation was different.

A Bloody Twentieth Century

In the interwar period, the West tried to engage with both Soviet Russia and Nazi Germany. Initially, Mussolini and Hitler were favored for their anti-communist orientation. Subsequently, the West settled on Stalin in a war that he and Hitler had begun. Ukrainian nationalists between the two world wars viewed the USSR as the greatest existential threat to Ukraine: the communist system wrapped itself around Russian imperialism and manifested itself in policies of genocide and mass terror, putting in question the very physical survival of Ukrainians.

However, the Entente operating at that time decided to ignore the Ukrainian question. With the exception of Czechoslovakia, the newly created states after World War I—Poland, Romania, and Hungary—pursued an aggressive policy of denationalizing the Ukrainian lands that had come under their control. They diverted the attention of the Entente countries by engaging in cynical reasoning: since there is no Ukrainian state, there is no nation and hence there is no problem. Therefore, the Ukrainian liberation movement had little choice but to cooperate during the interwar period with the anti-communist military and intelligence services of Lithuania, Finland, Italy, and Germany.

Later, when the Western Allies united with the Soviet Union against Hitler, Ukrainians were once again in a fateful predicament. According to the British historian Norman Davies, the problem was

---

[93] Andreas Umland, ЗА ЧАЙ.COM, TV Channel 5, March 8, 2018, https://www.5.ua/polityka/za-chaycom-ekspert-z-henezy-putinizmu-andreas-umland-u-efiri-5-kanalu-o-2310-140324.html

that Ukrainian nationalists fought not only against Hitler but also against Stalin,[94] whom many in the West regarded not as a necessary evil in the fight against another evil but as a "great ally" of the West in World War II.[95]

From the very first days of the Nazi occupation of Ukraine, mass arrests of OUN members began, including its top leaders. Transcripts of the interrogations of Stepan Bandera (imprisoned from 1941 to 1944 at the Sachsenhausen concentration camp) make it clear that there was no common ground between the OUN and the Nazi regime.[96]

> "If you really want to understand what made such Ukrainian nationalists as Stepan Bandera and Roman Shukhevych", Alexander Motyl says, "don't compare them to Adolf Hitler, Benito Mussolini, or Francisco Franco, but to George Washington, Jefferson Davis, Giuseppe Mazzini, Giuseppe Garibaldi, Menachem Begin, Vladimir Jabotynsky, Theodor Herzl, Ahmed Ben Bella, Ho Chi Minh, Mao Zedong, Josip Broz Tito, Simón Bolívar, and Emiliano Zapata. Personally, if I were doing comparative biographies, I'd do one on Bandera and Begin as political leaders and another on Shukhevych and Tito as military leaders. And then I'd compare the Ukrainian nationalist theorist Dmytro Dontsov with the Zionist theorist Jabotynsky".[97]

The Ukrainian liberation movement envisaged the overthrow of the Soviet Union as a "prison of nations" and the establishment in its place of independent nation-states, which is what happened in 1991. Ukrainian armed resistance lasted until the end of the 1950s. Subsequently, Ukrainians became the most numerous and active political prisoners in the GULAG.

---

94 Norman Davies, *Europe: A History* (Oxford: Oxford University Press, 1998), 1032.
95 Norman Davies said this on April 30, 2012 in his open lecture at La Trobe University (Melbourne, Australia). See Serhiy Kvit. "Norman Davies on the subjectivity and objectivity of the historian", Personal Blog of Serhiy Kvit, May 9, 2012, https://goo.gl/mLuohA
96 Professor Taras Hunczak (Rutgers University) and Professor Volodymyr Kosyk (Sorbonne University, Paris and Ukrainian Free University, Munich) cite these documents in their publications.
97 Alexander Motyl, "On Nationalism and Fascism, Part 3", *World Affairs*, June 25, 2013, http://web.archive.org/web/20130809050553/http://www.worldaffairsjournal.org/blog/alexander-j-motyl/nationalism-and-fascism-part-3; also in: Alexander J. Motyl, *Ukraine vs. Russia: Revolution, Democracy, and War. Selected Articles and Blogs* (Washington, DC: Westphalia Press, 2017), p. 528

Among political prisoners of all nationalities in the GULAG, the leaders of the Ukrainian nationalist movement, Mykhailo Soroka and Zinovii Krasivskyj, commanded tremendous and undeniable respect. Thanks to the published correspondence between Krasivskyj and the American Amnesty International activist Iris Akahoshi,[98] he was known in the West as a civic and political activist, a poet and humanist, and as a leader in the international human rights movement. Again, in the 1960s and 1970s, Western political correctness focused on the universal human rights credentials of Krasivskyj and his fellow political prisoners, rather than on their credentials as activists for the freedom of their nations.

This generation of Ukrainian nationalist resistance includes the prominent figure of Yaroslav Dashkevych, a long-term political prisoner, an important historian and a respected intellectual. He observes that nationalism need not be opposed to democracy, since the former concept belongs to the ideological register, and the latter to the theory of the state.[99] According to Dashkevych, to be a nationalist means to work for one's people, or nation. Under conditions of statelessness, this means participating in the national liberation struggle.

Accompanying the transformation of Ukrainian society as it fights for its own state independence, approaches to the study of Ukrainian intellectual history are changing. This is illustrated by a Canadian scholar, Myroslav Shkandrij, whose book is dedicated to the history, ideology, and politics of Ukrainian nationalism.[100]

The author acknowledges the heroism of OUN leaders who refused to succumb to the German invaders after unilaterally declaring the independence of Ukraine in Lviv on June 30, 1941: "The Germans reacted by immediately arresting the organization's leaders. Bandera, Stetsko, and others were transported to Berlin. They

---

[98] Zinovii Krasivskyj and Iris Akahoshi, *Two Worlds, One Idea: Ten Years of Correspondence between Amnesty International Group 11 and a Ukrainian Political Prisoner, Zinovii Krasivskyj,* ed. and trans. Anna Procyk (New York and Kyiv: Smoloskyp, 2013).

[99] Yaroslav Dashkevych. *"... Teach to tell the truth with a truthful mouth": Historical Essays (1989 – 2008)* (in Ukrainian) (Kyiv: "Tempora" Publishing House, 2011).

[100] Myroslav Shkandrij, *Ukrainian Nationalism. Politics, Ideology, and Literature, 1929–1956* (New Haven and London: Yale University Press, 2015).

refused to retract the declaration or to curtail their activities, insisting that that they were speaking in the name of the Ukrainian people, who desired independence" (59). Shkandrij concluded "neither pursuit of ethnic purity, nor racism, nor acceptance of Nazi doctrine were central to the OUN's ideology, nor were they officially endorsed" (268).

Hence, the EuroMaidan Revolution, also known as the Revolution of Dignity (2013–2014),[101] initiated a transition from Dmytro Dontsov's concept of "from nation to state" to the concept of the conservative thinker Vyacheslav Lypynsky, "from state to nation", signaling the creation of a consolidated and forward-looking Ukrainian political nation and a modern civil society.

Matters of Interpretation

It is necessary to take into account the difference between academic discourse and public media-based discussion. Historical issues can and are a formidable weapon in Russia's post-truth, hybrid war against Ukraine, both in confronting the West around the world and in Russia itself.

During his lecture at Stanford University on November 3, 2017 Wim Coudenys,[102] a Belgian specialist in Russian history, noted that Ukrainians, having been deprived of their history for centuries must, must be allowed to access their past through popular, mass media-based, non-academic formats. This approach cannot and should not be considered as either a restriction or ideological pressure on professional researchers. As already noted, 'historical politics' are a main component of Putin's imperial mythology and part and parcel of Russia's information war against Ukraine.

---

101 Serhiy Kvit, "The EuroMaidan Revolution and the Struggle for Ukraine's Place in Europe", in *Jews, Ukrainians, and the EuroMaidan*, ed. Lubomyr Y. Luciuk (Toronto: University of Toronto Press, 2014), i–xvi.
102 Wim Coudenys, "Crimea has always been Russian. Or has it? Historical Arguments in Russian Political Discourse", Stanford Global Issues, https://sgs.stanford.edu/events/crimea-has-always-been-russian-or-has-it-historical-arguments-russian-political-discourse

Yaroslav Trofimov, in an essay bearing the distinctive title "Russia's Turn to Its Asian Past",[103] tracks Russia's ongoing radical geopolitical reorientation via history. Unable to offer a comprehensible future to his own society, Putin's regime offers instead an interpretation based on a longing for a seemingly better past. Trofimov notes that Russian "GDP is roughly the size of South Korea's or of the Guandong province of China. [...] Russia's political class naturally looks with nostalgia to the time of its youth, when Moscow was the feared and respected capital of one of the world's only two superpowers". In search of Russian "greatness", Putin himself went back into the depths of past centuries: from nostalgia for the Soviet Union to delusions of the Mongol Golden Horde. Historical matters are becoming part of the Russian propaganda project and largely shape the field of modern hybrid warfare.

Questions for a World Order in Transition

Dramatic changes in international political realities, exacerbated by ever more dramatic technological innovations in communication and social media, require new approaches, including the understanding of history and current political reality. In addition to direct chauvinist attacks by the Kremlin, different pro-Russian lobbyists are also acting against Ukraine.

It is worth mentioning the situation at the Kennan Institute[104] and the Carnegie Endowment for International Peace.[105] Graduates, scholars and experts at these institutions tried to caution their leaderships against engaging in the blatantly pro-Russian politics that

---

103 Yaroslav Trofimov, "Russia's Turn to Its Asian Past. As nostalgia surges for the eastern conquest of Genghis Khan, Putin maps out his own empire", *The Wall Street Journal*, July, 8, 2018, https://www.wsj.com/articles/russias-turn-to-its-asian-past-1530889247

104 "'Our disagreement with leadership's pro-Kremlin tendencies ignored': Ukrainian Scholars on closure of Kennan Institute Kyiv Office", http://Euro-Maidanpress.com/2018/04/15/statement-of-ukrainian-scholars-on-the-closure-of-the-kennan-institute-kyiv-office/

105 Yuriy Dzhygyr and Kateryna Maynzyuk "kindly requested" to be excluded from the list of experts and that their names be removed from the Carnegie website "because of irreconcilable methodological and worldview differences", https://www.facebook.com/kateryna.maynzyuk/posts/10213834366685856

portray a Ukraine seemingly falling into the abyss of "ethnic nationalism", in which freedom of speech under siege, and even has political prisoners behind bars. Of course, none of this is true.

We even can speak about Russia's targeted policy of corrupting Western think tanks. In her study, "Hybrid Analytica: Pro-Kremlin Expert Propaganda in Moscow, Europe, and the U.S.", Kateryna Smagliy claims: "To a significant degree, Russia is testing the Western intellectual community and its ability to resist the Kremlin's many temptations and co-optation strategies".[106] The Ukrainian question is not the only item on the agenda of Putin's propaganda machine, but it is certainly one of the main issues.

The Revolution of Dignity heralded the consolidation of Ukrainians as a political nation, encompassing all social, ethnic, and religious groups. For all strata, Ukraine must be protected by all available means. Importantly, the culmination of this collective aspiration organically adopted the historical heritage, rhetoric, and symbols of the Ukrainian liberation movement. Prior to 2014, no one would have guessed that one would once again see Jewish volunteer fighters in Ukraine, this time even under the red-and-black banner of the Ukrainian liberation movement of the twentieth century.[107]

Moreover, the Revolution of Dignity assembled a strong and demanding civil society, serving as the engine for essential right-liberal reforms, including freedom of speech, freedom of political choice, equal rights and opportunities for all, as well as free market economic development. Ukrainian civil society takes a universal attitude to deep systemic reforms, including conservative approaches (in particular, restoration of the national identity after the long and devastating imposition of denationalization), simultaneously

---

106 Kateryna Smagliy, "Hybrid Analytica: Pro-Kremlin Expert Propaganda in Moscow, Europe, and the U.S.", Institute of Modern Russia, Project "Underminers," Free Speech LLC. Research Paper, October, 2018, https://imrussia.org/en/news/2997-hybrid-analytica-pro-kremlin-expert-propaganda-in-moscow,-europe-and-the-u-s-a-case-study-on-think-tanks-and-universities%20

107 Bohdana Kostiuk, "Ukraine-Israel: from the Jewish subdivision (Ukr.—'kuren") of the UGA and 'Hagan' detachments to the Jewish unit (Ukr. 'chota') UDA" (in Ukrainian), *Radio Liberty*, May 5, 2018: https://www.radiosvoboda.org/a/29208755.html

seeking national unity and individual liberty. Co-equal left-liberal components include demands for social justice, in particular equal access to quality education and employment and an adequate socioeconomic safety-net.

Ukrainian society seeks justice in the broadest sense. The main threats to Ukrainian democracy lie not in some mythical fascism. The real threat is irresponsible populism, hybrid wars and the geographic proximity of Russia, where a fake reality created by Putin has been planted by a controlled media and academic community. Putin's greatest worry isn't war with the West. His nightmare is "infecting" Russia with Ukrainian democracy, which he sees as "fascism" and "anarchy".

It is important to note that the political agenda set out by the Ukrainian people for themselves contains no extremist, xenophobic, racist or anti-Semitic elements. On the contrary, according to a study by the American Pew Research Center, Ukraine is the most tolerant of all countries in Eastern and Southern Europe, with the lowest level of anti-Semitism.[108] In Russia, on the other hand, according to the Moscow Human Rights Bureau, there are menacing and growing levels of xenophobia and, in particular, of anti-Semitism.[109] These processes are grounded in many historical traditions associated with appealing to the "greatness" of the Russian Empire, including during the Soviet era.

Conclusion

The confrontation between Ukraine and Russia has not only a military but also a civilizational and value character. In addition, historical issues are important. To disagree with the tendency to

---

108 In some countries in Central and Eastern Europe, roughly one in five adults or more say they would not accept Jews as fellow citizens. SEE Pew Research Center, March 27, 2018, https://www.pewresearch.org/short-reads/2018/03/28/most-poles-accept-jews-as-fellow-citizens-and-neighbors-but-a-minority-do-not/
109 "Nonlinear radicalism. Aggressive xenophobia and intolerance in the Russian Federation", Moscow Human Rights Bureau, http://pravorf.org/index.php/news/2897-novom-doklade-mbpch-nelinejnyj-radikalizm-agressivnaya-ksenofobiya%20-i-neterpimost-v-rossijskoj-federatsii%20and%20nazaccent.ru/content/28300-experty-nacionalisticheskie-%D1%96ekstremistskie-techeniya-prisposablivayutsya.html

withdraw from genuine ideological discussions in favor of post-truth, which offers only populism and public trust in fake news, does not necessarily mean that we need to return to the ideological wars of the twentieth century.

On the contrary, this may be the right time to bring up the fundamental issue: the state as a set of values that are to be safeguarded and promoted through the rule of law. Including liberal, left, and conservative views in the discourse around setting the priorities of the national agenda is the sine qua non for strengthening social concord and for the growth and effective functioning of the state. Only an independent state can be a genuine guarantor of national freedom and individual liberty for its people.

Who Writes History?
National Memory in the Context of Network Revolutions and Social Networks[110]

My presentation focuses on the creation of a a modern Ukrainian historical narrative influenced, first of all, by the national memory ignited in the three recent Ukrainian revolutions, but also by scientific discourse and its specific textual methodological requirements and by the broad media context. In particular, the so-called new media create special opportunities for anyone wanting to be an author interpreting national history. How can these different approaches be combined, to what degree do they accord with each other, and what contemporary senses do they produce?

According to Yaroslav Dashkevych, at the moment that it gained independence Ukraine lacked a set of texts containing factual history that could be the basis for source study. This meant, in his opinion, that professional historians had to continue the work started by Mykhailo Hrushevskyi. Only the composition of a factual history by the academic community, and later accepted by society, would make it possible to develop different interpretive traditions, supported either by relevant philosophical concepts or by ideological doctrines entailed by a cursory representation of these concepts.

Therefore, our principal question may be put as follows: to what extent is the current writing of Ukrainian history conditioned by a fact-based approach and to what extent does it result from a clash of ideological doctrines? Or: to what extent is the understanding of Ukrainian history based on specifically historical science (historiography), that is, are we facing politics per se or what could be called a "battle for history"?

---

[110] Speech at the Forum "Revolution of Dignity. On the way to history. Modern media and revolutions of a new type in Ukraine and the world", Kyiv, November 18–19, 2021.

Clash of Discourses and Narratives

It is not only Ukrainians engaged in the struggle for the independence of their state who aspire to gain victory in this battle for Ukrainian history (which should here be understood as Ukrainian identity); various imperial or post-imperial (chauvinist) groups are also taking part. The latter are supported by political forces in some neighboring states whose political image is experiencing "phantom pains" for the lost "greatness" of their national dominance in previous historical periods.

At first glance, it may seem that only "left-wing" (left-liberal, neo-Marxist, communist) and "right-wing" (pluralistic, conservative, clerical) political discourses, with all their shades and branches, can claim a self-sufficient "ideological purity". In fact, however, they also serve different national narratives represented in global politics.

Such narratives are not always used as aggressive foreign policy tools against Ukraine. Sometimes they can be used to service domestic markets, and only in certain situations for the interpretation of Ukrainian history. There are a few examples.

Putin's personal historiography is the most universal, aimed first of all at Ukraine, based on both radical right-wing ("traditionally" Russian chauvinistic) and radical left-wing (an "alternative" to Western civilization) types of rhetoric.

Left-wing intellectuals in the United States offer another example. In the 1990s, their concerns about the threats of global dominance came close to the position of Ukrainian right-wing intellectuals. In particular, it is possible to compare the positions of Noam Chomsky and Yaroslav Dashkevych. However, the American professor and the former Ukrainian political prisoner spoke from different national standpoints (one belonging to the greatest world power and the other, as Joseph Stiglitz put it, to a "weakened and feeble" state then incapable of self-defense), which led to their different ideological self-identifications.

At the same time, traditional criticism of U.S. "imperialism" by the American left, its consciously or unconsciously related sympathy for the Soviet Union as an ally of the West in World War II, its identification of the Soviet Union with Russia, its attempts to understand "the choice of the Soviet people", its sympathy for pro-communist regimes, etc., entailed criticism of the Ukrainian national liberation movement as "undermining the unity" of the USSR.

The latter position significantly relied on the following simple logic: if Ukrainians were against Stalin, and Stalin was against Hitler, then Ukrainians were for Hitler. The fallacy was that, in the first place, Russian Bolshevik social experiments had not brought prosperity to any of the nations involved.

Secondly, at the beginning of World War II, Stalin's regime viewed Hitler's regime as its own mirror image. Only a combination of circumstances and God's Providence helped prevent the two totalitarian regimes from cooperating to jointly continue the war, bring down Western governments, and divide their spheres of global influence.

Thirdly, the American government's recognition of the USSR, after the Holodomor of 1933, made it clear that it thought it impossible to defeat the communist dictatorship at that time. In other words, in its opinion, the Ukrainian national liberation movement's struggle for an independent state was pursuing an impossible and irrational goal.

And finally, one should not forget that the coming to power of such figures as Lenin in the territory of the former Russian tsarist empire was also made possible by the moral, political, and financial support of leftist Americans who, probably, sincerely wished to see a successful struggle against the injustices of capitalism.

Nobody wanted to admit that, in fact, a reincarnation and modernization of the Russian empire was taking place: the same Russian chauvinists came to power. This is well illustrated by Putin's historical narrative, which combines totalitarian Marxism, Russian Orthodoxy, monarchism and fascism, all on the basis of a Russian imperialism in historical retrospect. Meaning that all its previous possessions are important and still "ours".

Ukrainian Network Revolutions

Returning to the matter of professional writing and the broad public understanding of Ukrainian history, as well as its appropriate popular representations, it is important to build a national memory discourse that would rely on a policy of openness, making all archival sources available, as well as on an attentive attitude to living national memory and its related national mythology. This is what has been happening in Ukraine since the Revolution of Dignity.

The present political situation, which includes the strengthening of the Ukrainian political nation and an active civil society, was generated by three successive recent revolutions: the Student Revolution on the Granite (1990), the Orange Revolution (2004), and the Revolution of Dignity (2014–2015, whose name was proposed by Yuri Syrotiuk). What is more, the latter two were network revolutions. That is, that they unfolded without a centralized leadership, a unified plan, or single concept. The decentralized nature of network society involves high-speed responsiveness and the persistence of protest movements.

This means that Ukrainians did not need any special instructions to go out to protest, to take part in tactical actions, to formulate ideological principles and requirements in the framework of the revolutionary movement. The amazing self-organization of huge masses of protesting people reached its peak in the EuroMaidan. These masses of people constantly self-personified to ensure their leadership through the authorized exchange of information in social media, as well as in situational consolidations, to successfully implement different projects and tasks.

Social media activity exploded after the creation of Facebook (2004). In the Revolution of Dignity it provided the Ukrainian national liberation movement with new organizational opportunities. Commentators pointed out the movement's ideologically universal nature. In particular, as Volodymyr Yermolenko wrote, the Revolution of Dignity included right, left, and liberal components all at the same time. This very polyphony was essential for Ukrainian society. It became the keystone of national unity and laid new foundations for the development of political culture.

Mychailo Wynnyckyj rightly suggested that, perhaps, the Ukrainian Revolution actually began when Yanukovych fled. The influence of Ukrainian civil society, its desire to implement reforms, build strong institutions, and protect the state inseparably, displayed a very great interest in the historical agenda.

In this context, it needs to be understood that the latest Ukrainian revolutions were all a continuation of the Ukrainian people's national liberation struggle for its own independent state. That is to say, there is a deep attention to historical issues, but more especially to the proscribed Ukrainian history that was expropriated, distorted, and seemingly forgotten forever.

These circumstances gave rise to new historical research, publications of archival documents, recordings of oral history, public discussions, the dissemination of popular science information, and the fight against fakes. They also led to the vivid embodiment of archetypal national myths in social behavior.

A large number of the Maidan participants manifested their need for ideological self-identification through means of social interaction like *Viche* ("council"), borrowed from Kyivan Rus. The *Viche* operated actively throughout the entire Revolution of Dignity, and in the vote on the membership list of the first coalition government in late February 2014. Maidan-Sich, which arose in response to attempts to forcefully disperse protesters, was rooted in Cossack tradition. In a similar vein, the Maidan Self-Defense *sotnias* ("hundreds of defenders") were organized on the living historical memory of the Ukrainian Insurgent Army and in analogy to it.

Finally, social media functionality features allowed the participation of a lot of activists from intellectuals, who had previously not been able to speak publicly to a mass audience, to popular authors of political and historical texts. Social media also permitted the dissemination of large amounts of archival historical information, whose impact was comparable in importance to the regular news.

Such a strong public demand for historical information is comparable to that during Gorbachev's perestroika. Yet, if in the latter case it was largely to undermine the Soviet Union, now it contributed to forming the factors needed to strengthen Ukrainian statehood, such as modern Ukrainian identity and national mobilization. In this way, society assimilates a new narrative of Ukrainian history. So, it is time for professional historians to address not only the representatives of their own professional community, but the whole of society as well.

Theoretical Background

The special social significance of historical information in today's Ukraine provides grounds for seeking a theoretical basis not only in Carl Gustav Jung's theory of archetypes, but also in Albert Bandura's theory of social learning. The historical agenda is present in the behavior of both the broad masses of the people and in politicians. It affects interstate relations. Opinions may differ about historians leaving their studies and going out to the people who have called on them. Yet the fact cannot be denied.

The need for the above-mentioned fact-based approach to creating historical texts was advanced by Yaroslav Dashkevych, as part of his criticism of postmodern interpretations of Ukraine's history, made in the absence of any "fact-based standard" of Ukrainian history. This means that postmodernism can only deconstruct existing texts and discourses.

It must be noted that, in recent decades, a substantial number of texts have been added to the body of "fact-based history". At the same time, it is necessary to acknowledge the fruitful results of deconstruction in relation to all dominant narratives.

We must recognize the manipulative uses of a superficially similar rhetoric of the "relativity" of various views, opinions, and interpretations. For instance, the phenomenon of "post-truth", associated with social media, presents a different kind of manipulation, unconnected to any pressure on mass consciousness initiated and organized by some "dominant centers". In this instance, we are witnessing a claim for fake news (from a certain point of view, comfortable and convenient news) from the mass audience itself.

The new social media that appear to have grown out of "impersonal" Internet platforms, like other media technologies before them, are ambiguous as concerns the public interest. That is, they are neither good nor bad, but they can be used for any purpose. When responding to a great public demand for historical knowledge, social media can distribute genuine information and become a platform for fruitful professional discussions, but they can also disseminate fake news, unreliable and unverified information.

Need for Fruitful Discussion

The best way out of these tangled historical, social, political, and methodological circumstances surrounding the writing of Ukrainian history is to support a broad public discussion, one that would not simplify matters, but, on the contrary, keep the whole range of complex and unresolved issues in focus. Moreover, in terms of content, instead of a dialectical exchange aimed at proving one's position right, there should be a fruitful hermeneutic conversation (in Hans-Georg Gadamer's terms), a search for the truth that involves all the participating parties.

One Hundred Years of the Ukrainian Liberation Struggle[111]

To understand historical processes, it is not nearly enough to take into account only distant, objective social, political, and economic factors. We also need to pay attention to different well-established traditions, stereotypes and myths/archetypes, which invariably accompany and overrun historical memory. In time, some of the latter become canonized by historiography or, more accurately, by different competing historiographies. These unwritten traditions help us understand social phenomena, which have some origin, and whose existence consists in outlining the dramatic differences between contemporary Ukrainian political culture and that of a number of post-Soviet countries, in particular Russia. It is especially interesting when considering the global importance of the events happening in contemporary Ukraine. During World War I, Ukrainians tried to create an independent state, even as they sought to fit it into the geopolitical context of the time. The defeat of that Liberation Struggle, and all of Ukrainian history up to the collapse of the Soviet Union and our present moment, compel us take a closer look at historically remote events.

How Many States Did the Ukrainians Create through Their Liberation Struggle?

Much has already been written about the benign character of the Ukrainian language, which uses affectionate diminutive forms even for deadly enemies in folklore, calling them *vorizhenky*. In a similar manner, the concept of a "Liberation Struggle" ("competition", "effort" are more literal translations) has a substantial romantic sense, which, to some extent, poeticizes the attempt of Ukrainians to found and consolidate their state at the beginning of the twentieth century. This poeticization focuses on the process, rather than the result, which has to be concrete. In this way, those who

---

111 *Kyiv-Mohyla Humanities Journal* 4 (2017): 145–152.

fought but did not achieve the desired result (who were killed or captured) became historical role models, like figures in a new heroic folklore composition. In the case of the Liberation Struggle of 1917–1920, it is not only national memory, but also the Ukrainian political tradition and historiography that have described this unaccomplished formation of a state in similar poetic terms.

It is impossible even to count how many states Ukrainians created at that time. Besides the Ukrainian People's Republic (1917–1920) with its capital in Kyiv, there were also the Western Ukrainian People's Republic (1918–1919) with its center in Lviv, and the Ukrainian State (1918) also with Kyiv as its capital. The large part of Ukrainian territory controlled by Nestor Makhno (1888–1934), with its center in the town of Huliai-Pole in today's Zaporizhzhia region (1918–1921), was another attempt by Ukrainians to create their own state. Finally, almost all the big villages or groups of villages in the territory of so-called Great Ukraine (less Galicia, Western Volyn, Transcarpathia and Bukovyna) created their independent republics, too. The Cold Ravine (*Kholodnyi Yar*) Republic (1919–1922) with its center in the village of Melnyky became the most famous of the latter. The Medvyn Republic (1920–1921) showed amazing resolve, and included only two villages: Medvyn and Isaiky. Almost every region of Ukraine had its military leaders, or *otamans*, each doing his best in the fight for an independent Ukraine. In the Transcarpathia region, in 1919, the Hutsul Republic, with its center in the village of Yasinia, came into existence. Of course, none of these can claim to be regarded as genuine states. Yet they are evidence of the great scope and energy of the Ukrainian revolution. They also indicate that state formation was not a single common project of Ukrainians. That is why it is more appropriate to use the plural: the age of the Liberation Struggle included many different Ukrainian revolutions, and their plurality was the reason for their defeat.

Each understood the goal of the struggle differently and their understanding was itself rather unclear. The list of their main objectives would include the following: liberty, justice, property, and, finally, an independent Ukrainian state as the basic demand. In this we see the so-called unwritten or folkloric tradition at work, one rather remote from the modern ideological demands, made by a narrow circle of the political elite, which arose in the times of the Liberation Struggle. Most important to Ukrainians was the revolt against injustice itself, understood as a process. The form and rhetoric of struggle almost always appealed to the Cossack period (most likely dating from the end of the fifteenth century) which also has a place in the collective national memory.

Between East and West

Let us speculatively claim that the strength of contemporary Ukrainian civil society is rooted in traditions of a borderland military culture between East and West, on the Wild Field's frontier. Although Ukraine was organically part of both the West (the Kyiv-Mohyla Academy phenomenon) and the East (the Wild Field, which is today part of Southern and Southeastern Ukraine) and came under the influence of Islam (the Crimean Tatars and Turks), it was autonomously developed militarily, economically, and culturally by Ukrainian Cossacks. Ultimately, in the time of the Cossack state, Bohdan Khmelnytskyi's "Zaporizhzhian Army" (*Viisko Zaporozke*) and, later, other Ukrainians were pulled into ongoing wars against the Crimean Khanate, Poland, Turkey, and Russia. Almost all military actions had important social implications.

The national struggle for independence in Ukraine has always occurred in tandem with social emancipation. In the national memory, the struggle is imprinted in the same terms as upholding liberty, justice and property, although in the early modern sense of these words operative in the period. Since those times, which also coincide with the flourishing of Ukrainian baroque culture, myths about the Golden Age of Ukrainian history have been formed. These myths are linked to the idea that every Ukrainian is personally a free individual and that together Ukrainians make up the Cossack nation. This collective belief has held a special place in the system of the national culture.

For example, my grandmother, who came from Lykhvari, a small Cossack village in the Reshetylivka district of the Poltava region, explained to me, a primary school student in the mid-1970s that I am a free person because I am of Cossack origin. We need to note that her concept was not only romantic, but legalistic as well. She said, "Remember, none of your family was ever a serf". So, it is important that my rights as a free person were defended and affirmed by centuries of Ukrainian history, and that this is the basis for my life in the future. These "natural" Ukrainian rights cannot be questioned: if there is something wrong in the present, it will be corrected and resolved in the future.

Ukrainians have always collectively expected a successful final rebellion, deferred in time, when justice will be done and all brought to account. The absence of modern and political demands, relevant to the times, occasionally led to odious murderous attempts to impose justice, as during the Koliyivshchyna revolt (1768–1769). Similar traditions, connected to the "Golden" Cossack age, later had various effects in different modern political cultures.

My father, who was born in Pomoriany, a town in today's Lviv region, recounted as story he heard from relatives and neighbors. A confrontation took place between two different political cultures belonging to the same ethnicity during World War I, just before the Liberation Struggle. In 1916, the Russian army advanced into the territory of Galicia. A cavalry unit, consisting of Kuban Cossacks, was quartered in Pomoriany. These were ethnic Ukrainians who spoke no Russian at all. They sang the same songs as the Galician people, were portly, wore large *papakhas* (wool hats), special Kuban sabers, and a gold earring in one ear. The townspeople could see that these were Ukrainians, but did they look like Bohdan Khmelnytskyi's Cossack army, which had also crossed into Galicia in the seventeenth century? The Ukrainian community had preserved heroic memories of those earlier times because two hundred locals had joined Khmelnytskyi. And as the stories said, my relatives were among them.

The Kubanians did not look the way Galicians wanted them to look—every morning they fell into a column, took off their papakhas and, raising a Russian flag, sang "God save the tsar!" But "true" Ukrainian Cossacks were supposed to serve the people, not the authorities, certainly not the occupying authorities. Furthermore, the townspeople were struck by the low anti-Semitism of the

Kubanians, who would stop a group of Jews in the street and laughingly drive them to a watering hole, as if they were animals (to make it look even uglier) — all this to get some money from them, which would conclude the "joke". The locals only experienced such stress again during World War II, when two Germans in the field gendarmerie shot down two small Jewish girls in the street in broad daylight. That is why the townspeople would consistently doubted that the Kubanians were "our people".

A solution to the problem presented itself. The Kuban unit moved on, fell into an Austrian ambush, in which all its soldiers perished. A firman[112] picked up their *papakhas* and brought them to Pomoriany. Local Ukrainians solemnly buried those *papakhas* instead of the soldiers. They decided that the soldiers were really "theirs", Ukrainians, yet made wild and destroyed by the tsar's power. So, in the context of one Ukrainian ethnic culture, two political cultures came into collision: one from the area of Austro-Hungarian Galicia and the other from Kuban, wholly incorporated by Russia.

The Ukrainian Revolution

Returning to the time of the Liberation Struggle, we see that it involved an even more tragic collision of orientations, and not just of political cultures. The Democratic February Revolution of 1917 in St. Petersburg started with the uprising of a Ukrainian Volyn regiment in the Russian army, going into the streets under Ukrainian blue and yellow flags. The all-Russian revolution evolved into national revolutions on the empire's "fringes", including, in that same year, the announcement of the above-mentioned independent Ukrainian People's Republic under a progressive socialist government, as well as the truly Ukrainian Kuban People's Republic (1918–1920). Independence movements sprang up in other territories of the Russian Empire previously colonized by ethnic Ukrainians (specifically, the so-called Siryi Klyn in Central Asia and the Zelenyi Klyn in the Far East).

---

112 Firman means driver, who drove a cart pulled by a horse.

However, this enormous energy ran along different vectors and was divided by political party characteristics. Thus, Ukrainian socialists, who formed the majority, refused to collaborate with Hetman Pavlo Skoropadskyi (1873–1945), seeing him as a reactionary monarchist. The anarchist Nestor Makhno, one of the most charismatic Ukrainian military leaders of the time, was ironic about the state intentions of the socialist guides of the Ukrainian People's Republic, first concluding treaties with them, and then with the Russian Bolsheviks who were also "not strangers" to him (at one time he had shared tsarist prison cells with them). The partisan chieftains (*otamans*) of the numerous village republics most often fought against everyone, confining themselves to their local territories. The brilliant Kuban Commander-in-Chief Andrii Shkura (Shkuro, 1886–1947) became a stalwart supporter of General Denikin, Commander-in-Chief of the Volunteer Russian Army, and was keen to restore the "one and indivisible" Russian Empire.

Yet we can also list examples of the merging of state formations and their powers. Unfortunately, these were mostly symbolic. On January 22, 1919, the Ukrainian and the Western Ukrainian People's Republics united, one day after the All-National Assembly in Khust resolved to add Transcarpathia to the Ukrainian People's Republic. A similar Bukovynian assembly took place in Chernivtsi on November 3, 1918. However, the political and military disintegration of the Ukrainian powers finally led to the defeat of the young state, which left only positive precedents of democratic ambition behind. The problem was that nobody valued those achievements. Ukraine was occupied by new Russian imperialists, the Bolsheviks, who would organize the Holodomor (1932–1933) ten years later. Major international players, demoralized by the success of the Bolsheviks, barely noticed the emergence of a new state with the unknown name "Ukraine" on the political map of Europe.

Concept of National Interests

All non-Soviet Ukrainian sources made an effort to gain a deeper understanding and document events: they continued the unfinished business of state formation. In other words, they contained a distinctively journalistic tendency. Consider, first of all, the completion of the formation of Ukrainian political identity. The academic and essayistic works of leading Ukrainian intellectuals — Mykhailo Hrushevskyi (1866–1934), a historian; Volodymyr Vynnychenko (1880–1951), a writer; Serhii Yefremov (1876–1939), a literary critic; Symon Petliura (1879–1926), a theater critic; Hetman Pavlo Skoropadskyi, a professional military man; Dmytro Dontsov (1883–1973), a journalist and an essayist; as well as the historians Dmytro Doroshenko (1882–1951) and Viacheslav Lypynskyi (1882–1931) — demonstrate clear differences in ideology and evidence. All these authors played an important part in the Ukrainian liberation movement.

The main conclusion drawn by the political leaders who continued to fight for Ukrainian state independence after the defeat of the Liberation Struggle was to unite around the national interests of Ukraine. This political concept was proposed by Dmytro Dontsov, an ideologist of Ukrainian nationalism. He had a huge impact on the formation of a new generation of leaders connected with the Organization of Ukrainian Nationalists, founded in 1929, and the Ukrainian Insurgent Army created in 1942. Dontsov was deeply critical of the leaders of the Ukrainian People's Republic associated with the Liberation Struggle.

Appealing to the fate of the whole nation, Dontsov rejected party affiliation. His ideology concentrated on the Ukrainian revolution as an armed struggle for the creation of an independent Ukraine. At the front, there is no place for talk of democracy or authoritarianism because an army must have a common strategy to win. However, his views of the state were based on American and British models. This fact alone makes the ideologized interpretations of the neo-Soviet historical school representatives, who have built their academic careers on anti-Ukrainian activities or are ideological fanatics, a much more difficult proposition.

Actually, if we look at Ukrainian military victories from a detached and humanistic point of view, we can divide the reasons for most of the bloody battles into four groups: (1) those motivated by the struggle for state independence; (2) those pursuing social emancipation; (3) those sorting out relationships with national minorities, who rejected Ukrainians' right to statehood and supported colonial metropolitan countries; (4) and those whose political discourse was mainly based on traditional patriarchal categories of "our own" and "the other", thus retarding modern forms of political culture. Worse still, all these factors often became entangled. However, when Ukrainians were able to attempt to restore their state, they always proposed coalitions and democratic models. In the twentieth century, this could be seen in all the above-mentioned republics in the age of the Liberation Struggle, and also in Carpathian Ukraine (1939), with its capital in Khust, in the Ukrainian State Government in Lviv (1941), and in the State of Ukraine (1991).

The positive political capital of the age of the Liberation Struggle, the aspiration for a democratic state governed by the rule of law, was partly realized in the first years of a colonial body called the "Ukrainian Soviet Socialist Republic" (1919–1991). After Russian communists occupied Kyiv in 1921, the head of the Ukrainian Central Council (the parliament of the age of the Liberation Struggle [1917–1918]), Mykhailo Hrushevskyi, even managed to return from emigration. Later, Ukrainian dissidents (from the 1950s to 1991) and nationalists (thinking that "social emancipation can only come about only through national emancipation") turned their attention to ideas of social justice. The ideological and political heritage of the Ukrainian People's Republic was especially relevant with the renewal of Ukrainian statehood after the collapse of the Soviet Union.

Special attention should be paid to the history of Ukrainian socialism which, contrary to imperial Russian socialism, was characterized by a national liberation and anticolonial nature. From this perspective, Edward Said's *Orientalism* (1978) is also about Ukraine as a former colony.

Under conditions of occupation, the Ukrainian nation existed with an incomplete social structure, mainly composed of the peasantry. When a famous Ukrainian intellectual, Mykhailo Drahomanov (1841–1895), reflected on the ideas that would appeal to the vast majority of Ukrainians, he came to the conclusion that these would be socialist. Thus, in the Ukraine of modern time, for the first time since the Cossack state, programs of social and national liberation were again combined. At the beginning of the twentieth century, almost all politically active Ukrainian intellectuals — with the exception of the wealthy and some landlords who had Ukrainian cultural sentiments — allied themselves to the socialist movement. Meanwhile, in an all-Russian context, Mykhailo Drahomanov was disseminating the ideas of liberalism and constitutionalism.

Mykhailo Drahomanov also deserves credit for the impact he made on the most influential figure in Ukrainian intellectual history, Ivan Franko (1856–1916), who turned away from his Moscowphile orientation to the Ukrainian socialist movement. Later, in his essay "Beyond the Limits of the Possible", written in response to the epochal work by Mykola Mikhnovskyi (1873–1924), *An Independent Ukraine* (1900), Franko also turned away from Marxism to the principles of Ukrainian nationalism. Before its publication as an article in Lviv, this was the text of a speech Franko gave first in Poltava and then in Kharkiv. Mikhnovskyi was the most mysterious figure in the Liberation Struggle and influenced the worldview of Dmytro Dontsov. Mikhnovskyi was "right-wing", devoted attention to the military independence movement, and worked with Dontsov in Hetman Skoropadskyi's government.

After the defeat of the Liberation Struggle, ideological fashion gradually moved from the left to the right, in the case of the majority of active politicians, consolidating at the start of World War II. We often witness with the replacement of ideas because, first of all, the ideas of social justice associated with Marxism were never alien to the Ukrainian peasant nationalist movement. Because nationalists expressed their opinions in the terms of Dontsov's doctrine of protecting national interests, aimed at the creation of the Ukrainian Independent United State, they were considered to be exclusively "right-wing". In the Soviet Union, the nationalist label was applied not only to true representatives of the organized opposition of that name, but also to dissidents, independent-thinking Ukrainian intellectuals, and, later, even to those who used the Ukrainian language as a matter of principle.

The nationalist resistance included elements from various parties, among them former national democrats (Nil Khasevych, an artist, 1905–1952) and Marxists (Mykhailo Stepaniak, a former member of the Communist Party of Western Ukraine, later a member of the leadership of the Organization of Ukrainian Nationalists [OUN], and a soldier in the Ukrainian Insurgent Army [UPA, abbreviation following the original, *Ukrayinska Povstanska Armiia*], 1905–1967). The UPA became a broad liberation movement including representatives of various national minorities of peoples enslaved by Soviet Russia. It was dominated by the expressions of the icon of Ukrainian intellectual history, Taras Shevchenko (1814–1861), who called Russia "a prison of nations", and whose main motto was: "Liberty to the nations, liberty to the person".

Today, the Ukrainian political class again faces the challenge of creating a broad political spectrum, including ideological right-wing, left-wing, and liberal parties. The Ukrainian political vocabulary needs to bridge the distance between the state and society. Still unresolved is the problem of the pro-Communist, pro-Russian and pro-Putin orientation of left-wing political groups. The new leftists, ideologically allied to active neo-Marxist movements in the Western world, have no organized political power. Yet they continue to ignore the post-colonial state of Ukrainian society. In the tradition of the Liberation Struggle, they oppose various social values to the state, seeing no value in the state itself, although it enables the existence of a free society.

New Ukrainian Revolutions

Usually, there are four revolutions named in connection with an independent Ukraine. These are the students' Revolution on Granite (1990), the "Ukraine without Kuchma" protest (2000), the Orange Revolution (2004–2005), and the Revolution of Dignity (2013–2014). All contributed to the gradual development of the political culture of Ukrainian society. The gap between modern and traditional mythological Ukrainian discourses has grown much narrower. Indeed, the most ideologically advanced of these revolutions, the Revolution of Dignity, "organically", rather than simply conceptually, absorbed several historical myths and linked them to new networking technologies.

The Revolution on Granite was attuned to the explosive dissemination of printed self-published works (*samvydav*). In contrast, the Orange Revolution, as Timothy Garton Ash said in his speech at Kyiv-Mohyla Academy, was a "TV revolution", one in which a television image broadcast the proposition that "Together we are many, no one can defeat us" ("*Razom nas bahato, nas ne podolaty*"). The success of the Revolution of Dignity, on the other hand, is connected with social media, the entry into global processes, and the development of Ukrainian civil society. It should be noted that the EuroMaidan occurred simultaneously with the crisis of values of the West as it faced new global challenges. The greatest of these dangers is the hybrid, renewed Russian "evil empire" with its fake reality. For many centuries, Ukrainian liberation discourse with all its aspirations to liberty and justice has opposed it.

It looked as though Ukrainians were always ready to live "in the field", to build a Sich settlement (a Cossack archetype) in the center of Kyiv, to resolve important civil issues at the Maidan (at a *Viche*, a popular assembly inherited from the times of Kyivan Rus), to create independent media and social networks, to arm, to provide medical treatment, to teach people, to defend the barricades encouraged by the bells of St. Michael's Golden-Domed (*Zolotoverkhyi*) Monastery (which sheltered Kyivans during the assault by the Mongol army in the twelfth century), to create volunteer organizations, to bolster the high morale of the Ukrainian army, and, later, to counter the attacks of the Russian army. No single center commanded or carried out strategy planning. However, everyone knew his or her place and cooperated with other members of the Revolution. The coordination of actions was not the same as the rule of one. On the contrary, the power of resistance lay in a decentralized network and the self-sufficiency of its autonomous elements.

The Revolution of Dignity finally assuaged the old collective anxiety which arose due to a lack of leadership and unity. Leadership finally became a team concept, rather than simply the expression of individual charisma. The Maidan made demands and symbolized unity, regardless of political, national, religious or social affiliation. Everyone made their contribution to victory. This was a celebration not only of civil society, but also of the Ukrainian political nation, the first time in history that all national minorities rose to defend the Ukrainian state as their own. As a result, ancient myths and grievances, accumulated over centuries of wars and confrontations, vanished from the collective mind.

After the Revolution of Dignity, the Ukrainian liberation movement stopped being merely an alternative. Post-revolutionary governments are no longer perceived as an occupying power. The strong demands made by Ukrainians to the government, in spite of some efforts to continue cultivating hostility, have translated into activity through the development of civil society. However, we are still far from the total erasure of the difference between society and the state. The Ukrainian government does not yet enjoy sufficient trust because of corruption.

Conclusions

Only ruin and fiery destruction can be swiftly accomplished. Building new social relationships, disseminating new practices of governing, and creating an effective state require time. Yet Ukrainians are not ready to delegate all responsibility for the protection of national interests to the state. If we hear of a person with a Molotov cocktail, we call him or her an activist; during the Revolution of Dignity and the war with Russia, Ukrainians took up arms; they want to preserve the special status of volunteer battalions, relying on the value of personal courage.

After the victory of the Revolution of Dignity, it is the task of the present generation to draw attention to the experience of the Liberation Struggle with all of its successes and fatal failures. Now, as it was a hundred years ago, the need is not to create an alternative movement, a partisan detachment, or to avenge injustice. On the contrary, the need is to build an effective modern state to which all citizens can delegate their rights and responsibilities, trusting in its commitment to protect national interests and having confidence in its professional competence. The transition from timeless mythological and archetypal existence to the real, lived time of the nation requires turning attention away from the revolutionary process to the concrete goals and consequences of the struggle.

The Ukrainian Liberation Movement in the Interwar Period (1923-1939)[113]

It is extremely difficult to gain a conceptual hold of the complexities of the Ukrainian element in the interwar period, despite the relatively short time frame involved. We see this in the current historical discussion, which is taking place mostly in the mass media, as an integral part of contemporary political discourse. We have two main problems concerning methodology. First, today's political correctness is often used to interpret the events of the interwar period and World War II, even though the political context has changed dramatically since 1945. The second problem is related to the long traditions of Russian propaganda, which under Putin's direction have gained new strength through fake news and historical revisionism, an undertaking that could be described as hybrid post-truth information aggression on a global scale.

The key point of Putin's propaganda is the thesis that the modern Ukrainian state is not the result of Ukrainians' struggle for independence, but a consequence of the "evolution" of the Soviet system. That is, an independent Ukraine was produced completely by accident in 1991. However, to arrive at this conclusion the logical sequence of events had to be changed. Although, in fact, the collapse of the Soviet Union was largely caused by Ukrainians' unwillingness to live in the evil empire, the neo-Soviet school of history attempts to present Ukrainian efforts to gain independence in a peculiarly racist way: as a manifestation of their "natural" (innate) brutality, cruelty, treachery, and anti-Semitism, or as the result of intrigues by Austro-Hungarian, Polish or German secret services. Hence, Ukrainians are not fit to be considered a political nation, much less an independent state worthy of a place in the comity of the nation-state system.

My exposition will focus on discussing how, under the conditions of statelessness, Ukrainians sought to defend their national

---

113 The text of a speech given at the conference "Ukraine's Century of Struggle to Secure Independence", December 7-8, 2017, Washington, DC.

interests on the eve of World War II. My task is to trace the general logic of their processes and ideas.

Characterization of the Interwar Period

The defeat in the Liberation Struggle of 1917–1923 compelled Ukrainians to reconsider the organizational forms and methods of their struggle for an independent state. The ideological principles unpinning the struggle were of particular importance. In order to evaluate the events of that time, it is important to properly understand not only the circumstances and processes influencing Ukrainian political life, but also the situation in Europe and in the world as a whole. There are five main considerations:

First. Dissatisfaction at the end of World War I in the countries that suffered defeat (primarily Germany, Austria, and Turkey), as well as in those nations that did not gain an independent state independence (among them Ukrainians, Croats, and Slovaks). The former group sought revenge, the latter to complete the process of establishing their own states.

Second. The colonial policy of the victorious European states, among which we must number not only Great Britain, France, and Belgium, but also Hungary, Poland and Romania. For Ukrainians the key point was not only a brutally enforced policy of denationalization pursued by the aforementioned newly independent states in the territories inhabited by Ukrainians. We also have illustrative examples of expansionist ambitions such as the appeals by Poland to be granted overseas colonies seized from the Entente.[114]

Third. The isolationist policy of the United States. During the interwar years, America suffered from the Great Depression and the growing fear sowed by Nazi propaganda. At that time, the theory of strong media effects, known as the Hypodermic Needle or the Magic Bullet theory, was a major concern. That is, through corruption and influence peddling, Hitler's propaganda was able to spread through the American press and convince Americans to abandon their freedoms in favor of a "comfortable" life under

---

114 Taras Hunczak, "Polish Colonial Ambitions in the Inter-War Period", *Slavic Review* 26, no. 4 (December 1967).

dictatorship. In any case, the United States could not and did not have anything new to offer Europe in terms of political ideas and models that could undermine the growing influence of militarism and authoritarianism.

Fourth. A widespread sense of the instability of the political situation and the inevitability of another war was the consequence of aggressive saber rattling by the Soviet Union, on the one hand, and the emergence of authoritarian regimes in Western Europe, in particular in Italy, Germany, and Spain, on the other. Authoritarianism was in a sense the political radio of the day. The idea that the most challenging issues could be best managed by charismatic leaders and a "strong hand" dominated political discourse. Paradoxically, this was the result of both the global spread of communist ideas, coupled with the rapid development of the Soviet economy, and by the organizational success of the opponents of communism, first Italian fascism, and then German Nazism. We need only consider how anti-communism aligned Churchill and Mussolini. There is ample evidence that they maintained a long correspondence. Churchill also took a personal interest in close contacts between British intelligence and admiral Canaris, chief of the *Abwehr*, the German military intelligence organization, a relationship that existed before the Allies adopted the doctrine of unconditional German surrender[115] Western democracies looked favorably first at Mussolini and then at Hitler precisely because of their anti-communist rhetoric.

Fifth. During those years, the whole world perceived international relations through the lens of nation-states and ethnic conflicts. This was true not only in the case of Europe's changing borders. The internment of American citizens of Japanese descent in the United States during World War II reflected the same thinking as Canada's internment of its Ukrainian-born citizens in World War I.

---

115 Richard Bassett. *Hitler's Spy Chief: The Wilhelm Canaris Betrayal: The Intelligence Campaign Against Adolf Hitler* (New York: Pegasus Books, 2013).

Lull before the Storm

In the interwar period, the Ukrainian liberation movement undertook a reassessment of the plight of the Ukrainian people, and of the consequences of the failure to establish an independent nation-state. They were prey to the same social tensions and faced the same stark geopolitical realities as all who lost World War I.

The remnants of various Ukrainian military formations, governments, political party factions, diplomatic missions, etc., which ended up as political refugees outside the newly created Soviet Union, could not continue the struggle through existing organizational forms and structures. Their military defeat also meant the collapse of their political models. Therefore, quite naturally, new proposals were advanced. Later, history would show that many of the political tasks assumed by the leaders of the UPR (Ukrainian People's Republic), could be properly addressed and implemented only after Ukraine gained independence.

Armed struggle for independence became the main task for the interwar Ukrainian liberation movement. However, Western democracies didn't understand, didn't see, and didn't want to see, the aspirations of Ukrainians. None of the newly-created states, with the exception of Czechoslovakia under Tomas Masaryk, recognized the right of Ukrainians to their own state.

Thus, the Ukrainian political elite was confronted by significant change in the geopolitical realm. One part of the political leadership pinned its hopes on the development of Soviet Ukraine. Those who aligned themselves with left (socialist or communist) ideology included the chairman of the Ukrainian Parliament (Central Council), Mykhailo Hrushevsky, and others who returned to Ukraine after the defeat of the Liberation Struggle. Another part, including Symon Petliura and the Hetmanate circle of Pavlo Skoropads'kyi, established the Ukrainian People's Republic in exile. Yet another group participated actively and legally in the political life of the newly created independent states, first and foremost in Poland.

A considerable number of leaders simply withdrew from political life, including Nestor Makhno, the most charismatic of

Ukrainian commanders and a professional revolutionary. He defended Petliura's honor at the trial of his murderer, the Bolshevik agent Schwartzbard, and afterwards lived a quiet life and died in Paris. Similarly, Volodymyr Vynnychenko, head of the UPR government, spent his last days in France.

However, there was a fifth group of Ukrainian political leaders that decided to abandon efforts to salvage defeated state structures. They founded various underground organizations. The greatest success was achieved by the outstanding organizer Yevhen Konovalets'. In 1920, a group of his political allies founded the Ukrainian Military Organization, and subsequently, in 1929, the Organization of Ukrainian Nationalists (OUN). Over time, the OUN became the most influential Ukrainian political force. At this stage, we will not delve into factional differences, as the political successes of the OUN during this period exceed others' efforts and allow us to talk about a new era in the Ukrainian liberation movement. Therefore, I will focus my remarks on the OUN.

The Role of the Organization Of Ukrainian Nationalists

To start with, efforts at state-building were no longer the primary focus. Matters concerning the political system of a future independent Ukrainian state were set aside. Instead, achieving Ukrainian independence militarily became the priority. This is not to say that discussions were not constantly going on in these circles in the interwar period. However, to assert that some publications indicated some finalized political vision of an independent Ukraine would be baseless. The nationalist movement evolved, taking various factors of sociopolitical life into account, first in interwar Europe, and then during World War II.

Secondly, on the basis of the main task of gaining an independent state through armed struggle, the ideology of Ukrainian nationalism was politically non-partisan and based on the concept of the national interest. This was a transformative new concept, practically absent during the Liberation Struggle of 1917–1923, during which various political forces fought for the implementation of their party program. Suffice it to say that the concept of the national interest was present in the political vocabulary of every modern democratic state. In the Ukrainian context, it first appeared under these extraordinary circumstances.

Thirdly, the political thinker and essayist Dmytro Dontsov played a special role in the development of the OUN ideology and is in fact the author of the very concept of Ukrainian nationalism. Almost all the leaders of the Ukrainian nationalist movement acknowledged the influence of Dontsov's personality and ideas, although this did not prevent them from treating Dontsov very critically, taking responsibility for the political agenda upon themselves. Dmytro Dontsov believed that under normal conditions a nation will decide for itself which political model would be best. He himself preferred the American and British version.

Fourthly, the OUN considered the Soviet Union a major and immediate threat to the future existence of an independent Ukraine and even to the Ukrainian nation as a whole (as witness the glaring example of the Holodomor, genocide by famine). Russian chauvinism was the first target of the OUN. Ukrainian nationalists considered communist ideology as the means Russian domination and aggression adopted at that historical stage. As a consequence, the fundamental principle informing all further organizational and diplomatic Ukrainian nationalist activity is: the enemy of our enemy can be our friend or companion. Furthermore, emphasis was placed on the creation of a political entity that would represent the interests of Ukrainians and Ukraine in the inevitable coming war.

Therefore, fifth, ties were established with the military of Lithuania, Italy, Finland, and Germany. It is important to note that this did not involve political cooperation with the ruling parties of these countries. The OUN sought to borrow certain organizational forms needed to create an effective underground organization, one able to raise a nationwide uprising for independence; it did not entail ideological alignment as such. Later, during World War II, this task was transformed into a mission to organize an uprising in the entire Soviet Union as the "prison of nations" (the Ukrainian poet Taras Shevchenko's expression). The lofty goal was to enable all nations occupied by communist Russia to create their own independent states.

Sixth, racism as a political ethos was alien to the OUN's ideology. The identification of potential allies and enemies was based on an assessment of the degree to which they would either contribute or hinder the creation of an independent state, rather than on their national or racial origin. Nowhere was ethnicity a determinative factor. The OUN's rhetoric of liberation was based on the need to build a Ukrainian state, a right enjoyed by every European nation.

Seventh, the claim that the OUN was a totalitarian organization, which opposed the democratic Ukrainian parties that functioned under the laws of those states where their operation was allowed, does not stand up to criticism. One cannot compare apples and oranges, or complain, for example, that an army has a hierarchical structure. The army's task is not to participate in democratic elections, but to protect the state in which different political forces can coexist. It is important to note that in the two attempts to restore Ukrainian statehood in which the OUN was involved (Carpathian Ukraine in 1939 and the revolutionary Ukrainian state in 1941), the nationalists' "politics" was based on the implementation of the coalition principle of shared political responsibility and cooperation with representatives of all existing political forces.

Conclusion

Since history is not a natural science, its conclusions are always subjective and contextual. At the same time, it is important that we take into consideration, if possible, the full spectrum of factors that influenced and characterized Ukrainian political reality in the interwar period. In doing this we must resist interpretations based solely on the priorities dictated by new political agendas. There is no need to idealize or to demonize. Along with documents and facts that speak for themselves, we must seek to contextually understand the main vector of the Ukrainian liberation movement between the two wars.

The Ukrainian liberation movement's goal was to establish the independence of Ukraine, not to exterminate all non-Ukrainians or even, unaccountably, the Ukrainians themselves. On the other hand, one cannot ignore the social realities that led to the sad fact of inter-ethnic confrontation and even local wars in World War II. These obstacles to the creation of some sort of idealized historical representation must not be ignored. Contextually, the long history of statelessness inevitably let to the accumulation of a host of vendettas and vindictive stereotypes. These negative factors should be considered alongside the strained relations with national minorities who lived on the territory of Ukraine, minorities whose leaders strove to form a ruling class or to act as surrogates for imperial colonial administrations, thereby ignoring Ukrainians' right to an independent state.

Given the fact that the Ukrainian liberation movement during World War II was mainly drawn from the rural social strata, it also bore certain traits of medieval peasant wars, and sometimes advanced not a modern ideology but a simplistic patriarchal identification of "us against them". In the interwar era, the pendulum of the political mainstream swung from left to right. However, it is impossible to treat the Ukrainian liberation movement of that period as exclusively right-wing considering the already mentioned social composition of its participants. Their understanding of social justice was: "no social liberation without national liberation".

The history of the Ukrainian liberation movement in the nationalist period merits deeper analysis in terms of its universal nature, rather than by comparing it with the radically xenophobic movements of Western Europe. After all, it was Dmytro Dontsov himself who protested against applying the term "integral nationalism" to Ukrainian nationalism, being more relevant to the French realities of the early twentieth century. Ukrainian nationalism, whose ideology was shaped during the interwar period, has no imperial, chauvinistic or racist component; it was the movement of a stateless nation seeking the creation of an independent state, and therefore its first task was emancipation. That is why it is neither Nazism nor fascism. In its content, it was more closely related to the conservative forces of Western Europe. Indeed, later, in World War II, the Ukrainian liberation movement made a significant contribution to victory over German Nazism and, later still, to the defeat of Russian communism.

A separate issue that needs special consideration is the role played by the millions of Ukrainians serving in the Soviet Army, who contributed to victory over Hitler's Germany. This was a truly great sacrifice by the whole Ukrainian nation. To grasp the complex nature of this issue, we need only observe that, having destroyed Nazism, they contributed to bringing a new invader into Europe—Russian imperialists—just as in the Soviet-Finnish War of 1939-1940, in which a large number of Ukrainians also fought. These issues should not be depreciated, but rather given decent consideration.

We have evidence of the reluctance of Ukrainians to fight the Wehrmacht in 1941 because, remembering the Holodomor, they could not imagine anything worse than Soviet power. However, we also have every reason to assert that the turning point in the course of the war, in favor of the Soviet Union, was largely due to the fact that Ukrainians in the USSR massively changed in this regard and began to identify Nazi Germany as their main enemy. As Professor Timothy Snyder emphasizes, we need to better understand that World War II may have begun with Hitler's desire to seize Ukraine to expand the "living space" of his Reich. Also, Professor Norman Davis pays special attention to the fact that Stalin, other than in his ability to become a "major ally" of the West, was no better than Hitler. This Soviet alliance was forced by circumstances, yet somehow continues to nourish the self-deception or worse of some Western politicians and intellectuals, who continue to talk about the "progressiveness" of the Soviet Union and even about some "special path" for Russia.

The liberation ideology and revolutionary rhetoric of the Ukrainian nationalists and their more than a decade long struggle against impossible odds ultimately affected the whole of Ukraine, making it the most volatile part of the Soviet Union, exhibiting the most powerful resistance in every imaginable form (nationalist, dissident, and spontaneous) to the communist system. History has shown the importance of the anti-imperial orientation of the Ukrainian liberation movement. And its importance is no less today, in the midst of the reawakening of a Russian imperialism that uses new hybrid tactics to spread its ideological justifications for a "sovereign democracy", "Orthodox civilization" and "Russian world".

After the victory of the Revolution of Dignity, we can speak of the further consolidation of the Ukrainian political nation, in which not only ethnic Ukrainians but all national minorities and other social groups defend the Ukrainian state as their own, using the ideas, rhetoric, and symbolism largely shaped by the Ukrainian liberation movement between the two world wars of the twentieth century.

Ukrainian Nationalism, Ustashism, and Fascism
The Matter and Context of the Discussion[116]

What Is the Discussion About?

In an attempt to resist the mechanical identification of the nationalist movements of stateless nations — primarily Ukrainians, Croats and Slovaks, who, after World War I and the collapse of the Austro-Hungarian, Ottoman, and Russian empires, were not able to create their own states — with fascism, Oleksandr Zaitsev proposes the term "Ustashism" (after "Ustaša", the Croatian Revolutionary Organization [*Ustaša – Hrvatska revolucionarna organizacija*, UHRO]).

Specifically, Zaitsev believes that the Organization of Ukrainian Nationalists (OUN) was never a fascist organization in its essence. At the same time, the OUN belonged to political movements whose ideology could be called "revolutionary integral nationalism developing under conditions of perceived foreign oppression and using violence for the purpose of national liberation and the creation of an independent authoritarian state".[117]

The concept of "integral nationalism" dates back to the monarchical political organization *Action française*, founded by Charles Maurras in 1899. It is worth noting that this was the year of the first appearance of Mykola Mikhnovsky's *An Independent Ukraine*, initially delivered as a public lecture in Poltava and Kharkiv, and published as a pamphlet the following year in Lviv.[118] No evidence of any connection between the two events exists, except for one striking fact, namely, the similarity of the basic principle of "France for the French" in Maurras and the slogan "Ukraine for Ukrainians" in Mikhnovsky.

---

116 *Journal of Soviet and Post-Soviet Politics and Society* 7, no. 2 (2021).
117 Oleksandr Zaitsev, "Fascism or Ustashism? Ukrainian integral nationalism in comparative perspective, 1920s–1930s", *Communist and Post-Communist Studies* 48, no. 2–3 (2015): 184.
118 Mykola Mikhnovsky. Самостійна Україна [An Independent Ukraine] (Львів: Вид. Косевича, 1900).

Zaitsev notes that the concept of "integral nationalism" was later adopted and further explored by Carlton Hayes, Peter Alter, and John Armstrong in order to typologize radical nationalist movements, especially in state and stateless nations. In other words, this is the continuation of a great debate in which Anthony Smith, notably, considers Nazism and fascism as alternatives to the tradition of European nationalism, which is based on the idea of unique and plural free nations, and for whom French integral nationalism acts as a link between nationalism and fascism.[119]

Thus, the concept of "ustashism" is meant to open a distance between the political organizations of stateless nations and their ideologies, on the one hand, and such phenomena as (Italian) Fascism, (German) Nazism, and (Spanish) Falangism, which emerged in independent states and are usually assimilated into "generic fascism" in the scholarly literature, on the other.

On the other hand, Tomislav Dulić and Goran Miljan criticize Zaitsev's approach because "by the late 1930s ustaštvo was basically another iteration of fascism that contained the usual specificities to suit a local historical, political, and cultural context".[120] These authors also deny the existence of any fundamental difference between nationalist organizations and their ideologies in state and stateless nations. Most interestingly, they mention the subject identity (state independence) of the Ukrainian Soviet Socialist Republic within the Soviet Union in the context of its membership in the UN,[121] as if this identity were related to the Ukrainian nationalist movement, and imply that this relation somehow makes the latter fascist.

It is important that Zaitsev does not insist on "ustashism" as a term ("if anyone can suggest a better one, I am ready to accept it"); however, he insists that "ultra-nationalist (integral nationalist)

---

119 Oleksandr Zaitsev. "Інтегральний націоналізм" як теоретична модель для дослідження українського націоналістичного руху ["'Integral nationalism' as a theoretical model for studying the Ukrainian nationalist movement"]", *Український визвольний рух: науковий збірник* 15 (2011): 5–25.
120 Tomislav Dulić and Goran Miljan, "The Ustašas and Fascism: 'Abolitionism', Revolution, and Ideology, 1929–42", *Journal of Soviet and Post-Soviet Politics and Society* 6, no. 1 (2020): 305.
121 Ibid., 281.

movements in stateless nations are typologically different from ultra-nationalist, in particular fascist, movements in nation-states and, therefore, they should be considered a separate genus of ideological movements".[122] This proposal looks eminently rational and aims at the comparative study of various nationalist movements in interwar Europe.

At the same time, in my opinion, academic attempts to introduce new typological characteristics of certain historical phenomena enter into conflict with the ideological assessment of such phenomena, and, perhaps most importantly, with media representations of judgments of this kind.

The Deeper Subject of the Discussion

As we can see, the complexity of the discussion lies in the ambiguity of any typology of nationalist movements resulting from the innate features of each distinct national phenomenon and the circumstances of its functioning. For example, it is extremely problematic to apply "integral nationalism" to the Ukrainian context precisely because the concept originates with *Action française*, and is shaped by its distinct origins in the French situation.

If we return to the ideological legacy of the Organization of Ukrainian Nationalists (OUN) and Dmytro Dontsov, it immediately becomes obvious that the Ukrainian nationalist movement—whether its nationalism is characterized as "active", "volitional" or "organized"—never relied on ethnic exclusiveness. We even find the opposite in Dontsov's works—"Ukrainians for Ukraine"[123] is closer in spirit to the concept of responsible leadership in the struggle to create one's own state.

It would appear that the slogan "Ukraine for Ukrainians" (which originates with Mykola Mikhnovsky), seemingly quite in line with the principles of *Action française*, is, in fact, almost completely denied in the Ukrainian context. After all, the draft constitution of the Ukrainian state—which, unlike France, did not then

---

122 Oleksandr Zaitsev, "On Ustashism and Fascism: A Response to Critics", *Journal of Soviet and Post-Soviet Politics and Society* 7, no. 1 (2020): 125.
123 Dmytro Dontsov, "На два фронти" ["On the Two Fronts"], *Заграва* 9 (1923).

exist on the map—published in the single (September 1905) issue of the Ukrainian People's Party newspaper under the title "An Independent Ukraine", guaranteed the rights of national minorities.[124]

Therefore, we should interpret Mikhnovsky's position starting in 1899 as a call to fight against the occupiers, to restore the independent Ukrainian state and exercise the nation's right to self-determination. As a lawyer, he devoted much attention to the legal justifications for Ukrainians' right to state independence, in particular through revising the 1654 Pereyaslav Agreement between Ukraine and Russia.

In contrast, the strong state context of the French monarchical nationalist movement linked it to the colonial traditions of France's global empire and indicated a willingness to dominate all the different and weaker social elements that did not fit the concept of national exclusiveness.

Indeed, the very idea of the national "integrity" of the Ukrainian liberation movement, which places national priorities above all else, derives from a romantic perception of the nation, one initiated by Taras Shevchenko in his poem "To the Dead, the Living, and to the Unborn Compatriots of Mine in Ukraine and Not in Ukraine, My Fraternal Missive", written on December 14, 1845. In this poem we can see the nation as a community existing beyond time and space.

Taras Shevchenko's vision was influential in shaping the ideology of Ukrainian nationalism. In particular, the OUN adopted another of Shevchenko's statements, describing the Russian Empire/Soviet Union as a "prison of nations" that must be destroyed by any means. Starting in 1940, the Ukrainian nationalist movement officially used the slogan: "Liberty to the nations, liberty to the person". Such a statement would be absolutely impossible for fascist movements with their deep etatism.

---

124 Mykola Mikhnovsky, "Основний Закон «Самостійної України» спілки народу українського" ["The Principal Law of 'An Independent Ukraine' by the Union of Ukrainian people], *Самостійна Україна* 1 (1905). Article 117 states: "The foreigners who settled in Ukraine 10 years before the proclamation and enactment of this principal law shall be considered as having lived continuously and along with native Ukrainians …".

National "integrity" was also supported by Ivan Franko, a prominent Ukrainian intellectual, in a debate provoked by the publication of Mykola Mikhnovsky's *An Independent Ukraine*. In his essay "Beyond the Limits of the Possible", Franko takes Mikhnovsky's side, reflecting on the "ideal of political independence" and the "ideal of national independence".[125] He expresses no reservations about the slogan "Ukraine for Ukrainians" because he perceived it as a call for national liberation, and not through a xenophobic lens.

So, Who Was Really Whom?

When considering the characteristic features of the Ukrainian nationalist movement, we should question the widespread thesis about the authoritarian nature of the Organization of Ukrainian Nationalists. The OUN was authoritarian in that it was a military organization. Its purpose was the armed struggle for Ukrainian state independence, but it also undertook preparations for the coming war, like the European states and other nationalist movements in stateless nations.

The authoritarianism of interwar Ukrainian nationalism did not intend to accomplish any particularly authoritarian/totalitarian project in an independent Ukraine. Taking quotes out of the context, as has unjustifiably been done in several dozen institutional publications, does not benefit the truth.

Likewise, claims about Dmytro Dontsov's "fascination with fascism" look very dubious. He also "admired" Bolshevism, the Zaporizhian Cossacks, Crusaders, and the figure of Muhammad — any and all examples that could "technically" bring "success" to the Ukrainian liberation movement. Similarly, Western democracies also once "admired" the anti-communist stance of Benito Mussolini, a fascist.

---

125 Ivan Franko, *Поза межами можливого* ["Beyond the Limits of the Possible"], Зібрання творів у 50 томах [Collected Works in 50 volumes] (Київ: Наукова Думка, 1976–1986), 45: 279, 280, 285. See Ivan Franko, "Beyond the Limits of the Possible", in *Towards an Intellectual History of Ukraine: An Anthology of Ukrainian Thought from 1710 to 1995*, ed. Ralph Lindheim and George S. N. Luckyj (Toronto: University of Toronto Press, 1995), 196, 198.

Even in Soviet Ukraine, under Russian Bolshevik occupation, when intellectual discussions used the rhetoric of "Get away from Moscow!", the writer Mykola Khvyliovyi, who coined the slogan, wrote in 1926 that "the hot temper that spawns fascism cannot but evoke sympathy".[126] Such a statement would receive very harsh treatment after the Nuremberg trials, but in the interwar period it had quite a different contextual meaning.

Incidentally, in that period, Dmytro Dontsov expressed sympathy for the political system of Great Britain (in 1933, in a letter to the writer Yuri Klen, he said: "I consider England the best creation of modern civilization")[127] and, in 1929, he expressed admiration for the United States of America.[128] In no way does this indicate his adherence to contemporary liberal democracy. Yet neither does it mean that we can today ignore the interwar geopolitical context. In other words, on the eve of World War II, the Ukrainian nationalist movement was focused not on the political system of a future Ukraine, but on the struggle for independence.

One should remember here that the OUN gave rise to three attempts to declare an independent Ukrainian state and create Ukrainian governments. They were Carpathian Ukraine (1939), the Ukrainian State (with the Ukrainian State Council as its government, 1941), and the Ukrainian Supreme Liberation Council (1944). The latter was the prototype for the Ukrainian government's political leadership during the armed struggle of the Ukrainian Insurgent Army. These all provide important evidence for understanding the OUN's intentions regarding the future political system of an independent Ukraine. All three governments contained signs of a coalition structure.

---

126 See Serhiy Kvit. "The Ukrainian liberation movement in the interwar period (1923–1939)", Конференція Дмитра Штогрина [Dmytro Shtohryn Conference]. Збірник матеріалів [Collected Works], (Вид. дім «Києво-Могилянська академія», 2020), 169.

127 R. Rakhmannyi, *Дмитро Донцов і Юрій Клен: 1933–1939*, Україна атомного віку: есеї і статті, 1945-1986 [Dmytro Dontsov and Yuri Klen: 1933–1939, Ukraine in the Atomic Age: Essays and Articles] (Торонто: Гомін України, 1988), 21.

128 Dmytro Dontsov. "Дух американізму" [The Spirit of Americanism], *Літературно-Науковий Вістник*, 4 (1929).

It should be noted that only the government headed by Augustyn Voloshin was actually a coalition government, as Carpathian Ukraine was proclaimed just before World War II. After the war started, legal Ukrainian political parties ceased to exist. However, whenever possible, well-known public opinion leaders, experts, scholars, and individuals holding different political views were involved in the Ukrainian State Council (under the premiership of Yaroslav Stetsko).

Finally, the Ukrainian Supreme Liberation Council was symbolically headed by Kyrylo Osmak, a former member of the Central Council of Ukraine (1917–1918), which emphasized the continuity of Ukrainian statehood with the Ukrainian People's Republic period. That is, all the three precedents for creating national governments were attempts at making the latter attractive to society as a whole, shared political responsibility with activists who held different political views, but who all stood on the platform of an independent Ukraine.

Returning to the features of the Ukrainian and Croatian nationalist movements, it can be observed that they had much in common. Oleh Bahan points out that "for the first time in the discourse of the emerging Ukrainian nationalist movement of the twentieth century, the subject of Croatian arose in 1913 at the Second Student Congress in Lviv in the famous speech of Dmytro Dontsov (1883–1973) titled 'The Present Political Situation of the Nation and Our Tasks'".[129]

Bahan writes about political and institutional cooperation, the exchange of ideas, and artistic contacts taking place in the context

---

129 Oleh Bahan. *Хорватська тема в українській націоналістичній пресі 1930 – поч. 1940- х років*, Україна і Хорватія: Історичні паралелі. [The Subject of Croatia in the Ukrainian Nationalist Press of the 1930s and early 1940s, Ukraine and Croatia: Historical Parallels] Матеріали Другої міжнародної українсько-хорватської наукової конференції [The Proceedings of the Second International Ukrainian-Croatian Research Conference] (Дрогобич: Бойківське етнологічне товариство, Кафедра української мови та літератури Sveučilište u Zagrebu, 2019), 366. Dmytro Dontsov. Сучасне положення нації і наші завдання [The Present Political Situation of the Nation and Our Tasks] (Львів: Видавництво Українського Студентського Союза "Молода Україна", 1913).

of the very similar historical tasks facing Ukrainians and Croats: to create their own independent states. In the OUN, Bohdan Kravtsiv played a special role in the development of Ukrainian-Croatian dialogue.

Studying the typological similarity between the OUN and the Ustašas is fruitful. However, according to Bahan, it is important to remember how the two political traditions differ. Unlike the Ukrainians, the Croats had for a long time enjoyed state autonomy, possessed their own idea of monarchy, and were more deeply immersed in the Western European cultural and political context. Probably, in the interwar period, the Ustašas were as popular among the politically active part of Ukrainian society, as Mladočeši had been in the late nineteenth century.

At the same time, Ivan Patryliak reminds us that "firstly, until 1941 the Ustašas were mostly an émigré organization, which had little influence in Croatia after the 1932 Lika uprising and which, unlike the OUN, could not boast an extensive underground network back home. The Ustashas were truly 'granted' their statehood by the Nazis and fascists whose example they followed in nation-building. Secondly, in 1941, OUN members (the Bandera) strongly rejected the Slovak or Croatian type of ersatz statehood (and informed Berlin of this in a special memorandum of June 23, 1941)".[130]

That memorandum was prepared by Ukrainian nationalists on June 15, 1941 and handed to the Reich Chancellery on June 23. The text was full of strong criticism, exhortations, and even threats to the Third Reich, as well as demands for complete state independence and the creation of a full-scale Ukrainian army. The document utterly rejected the Croatian and Slovak "models":

> "It must be stated that there is no analogy for resolving the Ukrainian issue. Since 1938, two new states have emerged in Europe: Slovakia and Croatia. Without taking into account the difference in area and population of the countries, the Ukrainian problem is far more pressing […] Not only do

---

[130] Ivan Patryliak. Відгук офіційного опонента на дисертацію Олександра Зайцева «Український інтегральний націоналізм (1920–1930-ті роки): генеза, еволюція, порівняльний аналіз» [Review by an official opponent to the dissertation by Oleksandr Zaitsev, "Ukrainian Integral Nationalism (1920s–1930s): Genesis, Evolution, and Comparative Study], 2014.

further German-Ukrainian relations depend on the final solution of the problem, but so do the methods to be used from the very beginning. [...] The Organization of Ukrainian Nationalists, which has for many years been leading the vibrant part of the Ukrainian people in its revolutionary struggle for the state independence of Ukraine and educating the entire Ukrainian people of this duty, is ready to lead this struggle to achieve its national ideal".[131]

After the proclamation of the Ukrainian State in Lviv on June 30, 1941 (as part of the so-called "policy of accomplished facts" pursued by the OUN), the German occupation authorities imprisoned many OUN leaders and initiated a mass repression of the nationalist movement. In response, the OUN, keeping the promises communicated in the memorandum, launched an insurgent movement and created the Ukrainian Insurgent Army. These events have been substantially highlighted by Volodymyr Kosyk, who relies on German archives.[132]

More about the Context

After World War II was over, the Ukrainian community was left with two possible choices: either accept defeat and abandon any intention of creating its own independent state or continue the armed struggle. All the major players in the European arena had denied Ukrainians the right to their own state.

The refurbished Russian Empire—the Soviet Union—organized the Holodomor in 1932–1933 on the territory of the quasi-state called the Ukrainian Soviet Socialist Republic, threatening the physical existence of the Ukrainian nation. The Entente collaborated with newly created states that also pursued a policy of denationalizing the Ukrainian population in their territories (Poland,

---

[131] Ivan Patryliak. Визвольна боротьба ОУН й УПА (1939–1960 рр.) [The OUN and UPA's Liberation Struggle (1939–1960)] (Київ: ВД АДЕФ-Україна, 2019), 117.

[132] Wolodymyr Kosyk, L'Allemagne national-socialiste et l'Ukraine (Paris: Publ. de l'Est Européen, 1986); Україна в Другій світовій війні у документах. Збірник німецьких архівних матеріалів (1944–1945): в 4 томах [Ukraine in World War II, Documents: A Collection of German Archive Materials (1944–1945), 4 vols.]; Упоряд. Wolodymyr Kosyk. — Львів: Львівський національний університет імені Івана Франка; Інститут української археографії та джерелознавства ім. М. Грушевського НАН України, 2000.

Romania, and Hungary first of all). Taken together, those countries treated the "Ukrainian question" according to the formula "no state, no problem". Only Czechoslovakia, under Tomáš Masaryk, was the exception.

As a consequence, the Ukrainian nationalist movement had little choice but to cooperate with Italy, Lithuania, Finland, and Germany (with the *Abwehr*) on a joint anti-communist platform. The latter, incidentally, is the same reason that the Entente countries also engaged in similar cooperation. This period of history saw a sort of "fashion for authoritarianism", a massive preparation for the coming war. The OUN also undertook the task of national mobilization as Ukrainians faced mortal danger, having neither an army nor a state.

To treat the European national liberation movements of the interwar period, in particular the Ukrainian movement, according to the rhetoric of the 1945–1946 Nuremberg trials is inappropriate. The Entente countries' refusal of aid turned Finland into an ally of Hitler's Germany after the Soviet invasion. Stalin entered into the war as a natural ally of Hitler, but then situationally continued it within the anti-Hitler coalition. That allowed him to avoid international condemnation for crimes against humanity.

Norman Nymark points out that almost all the members of the Soviet delegation to the Nuremberg trials were involved in mass repression within the USSR and therefore deserved to be put on trial alongside the Nazi criminals.

> "After having demonstrated his worth as a vicious and unrelenting attack dog of Stalin's during the Moscow trials, where he abused the defendants and shouted down their attempts to clear themselves of impossible charges, Vyshinskii was deputy foreign minister in 1946 during the Nuremberg trials and head of a secret special commission on Nuremberg that reported directly to Molotov and Stalin. The main job of the commission [...] was to make sure that there was no public discussion of Nazi-Soviet relations (not to mention cooperation!) during the period of the pact, 1939–1941. The Soviet government was especially concerned that the secret protocols of the Nazi-Soviet Pact were not mentioned at all". [133]

---

[133] Norman M. Naimark, *Stalin's Genocides* (Princeton: Princeton University Press, 2010), 18.

Finally, according to Norman Davies, the problem was that the Ukrainian nationalists fought not only against Hitler but also against Stalin,[134] whom many in the West continue to regard not as a necessary evil in the fight against another evil but only as an ally of the West in World War II.

Conclusion

Discussion of the typology of European interwar nationalist movements in the twentieth century is rooted in the "presumption of guilt" of the OUN in terms of its alleged pro-fascist orientation, one that only by mere accident did not materialize into a quasi-state on the model of Croatia and Slovakia. Such a view derives from an incorrect interpretation of an observation made by Alexander Motyl: "Paradoxically, repression proved to be the best thing that could have happened to the OUN, saving it from the collaborationist fate of the Croatian Ustasha or the Slovak People's Party".[135]

Such a collaborationist quasi-state did not materialize because it was fundamentally impossible. On the one hand, Hitler unleashed World War II, intending to expand the Germans' "living space" in the East: *Lebensraum im Osten*. This affected Ukraine first of all. Ukrainian territory was to be for the Third Reich, not for Ukrainians.

On the other hand, the facts prove that the OUN would not agree to Hitler's projects. The OUN was fighting a war on all fronts, against literally everyone who opposed Ukrainian independence. First of all, against Nazi Germany and the Soviet Union (a new iteration of the Russian Empire, as it was). It is this anti-imperial focus that makes the ideological heritage of the Ukrainian liberation movement so relevant today.

In particular, when trying to better understand Putin's Russia, which has made the "Great Patriotic War" narrative the main ideological basis for the world's largest "fake news factory", an integral

---

134 Norman Davies, *Europe: A History* (Oxford: Oxford University Press, 1996), 1032.
135 Alexander J. Motyl, *Dilemmas of Independence: Ukraine after Totalitarianism* (New York: Council of Foreign Relations Press, 1993), 95.

part of the post-truth phenomenon.¹³⁶ What is the "Great Patriotic War"? In fact, it is almost the same as World War II. Only without its beginning (1939–1941), when the Soviet Union collaborated with Nazi Germany. Today, the unpunished crimes of the "communist paradise" have sprouted as the generic fascism of Putin's Russia.

Finally, I would like to mention two publications that are conceptually important for discussion of the typology of nationalism and fascism. The first is Alexander Motyl's article "Ukraine, Europe, and Bandera", in which he offers extremely valuable thoughts on the nature of both phenomena:

> There is no reason that nationalism must have fascist components. The striving for national liberation is perfectly compatible with every philosophy, political ideology, culture, and economic theory. Unsurprisingly, nationalist ideologies and movements have spanned the political spectrum, being found among democrats, liberals, authoritarians, militarists, fascists, Communists, Catholics, Islamists, Jews, and capitalists. Interwar nationalist movements tended to be influenced by the prevailing fascist ethos just as post-World War II national liberation struggles tended to be influenced by the prevailing Communist ethos — which is simply to say that nationalism is malleable and can adapt itself to a variety of political ideologies, even, as in the nineteenth century, to liberalism.
>
> Fascism, meanwhile, presupposes an independent nation state and proposes to reorganize it along specifically fascist lines. In that sense, fascism is not about national liberation per se; instead, it assumes that national liberation and the attainment of a nation state has already taken place. Logically, this means that nation-statehood is a necessary condition of fascism: that is, fascist ideologies, movements, and systems of rule can exist if and only if an independent nation state is already in existence.¹³⁷

The second publication is a book by Myroslav Shkandrij, *Ukrainian Nationalism: Politics, Ideology, and Literature, 1929–1956*, which gives a broad picture of the political and intellectual history of the Ukrainian nationalist movement and its values: "This generation, whatever its political colors, exhibited a remarkable enthusiasm for, and faith in, political struggle. It refused to reconcile to the existing political situation and continued to dream of an

---

136 Serhiy Kvit. "A perspective on 'fake news'", *Kyiv Post*, May, 8, 2021.
137 Alexander J. Motyl. "Ukraine, Europe, and Bandera", Cicero Foundation Great Debate Paper, No. 10/05 (March 2010): 3–4.

independent state, even when the odds against such a state emerging seemed overwhelming".[138]

Shkandrij also recalls the OUN's later influence on the dissident movement:

> "The imprisoned dissident [Mykhailo Horyn], like other Ukrainian and Jewish prisoners of conscience who at this time found themselves in the camps, came to admire the steadfastness of these old prisoners, their discipline, solidarity, and commitment to national rights".[139]

When studying the Ukrainian liberation movement of the twentieth century one must throw out the habitual condemnatory mythology created by the opponents of Ukrainian independence. Shkandrij concludes that "neither pursuit of ethnic purity, nor racism, nor acceptance of Nazi doctrine were central to the OUN's ideology, nor were they officially endorsed".[140] Methodologically, this book is related to Alexander Motyl's principles.

The main conclusion is the following: along with independence itself, Ukraine has gained the right to the history of the struggle for it. In time, the work of professional researchers and the media representation of the history of the Ukrainian liberation movement will grow more responsible.

---

138 Myroslav Shkandrij. *Ukrainian Nationalism: Politics, Ideology, and Literature, 1929–1956*, (New Haven and London: Yale University Press, 2015), 12.
139 Ibid.
140 Ibid., 268.

The Process, Meaning, and Consequences of Ukraine's Revolution[141]

This review briefly summarizes the contents of the book *Ukraine's Maidan, Russia's War: A Chronicle and Analysis of the Revolution of Dignity* by Mychailo Wynnyckyj, a professor at the National University of Kyiv-Mohyla Academy and at the Lviv Business School of the Ukrainian Catholic University. The book was translated from English into Ukrainian by Roman Klochko and published in 2021 by the Old Lion Publishing House.

This book is significant as a contribution intended to educate Western readers, like Timothy Garton Ash and Timothy Snyder's earlier "The Orange Revolution".[142] Both texts broadly present a Ukrainian context that is often still unknown to Western audiences either as a result of plain ignorance or due to the hyperactivity of Russia's fake news factory (along with "the world's largest gas station", this metaphor accurately describes the Russian state system).

Mychailo Wynnyckyj's book about the Ukrainian Maidan and Russian war is of great interest to Ukrainian readers because of the distinctive emphases made by the author, who was intellectually raised in various research traditions and is well versed in the relevant terminology, rhetoric, and public discussions.

Serhii Plokhy, in his foreword, calls Wynnyckyj "an activist and a scholarly analyst".[143] However, Mychailo is not a typical participant in the Revolution of Dignity: he was born in Canada, defended his PhD in Great Britain, moved to Ukraine, and ultimately contributed personally to the events he describes.

---

141 *Den'* [The Day], 2021.
142 Timothy Garton Ash and Timothy Snyder, "The Orange Revolution", *The New York Review of Books*, April 28, 2005; rpt. in Timothy Garton Ash, *Facts Are Subversive: Political Writing from a Decade without a Name* (New Haven and London: Yale University Press, 2011), 31–45.
143 Serhii Plokhy, "Foreword: Making the Revolution Happen", in Mychailo Wynnyckyj, *Ukraine's Maidan, Russia's War: A Chronicle and Analysis of the Revolution of Dignity* (Ibidem: Stuttgart, 2019), xv.

To some extent, Wynnyckyj's book is a follow-up to his chronicle "Thoughts from Kyiv", which was published on his Facebook page and disseminated by his brother Roman via e-mail to an "off-Facebook" audience. That is, the book presents the subjective narrative of someone personally involved in revolutionary events, and this is what makes it so valuable. "To hell with academic distance. Evil must be stopped", the author writes in his diary entries from the Maidan.

Such an emotional response does not exclude some extremely engaging theoretical suppositions and rational observations. Wynnyckyj goes deep into the meaning of events, finds reliable sources, and analyzes what took place not only during the Ukrainian Maidan, but also before and after it. He also emphasizes that "This book is about the indestructible Ukrainian nation. It is about a people transformed through revolution, and about the broader civilizational consequences of these events".[144]

Mychailo Wynnyckyj, who believes that his work needs to represent different points of view, "for" and "against" the Ukrainian Maidan, feels obliged to mention such authors as Ivan Katchanovskyi and his completely irrelevant, not to say fantastic, interpretations of events. Thanks to this balance, we gain an understanding that the Maidan actually contained real discussions and a pluralism of opinions.

In the context of Wynnyckyj's reflections on the postmodern nature of the Ukrainian Maidan, it is worth recalling the widely quoted idea from Lee McIntyre's *Post-Truth*: "The goal of objectivity is not to give equal [journalistic] time between truth and falsehood — it is to facilitate the truth".[145]

The Ukrainian Maidan has forced the Western world to acknowledge the need for a real response to the challenges emanating from Russia, including the threat of the complete destruction of the postwar international security system, the destruction of the Western way of life in both institutions and values. At the time of the Revolution of Dignity, to declare that Ukrainians have a

---

144 Mychailo Wynnickyi, *Ukraine's Maidan, Russia's War*, 5.
145 Lee McIntyre, *Post-Truth* (Cambridge, MA: MIT Press, 2018), 81.

European identity was almost the same as affirming their national identity.

Perhaps this is why Ukrainians' struggle for independence at the beginning of the twenty-first century was so broadly attractive to Ukraine's minorities: practically all national and social groups living in the territory of Ukraine supported the struggle. Wynnyckyj draws attention to the territorial, and not simply ethnic, nature of the emerging Ukrainian political nation, united by the values of dignity and freedom and the European choice of Ukrainians: in contrast to Putin's Russian "mordor", associated with evil and injustice.

The book advances the idea that the Maidan's victory and Yanukovych's flight from power represented only the beginning of the Ukrainian revolution. This process must complete its mission and bring specific plans and promises to reality.

The author focuses on the question of the "authenticity" of the Ukrainian revolution, which, according to existing theories, could easily have descended into terror and dictatorship in its final stage. However, Ukraine appeared to be "saved" from this by Russian aggression, all revolutionary energy being redirected to saving the state through the initiatives of civil society, voluntary activity creativity, responsible leadership, and the volunteer movement, which made the victory of the Maidan possible.

It is extremely important that public attention be focused on the strengthening and fundamental reform of the Ukrainian state, which simply must be a just state. The author considers the idea of justice "cosmological", one which lays a philosophical (moral and ethical) foundation for the development of worldviews and institutions.

No less interesting are the author's philological explanations of the inconsistent conventional translation of the Ukrainian "*hidnist*" as "dignity" in English. He says that this is not fully accurate since the Ukrainian notion has no hierarchical connotations. Dignity is either present or not. Ukrainians earn their dignity as part of their valor in struggle. Here, there is a suggestion about Ukrainian military traditions, related to the ability of protesters to organize the Maidan-Sich and to the Maidan Self-Defense Forces' lightning-fast response to the escalation of violence by the authorities.

We must take into account the network-based nature of the Revolution of Dignity and virtually all its achievements. This network (horizontal) action, in addition to using social media and modern technologies, also relied on a large number of universally recognized historical symbols: the regular "*Viches*" (assemblies) of the Maidan return us to the democratic traditions of Kyivan Rus; St. Michael's Golden-Domed Monastery, a refuge for students beaten by the "Berkut" special police forces activates the memory of the last bastion of the defenders of Kyiv against the Mongol invasion in the thirteenth century; the Maidan-Sich reminds us of Ukrainian Cossack traditions; the Maidan Self-Defense Hundreds were organized in a way similar to UPA units; and so on.

Wynnyckyj highlights the epoch-making nature of the Revolution of Dignity, as it has conferred on Ukraine the status of being the "frontier of Europe". Similarly,

> "just as the Great Transformation from agrarian feudalism to industrial capitalism [...] was punctuated by several revolutions and wars in the course of its centuries-long progression, so too [...] will history record Ukraine's Revolution of Dignity as one of the 'great revolutions' that fostered new ideas, values, social arrangements, and proto-institutions that defined social development in the era that followed industrial society (i.e. 'modernity')".[146]

Just as thirteen peripheral British colonies became the United States of America, Ukraine, although peripheral from a Western perspective, has offered a fundamentally new value discourse in the context of a deep, specifically European, civilizational crisis. Indeed, Western rhetoric of a "Ukrainian crisis", as encountered in some references to Ukraine's Maidan and Russia's war, is deeply harmful and distorted.

Wynnyckyj speaks of simultaneously unfolding national, bourgeois, and postmodern revolutions. The national revolution was a follow-up to Ukrainians' long national liberation struggle for their own state. However, the Maidan became something greater for Ukrainians than simply the expression of their traditional

---

146 Mychailo Wynnickyi, *Ukraine's Maidan, Russia's War*, 300.

identity. This new Ukrainian identity had a new articulation: not fully "linguistic, ethnic, or political", but rather territorial, in the first place, and then civic (in the sense of the Ukrainian word "*hromada*"). No new "revolutionary dictator" or leader could possibly emerge in the context of this identity.

A bourgeois revolution is the second dimension of the Ukrainian Maidan. According to Wynnyckyj, the revolution primarily engaged Ukraine's new "creative class", which is not only capitalist but also idealistic. Not only did this class support the Revolution of Dignity; it was produced by this event. The bourgeois nature of the Ukrainian Revolution has nothing to do with confronting any "proletarian interests". Rather, it refers to Max Weber's "spirit of capitalism", embodied in qualitatively new social, technological, and civilizational conditions.

Finally, the author links the definition of a "postmodern revolution" to the historical period that comes after the age of "modernity", the latter including industrial capitalism, urbanization, the transition from collectivism to individualism, the division of labor and its impact on social relations, the principles of the rule of law, equality of rights, etc.

Here the author mentions such social phenomena as post-truth, horizontal connections, demanding respect for one's own dignity, the movement from individualism to personalism innately directed to truth, humanity, and justice ("a strange mix of western individualism with respect to rights, and Slavic collectivism with respect responsibility"),[147] and an idealistic system of values.

Wynnyckyj's book explains many things, but the author did not intend to provide comprehensive and final answers to all possible questions. In a certain sense, this book is a continuation of the great intellectual debate started by the Revolution of Dignity. Here one should mention the talks of Volodymyr Yermolenko, in particular "The Fluid Ideologies of the Maidan".

As I already mentioned, according to Yermolenko, the Maidan was an interesting ideological cocktail.

---

147 Ibid., 322.

"This fluidity," he says, "was a godsend for the Maidan since it turned the protests into something more than a narrow ideological project. Today, more than ever, Ukrainian politics needs to distinguish ideological boundaries, and to structure the political field around ideas, and not only around "financial and industrial groups".[148]

We should not treat the Revolution of Dignity as a completed historical event. Mychailo Wynnyckyj offers a long list of tasks that need to be accomplished. He talks about the need for institutionalizing the innovations created by Ukraine's Maidan. How can the State be governed in a horizontal way? How can the principles of "justice" and "dignity" be institutionalized? How do we institutionalize the pursuit of justice in Ukraine's judicial system? In what way can Ukraine's institutions become effective and overcome corruption?

And further: How can we make the Ukrainian state so strong that it will reliably protect these changes, without posing a threat to strong horizontal links? What changes must take place in Western perceptions of Ukraine? What are the adequate responses to the threats from a mainly "postmodern" and therefore even more aggressive Russian imperialism? Most probably, it is up to the readers of the book, and not only its author, to seek answers to these questions.

---

148 Volodymyr Yermolenko, Рідинні ідеології Майдану [The Fluid Ideologies of the Maidan], Флософська думка (2014) 6: 9.

A University Degree for Carlos and "Kyiv-Mohyla 2.0"
Three Criteria for a High-Quality Education[149]

Public discussions around reforms in higher education are targeted, as a rule, exclusively at the educational community and are much less correlated with the growing practical demand for high-quality education in society at large. Today, anyone who wants to can receive a higher education diploma in Ukraine. Therefore, it is increasingly recognized that such an education should be of the highest quality possible.

What is a High-Quality Education?

While visiting Stanford University a few years ago as a Fulbright scholar, I met a barber named Carlos, who was from Mexico. He did not have enough money to pursue higher education in the United States, but he read much and even spent his vacations visiting countries that had made key contributions to the development of European civilization. For example, he showed me photographs he had taken in Greece.

Carlos would be able to afford a Ukrainian university education. The question is whether he would get a high-quality education if he chose to do so. The question is more than rhetorical, given the large number of higher education institutions in Ukraine today (more than 1,200, according to the Single State Database of Education). We should first give a definition of what could be considered a high-quality one. I propose three main criteria.

First, when all the promises by a university to provide its students with various competencies, personal development, and other necessary services, are kept. That is if a university is one that is able to do so. [It's OK—S.K.]

Second, it is important to understand how confident a particular higher education institution is within the global context, and

---

[149] *Den'* [The Day], November 16, 2021.

how integrated it is into international networks of higher education and scholarly research. Since we live in a globalized world, we have to compare ourselves not just with other Ukrainian HEIs, but with the best of international universities.

Third, it is necessary to assess the reputation of a university, whether and to what extent its culture is responsive to its internal community (students, faculty, non-academic staff). What kind of values does it promote in daily activities and how does it see its graduates: as competent actors only, or as future leaders?

This is why discussions concerning reform in higher education and research, their relationship to labor markets, reflections about future professions, and other similar issues should be addressed to Ukrainian universities that regard high-quality education as a defining factor, universities that, I am sure, we will create in the near future. They will become independent platforms for the free circulation of ideas, centers of expertise and research, and, through relevant ecosystems, of innovation.

Leadership Issues

According to Roger Everett's diffusion of innovation theory, in order for a system to adapt to changes associated with innovations, "innovators" and "pioneers" must first emerge who will believe in the new ideas, implement them, and serve as an example for others.

In the stagnant Ukrainian system of higher education at the gaining of independence in 1991, then little more than a silent fragment of the Soviet system that had already ceased to exist, the National University of Kyiv-Mohyla Academy (NaUKMA) played this innovative role. Historically, it was the very first (founded in 1615) institution of higher education in Ukraine, and, importantly, the reborn *Mohylianka* had no Soviet heritage.

I have recently heard the term "*Mohylianka* 2.0" from a NaUKMA graduate. He has had a very successful professional career. Yet the unusual trajectory of his career draws the attention, as does the previous direction of his education. Neither could have been planned in advance.

According to the *"Mohylianka* 1.0" concept, such things occur as a by-product of the possibilities of a Liberal Arts Education system, introduced at NaUKMA in the early 1990s. This means not just the opportunity to freely choose academic courses and minors, specialized blocks of academic subjects, in particular from different fields of knowledge. Today, signing up for optional courses is done online. Moreover, the number of such courses usually exceeds the number of students able to enroll.

The possibility to choose is the basic principle of organizing the academic process, asking students: what would interests you, what would suit you most? Shaping one's own education means the opportunity for everyone to receive a unique and tailor-made education. Students are not pushed into a predetermined corridor during their student years. Instead, one's choices and life circumstances decide.

From the very beginning, Kyiv-Mohyla's success has rested on two pillars: the concept of a Liberal Arts Education, in the broad sense of this concept, and the absence of corruption. Subsequently, the adoption of external independent assessment in the form of a nationwide entrance exam was based on the successful example of NaUKMA's entrance testing. A tiny detail was omitted: when national testing was introduced, no one asked the Kyiv-Mohyla community for its opinion.

In a strange way, the borrowing of its innovations eventually lent a blow to the uniqueness of *Mohylianka*. In reality, NaUKMA's entry exam was much more demanding than its copy—it covered seven academic subjects and was uniform for all fields of university study. This meant that all applicants were tested in mathematics, the history of Kyiv-Mohyla Academy, Ukrainian, English, and law (two tests based on specialization were also included—one for the humanities and one for the natural sciences).

After the examination was over, answer sheets were automatically checked by a computer in the assembly hall of NaUKMA's Culture and Arts Center in the presence of the applicants, their parents, and journalists, so that applicants knew whether or not they had become NaUKMA students by 5 p.m. that very day. Applicants who passed entry requirements for two specializations (the first time that this possibility was offered in Ukraine) were given a few more days to make their final choice. The main goal of Kyiv-Mohyla's entrance exam was to build a community of students. Its anti-corruption character was important, but supplementary.

NaUKMA has become a platform for innovation in Ukrainian higher education after the gaining of Ukrainian independence in 1991. Here we can mention the first Bachelor's, Master's, and PhD (Doctor of Philosophy) programs; cross-disciplinary entry into Master's programs; the first university job center; the first policy provisions for academic integrity; effective student self-governance; the first center for quality assurance; the use of English as the second working language; and many other innovations.

Offering prestige, integrity, professionalism, possibilities for professional self-realization, influence on the democratic transformations in the country, and being a catalyst for public change became the hallmarks of "Kyiv-Mohyla 1.0". In this context, we are, first of all, interested in the institutional culture of quality and integrity, and in the ability to adjust to change and quickly change ourselves.

Ukrainian "Boutique" Universities

The common European Higher Education Area fosters the creation of so-called "boutique" universities, based on a unique mission, strategy, role in the labor market, significance for local communities, and other criteria. To date, in the Ukrainian context, such an appeal has been mostly seen as "not serious" and cut off from "real life". This is evidenced by the present cumbersome university accreditation process, consisting of self-assessment information prepared by higher education institutions.

Every congress of the European University Association that I have had the opportunity to attend opened with a review of still unsettled issues regarding the course of broadening the autonomy of higher education institutions (HEIs), allowing them to become even more autonomous and economically effective, approaching American universities in these parameters.

The Law of Ukraine "On Higher Education" (2014), which replaced the policy of "leveling the ground", encourages, first of all, a unique internal culture of quality—the starting point—for higher education institutions, based on the concept of comprehensive university autonomy. That is why, according to the NaUKMA graduate I mentioned above, it is high time for a *"Mohylianka 2.0"* project.

It is good when an employer can hire a highly qualified graduate to perform certain tasks. However, today it is no longer simply a matter of training a proactive and responsible specialist. Distinct from natural resources and material assets, a human mind endowed with a broad world outlook is becoming a principal form of capital, ready for non-standard interpretations of important problems and with a special ability to notice and predict unsuspected connections and trends in ordinary phenomena.

Here is where American approaches prove their advantage: first, in their ability to select the best applicants to their universities, then to attract the best graduates for scholarly research and for political leadership in the state, and also to seek out the best minds around the world for the development of their country. Other Western universities and states try to do the same.

After all, people with special abilities who are both advanced mathematicians and profound humanists will increasingly generate progressive shifts in current systems. On the basis of these conditions, Ukrainian higher education needs a university with the necessary relevant training principles embedded in its practices. In the current Ukrainian landscape of higher education institutions, let this be a compact and mobile *"Mohylianka 2.0"*.

This would be a place where it would be easy to reorganize, change concepts, go beyond strictly professional requirements, and walk one step ahead of everyone else. In the end, this environment would not only teach students to be lifelong learners, but also, and very importantly, to ask questions throughout their lives. This is the only way to ensure finding viable answers to questions.

Practical Steps for Domestic Higher Education

What concretely should be done considering present Ukrainian realities?

First, cease to invest in rich Western countries. They get graduates from Ukrainian universities free of charge. Such students lack the proper environment to complete the most advanced training at home, as well as professional opportunities upon graduation. The Ukrainian state spends money on training young people, starting from kindergarten, then later simply passes them on to richer countries that offer more possibilities.

Second, it is necessary to implement full financial autonomy together with corporate governance elements. This entails an increased role for supervisory boards, inviting interested businessmen and opinion leaders to participate in and develop university life. Higher education institutions must become subjects of economic activity. Only after gaining this scope and capacity will they be able to ultimately become centers of innovative ecosystems and leaders in prestigious university rankings.

Third, it is necessary to restore the funding of scholarly research, which was stopped in Ukraine in the final years of Soviet rule. Additionally, research and higher education must be integrated. The current level of funding only just allows the academic infrastructure to avoid complete breakdown. The lack of demand in the Ukrainian state for the development of domestic research is pushing gifted researchers to the West.

Fourth, special attention should be paid to learning and acquiring the experience of so-called teaching universities, particularly in the context of discussing ideas surrounding students' personal development and of being attuned to the labor market.

We will continue to experiment and at first attempt to reorganize the university entrance system — offering students the option to choose professional area and specialization later. These ideas were first raised in the early 1990s, back when "*Mohylianka* 1.0" was initiated.

Fifth, we should realize at last that up-to-date high-quality universities cannot appear in a country that is "suspended' in an uncertain condition with a "transitional economy", oligarchic monopolies, and a level of justice that threatens national security. The implementation of an authoritarian model of higher education in Ukraine is impossible, considering the country's active civil society. Reforming the economy and education in tandem is necessary to avoid political dependence on state sponsorship, as, for example, occurs in Russia, whose natural resources allow for the adequate state funding of universities in exchange for loyalty.

Ukrainian universities can become international "boutique" centers of research and innovation, provided that they turn into free platforms for the expression of independent opinion — an important component of civil society — and become drivers of social change. Ukrainian universities can only be reformed alongside the implementation of fundamental reforms in Ukrainian state institutions and the creation of the conditions for the development of a free economy.

Returning to the question raised above regarding the possibility for Carlos to obtain a high-quality education in Ukraine today: yes, it is possible. Still, a whole range of conditions need to be favorably arranged for this to occur. A person who wants to study in Ukraine can find the opportunities necessary to do so. However, our current system of higher education does not yet foster adequate quality.

Our country has excellent examples of high-quality educational programs, professional teachers who are leaders in their spheres, and successful administrators and experts in academic communities. There are also prestigious Ukrainian universities that would be happy to participate in system transformations. However, someone must be the first to walk this path to enable the required systemic change.

Josyf Zisels: "Yes, I am a Ukrainian Jew"[150]

I read everything I wanted to find in *You Will Hear From my Lips...* a book of conversations with Josyf Zisels, a Jewish-Ukrainian intellectual and dissident, with Iza Chruslinska, a renowned Polish journalist. The book was published by *Dukh i Litera* Kyiv-Mohyla Academy Publishing House in 2017. It has a foreword by another former dissident, the intellectual Myroslav Marynovych. It often happens that in encountering the writings of remarkable people, everyone can find something for themselves. These are not just words. As a literary critic, I know that it is better to tell people here and now what they deserve to hear rather than later regretting not doing so.

Inter-Ethnic Dialogue

The genre of the dialogue, or conversation, is quite specific, essayistic, and probably ideal for this book. Indeed, it is unknown whether Josyf Zisels would have found the time himself to recall all the vicissitudes of his life journey, leading to his current identity, if it had not been for the journalistic persistence of such an interested interviewer as Iza Chruslinska. She skillfully leads the conversations in a manner that would interest not only Ukrainian and Jewish readers, but also a Polish audience. In other words, the book is for everyone interested in modern Ukraine, the former "socialist camp", and post-Soviet space. What is especially important to us is the process of unfolding the Jewish-Polish-Ukrainian international dialogue itself, one that references key intellectual questions.

The best and the greatest that we can find in relationships between different peoples is mutual trust and respect. This is something that can very quickly and easily be lost, however long it took to achieve, and it is hard to restore. As for inter-ethnic dialogue, it can only take place through the mediation of independent intellectuals. They can always do much even in times of war, mutual misunderstanding, and irresponsible politics. Josyf Zisels talks at

---

[150] *Den'* [The Day], March 17, 2017.

length about the formation of different identities: his own identity, present-day Jewish identity (its Western, Israeli, and Eastern European varieties), as well as modern Ukrainian identity. This is because he has been forming his identity throughout his life. Moreover, in the conversations he mentions the philosophy of existentialism, which is based on the idea that individuals can form their own identities.

Josyf Zisels is a rationally thinking person, a professional physicist. He is able to analyze himself and the world around him under all circumstances. It is interesting that this rationalism is not aimed at material gain, but at reaching non-material and even romantic goals. He finds justification in Jewish traditions: in helping the weak and changing the world for the better. At the same time, he understands that key to the survival of the worldwide Jewish diaspora throughout its long and tragic history was its attempt to remain close to the powerful. Herein lies the main reason for the stereotypes and the accumulation of mutual distrust between Ukrainians and Jews who lived together under different empires. This includes competing before ruling power structures — to win favor — and misunderstanding each other in times when Ukrainians, with weapons in their hands, attempted to become a free nation.

The work of such intellectuals as Josyf Zisels contributes to the accumulation of goodness. Before reading his texts, I was fortunate to make the acquaintance of Marten Feller, a unique person not only completely devoid of evil, but seemingly unable to even have evil thoughts. Under the influence of Vasyl Ivanyshyn,[151] he publishes his books with long and almost baroque titles: *The Explorations, Reflections, and Memories of a Jew who Remembers his Grandfathers' Thoughts on Jewish-Ukrainian Relations, Especially on Languages and Attitudes Towards Them* (Drohobych, 1994) and *The Explorations, Reflections, and Memories of a Jew who Remembers his Grandfathers' Thoughts on Jewish-Ukrainian Relations, Especially on the Inhuman and Human in Them* (Drohobych, 1998). Professor Feller is committed to

---

151 Vasyl Ivanyshyn — noted Ukrainian intellectual, author of the best-selling books "Ukrainian Church and the Process of National Revival" (1990), "Language and Nation" co-authored with Ya. Radevich-Vynnytskyi (1990, 1991, 1992, 1994, 2004), "Nation. Statehood. Nationalism" (1992), and others.

the special mission of spreading humanism as the basis for mutual understanding. He was also a Soviet Jew, when Jewish identity, as Zisels ironically remarks, was largely sustained by state anti-Semitism.

The Path to Oneself

Josyf Zisels is a man of intense action. He does not wait for the world around him to change for the better by itself. Instead, he does something in the pursuit of this end every day. At some point, it appeared that he needed to understand what it really meant to him that he was a Jew. Zisels thus studied the history of his family and then turned to his language (or, more correctly, languages, because both are important here—Yiddish and Hebrew), history, culture, and religion. He had childhood memories related to traditional holidays and of those close to him who knew Yiddish; there were isolated contacts with relatives who had gone abroad—to Romania and America. His family was from Bessarabia. The destiny of relatives has become a topic for reflection in the recent history of Eastern Europe, "the bloodlands", according to Timothy Snyder.

Zisels' father's eldest brother became a merchant, married the daughter of Sava Morozov, a famous Russian millionaire, and moved to Moscow. In 1925, he was sentenced to death and executed by the new "progressive" authorities in Moscow. His older brother, instead, took the Bolsheviks' side and throughout his life served in the "CHK" [Extraordinary Committee]—NKVD [People's Commissariat for Internal Affairs]—MGB [Ministry of State Security], eventually settling in Leningrad. His children severed all contact with the Ukrainian branch of the family due to Josyf's dissident activity. Josyf's father (the youngest brother in the family) was "liberated" by Soviet authorities later [I mean, according to Soviet rhetoric, the territories that were annexed before and as a result of World War II were "liberated". That is, Zisels' father got into the Soviet occupation later—S.K.]—at first, he remained on Romanian territory and even served in the Romanian army in the interwar period. Later, in the USSR, he worked for the railway and at many other jobs—he had to feed his family. When the war began, the family evacuated to Uzbekistan, where Josyf was born.

The city of Chernivtsi played an extremely important role in Josyf Zisels' life. There he could meet and talk with the surviving members of families of German-speaking Jews who still remembered the former favorable and tolerant Austro-Hungarian times. Zisels' rational and, therefore, critical mind could not accept Soviet realities, which would have seemed comical if they had not been so cruel and inhuman. His disagreement with the regime was fundamental. Having stepped onto the dissident path, he connected his life to his Ukrainian environment. It should be noted that the Ukrainian language, Ukrainian history and culture were barely present in Josyf Zisels's life before turned 30. Ukrainian was a kind of "niche" culture, and not only in Chernivtsi. You could live your whole life in Ukraine without ever encountering anything Ukrainian, as though you had been living in a completely different country.

And here is the most interesting thing. The transformations of Zisels' identity led to his understanding that his path to Jewishness had to pass through a Ukrainian identity. At first, it was like an acquaintance. Then Josyf Zisels learned the Ukrainian language, read a lot, and discussed with Ukrainian political prisoners the price Ukrainians were paying for the right to dream of their own independence. At the same time, he was growing stronger in his Jewish identity which, for him, as for the entire Jewish community, was fostered by pride in the distant state of Israel.

It is important to note that Zisels served his sentence in Soviet penal camps for criminal offenders, not political prisoners. However, we find no complaints regarding this in his memoirs. The author is a strong and self-possessed person. His explanations are quite rational: he knew from the very start where he was headed. He perceives everything in his life as a new experience contributing to his personal strength and growth. He calls the dissident period of his life his "stellar time".

One area of Josyf Zisels' activities, along with his dissident practices (creating and disseminating *samvydav* [underground literature], exposing the crimes of Soviet psychiatry, supporting political prisoners, etc.), was to help Jewish families who wanted to leave the Soviet Union. And that was no easy task. As for himself, he never planned or tried to find another place of residence outside of Ukraine. This was also his choice, an act of self-realization. Gradually, he started to identify himself as a Ukrainian Jew, whose fate was connected primarily with Ukraine. In his opinion, creating the best conditions for the development of the Ukrainian Jewish community was closely connected with the success of the Ukrainian state itself.

For Your and Our Freedom

As for me, the deep ideological anti-imperial commitment of Josyf Zisels also originates, to a significant extent, in Ukrainian liberation discourse. He pays tribute to his fellow Ukrainians, in particular fondly recalling the nationalists, people "without fear or doubts": Yaroslav Dashkevych and Zinovii Krasivskyj. They and those like them were linked to the tradition of armed struggle for Ukrainian independence and significantly influenced the author. Answering the question about what he thinks of Ukraine's new decommunization laws, he says: "Decommunization had to begin, it has to be done, better late than never. (...) There is also the Ukrainian Helsinki Group, and there are also the OUN [Organization of Ukrainian Nationalists] and UPA [Ukrainian Insurgent Army], and others. Decommunization doesn't bother me because I know more about the OUN and UPA than others, but it bothers many other people, especially in Poland".

Together with Iza Chruslinska, Josya Zisels makes insightful forays into the history of anti-Semitism. Whereas medieval prejudices and their legal consequences were already overcome almost everywhere in Europe and America by the late nineteenth and early twentieth centuries, the Russian Empire continued to cultivate anti-Semitism at the state level, financing and ideologically justifying it. The book fully separates the Ukrainian liberation movement from the politics of anti-Semitism, and Symon Petliura is mentioned as a victim of circumstance.

In the context of the current Ukrainian-Russian war, including propaganda warfare, published materials held by the French secret service on the Petliura case should be mentioned. They prove that the agency knew that Petliura's killer, Schwarzbard, was an agent of the Soviet CHK (Extraordinary Committee) when he arrived in France. The French authorities monitored Schwarzbard, documenting all his contacts and links: everyone who came into contact with him was automatically regarded as part of the Bolshevik agent's network.

In other words, the entire affair about the "people's avenger", declared to be retaliating for pogroms committed by Ukrainians, was actually orchestrated in Moscow. The image of the Ukrainian anti-Semite was largely shaped by that incident, which received great international attention first in the 1920s, and then in the 1950s. We cannot help mentioning Putin's propaganda here.

It is normal for a people to defend its statehood with arms in hand. For Josyf Zissels, it was clear that the declaration of Ukrainian independence in 1991 was not the result of some macabre evolution of the Ukrainian SSR, but the fruit of the struggle of many generations of Ukrainians and people like himself, a Ukrainian Jew, for independence. Each era brings its own rhetoric, forms, and methods of struggle. So, the symbolic analogies between the UPA's armed resistance, the Revolution of Dignity, the volunteer movement, and the anti-Russian front in the Donbas are more than obvious. In this context we can also recall the Jewish volunteers thanks to whom the Star of David appeared on the red and black flag.

It is important that at the beginning of the twenty-first century Ukrainian liberation discourse unexpectedly turned out to be attractive to all citizens of Ukraine, the Jewish community included, primarily to the latter's intellectuals, activists, and EuroMaidan military instructors. We can say, without exaggeration, that Josyp Zisels' December 15, 2013 speech on the Maidan, "For Your and Our Freedom!", had historical significance. Not only did it outline the idea of the Ukrainian political nation in a new way, but it also called on national minorities to fight together for a common future in Ukraine. The title of the speech also brings us to the history of Polish-Ukrainian anti-imperial relations. The overall attractiveness of the Ukrainian liberation movement was closely related to it being correctly identified with a highly active civil society, where everyone wishing to do something for Ukraine could find a place.

The Ukrainian revolution generated many incredible stories. When I was going to a meeting with the students who had come from the Maidan on February 21, 2014 to seize the buildings of the Ministry of Education and Science of Ukraine, I was stopped by a man wearing a helmet, a bulletproof vest, and carrying a baseball bat at the roadblock near the entrance. He pronounced the magic words "Glory to Ukraine!" and looked intently into my eyes waiting for my response. After I answered with "Glory to the Heroes!" he shook my hand and allowed me into the premises of the Ministry. He was an Israeli citizen who was living in Western Europe before Maidan. When Maidan started he immediately went to Kyiv, and, following the Russian attack on the Donbas, volunteered to serve at the front. By the way, he is still there.

To Live is to Change the World for the Better

Returning to Josyf Zisels' book, it becomes clear to us that it is not revolution that he believes in; rather, it is evolution that, in his opinion, can bring about necessary social transformations and change the people. A revolution is extremely important. It breaks down what is no longer necessary and sets new hallmarks. However, a new kind of state is not created immediately after the removal of the previous state system. It takes time to change previous habits and ways of doing things, established practices, patterns of behavior, and eventually society. Here again Zisels' rationalism is evident, and helpfully prevents his reader from enthusiastically internalizing any sort of idealization. Zisels calls himself a skeptic and a de-heroizer. What he means is that one should never simplify: yes, much has been done, but we still have much to do.

His reflections on the importance of the survival and development of the state of Israel, which maintains itself within a democratic framework despite an ongoing state of war, are engaging. Josyf Zisels points to the lack of experience and sometimes even to the naïve attitudes of Ukrainians in defending their national interests. Indeed, only a very young state could permit the operation of mass media which oppose Ukraine and actually support the enemy in wartime. He regrets that current Ukrainian society does not demand moral authorities, or rather does not notice them. Amidst the very dramatic events and rapid changes taking place people tend to trust no one except for a narrow circle consisting of close friends and relatives.

Josyf Zisels never went into politics, although he had opportunities to become a member of parliament. He did not want to sit next to and shake hands with those stained with the crimes of the communist regime, and were never punished for them. However, we now have a list of officials and politicians scheduled for punishment for crimes related to the betrayal of national interests and corruption. Josyf Zisels remains a public activist and one of the leaders of civil society. Iza Chruslinska's interviewee has an opinion on all of Ukraine's painful issues.

He emphasizes the special importance of the Heavenly Hundred, who symbolize the unity, strength, and dignity of Ukraine, and the readiness of our people for an absolutely different and dignified life. He stresses the need of raising the importance of the Ukrainian language so that it truly becomes the state language. This is important not only for observing the principles of justice, but also for the further strengthening of Ukrainian society. He feels obliged to continue fighting for the rights of Crimean Tatars, primarily for their right to national and territorial autonomy. He also heads the Association of Jewish Public Organizations and Communities of Ukraine (VAAD), oversees the Master`s program in Judaic Studies at the National University of Kyiv-Mohyla Academy, and has many other plans and projects. Not to be indifferent and to care for good things are simple but important core truths for Josyf Zisels.

The Ukrainian Challenge by Professor Schlögel[152]

We are so used to explaining to foreigners the most elementary things about Ukraine, the Revolution of Dignity, the war with Russia, and where we are on the map of Europe that I was a little puzzled by Karl Schlögel's book *The Ukrainian Challenge: The Discovery of a European Country*, published in Munich in 2015. Last year, it appeared in Ukrainian, published by *Dukh I Litera* [Spirit and Letter] (Center for Studies in the European Humanities at the National University of Kyiv-Mohyla Academy; translated by Natalia Komarova; edited by Volodymyr Prykhodko) thanks to the energy and fine discretion of publishers Kostiantyn Sihov and Leonid Finberh, and support from the Embassy of the Federal Republic of Germany in Ukraine, the Konrad Adenauer Foundation, and the Goethe Institute).

Reading this book leads one to an extremely friendly attitude towards its author, who knows a lot about Ukraine and Ukrainians. It does not matter at all that readers may at times disagree with some of his opinions or that they may wish to clarify some of the information presented. The important thing is that Karl Schlögel has no intention to judge, teach, or even advise his readers. Instead, he strives to understand Ukraine's history, Ukrainian reality, and us Ukrainians. His delicacy prompts us to better understand the author himself, his position, and experience.

In the "Academic Editor's Afterword", Volodymyr Prykhodko points to three reasons that encourage us to read the book. The first concerns the literal translation of the title "Entscheidung in Kiew" — "Decision in Kyiv". That is, the author shifts the center of European concern from the European Union to Kyiv. It is now the outpost and even, to a certain extent, the beacon of European civilization, where things acquire their true meaning. The second reason is that Ukrainian readers will acquaint themselves with

---

152 *Dzerkalo Tyzhnia* [Weekly Mirror], March 10, 2017.

the text of a book written for Germans. The third concerns the specific spatial language for representing Ukraine, including places of memory, difference, and situational centers.

Karl Schlögel has extensive research experience—in the past in the Soviet Union and now in Ukraine. He says that he always wanted to understand this strange large country as a unique dimension of life. I have identified two examples where my own experience has intersected with Karl Schlögel's vision.

The first relates to Bavaria, where Schlögel spent his childhood and high school years. His father went to war in 1939 and returned in 1945, leaving behind old photographs in a tin box. Schlögel has childhood memories of his father fetching these photographs and perusing them with his neighbors, war veterans like himself.

It was then that Karl Schlögel heard for the first time about the bizarre and threatening East, generalized in the term "Russia", which was to fascinate him as a researcher. That is why, unlike many of his fellow students who were interested in the West, Schlögel learned Russian and traveled, in his own words, "far and wide" across the "indestructible" USSR.

The free land of Bavaria revealed a lot to me through the Ukrainian Free University in Munich and its fascinating professors from different countries and continents. It was my first travel abroad and my first encounter with a different lifestyle, particularly a different kind of university life. One of my professors headed the Society of Sudeten Germans who had been expelled from postwar Czechoslovakia, finding refuge in Bavaria. For me, this was a completely different world, with a largely unknown history, Gothic and Baroque churches, punctuality, cleanliness, and the philosophy of Heidegger, whose colleague Hans-Georg Gadamer, aged 98, passed on his greetings to us, Ukrainian students. At that time, he knew much more than I did about Kyiv-Mohyla Academy from his old friend Dmytro Chyzhevsky. We can also find reflections about *Mohylianka* and its meaning in Schlögel's book.

The second experience involves an unexpected meeting with Karl Schlögel in May 2014 at a conference organized by Timothy Snyder for Western intellectuals at the Diplomatic Academy in Kyiv. I saw Professor Schlögel then, but we did not get to know each other as there was no opportunity for that. It is clear from the book that he did not need explanations about what had happened in Ukraine during the Revolution of Dignity. After the annexation of Crimea, he refused to accept the Pushkin medal for extraordinary contributions in the promotion of Russian culture from Putin's hands. It is important that along with the transformation of Ukraine the author himself is undergoing change in his established views. That is why Professor Schlögel is attempting to explain these processes to his fellow citizens, who mostly accept the stereotypical illusions fostered by the rising demon of Russian imperialism in new propaganda incarnations, the Ukrainian-Russian war, and gloomy global trends.

"Europe's *Ukraina*: An Introduction" and the book's first chapters—entitled "Information War", "Farewell to Empire, Farewell to Russia?", and "Seeing for Ourselves: Discovering Ukraine"—include Karl Schlögel's reactions to Ukrainian events. It is his way of saying goodbye to Russia, to an almost ingrained German "enchantment" with it as a phenomenon, and hence the opening to a completely new and no longer alternative Ukraine. Putin appears not just as a thug who has brought Russia to a dead end, but as an international criminal, one with a positive image in certain circles and certain media, which represent him as a political figure with a way of thinking not consonant with the West. Since Karl Schlögel has always been familiar with a different Russia, represented by émigrés, intellectuals, and dissidents who disagreed with the Soviet authorities and now with Putin, he experiences a growing dissatisfaction with the current regime in Russia.

Follow-up chapters, written in different years, contain portraits of Ukrainian cities. These images were created using "urban archeology". They give us a view of a number of historical and political centers of Ukraine and its geographical and cultural diversity. Presented here are "Kyiv, Metropolis", "Ah, Odessa: A City in an Era of Great Expectations", "Promenade in Yalta", "Look upon This City: Kharkiv: A Capital of the Twentieth Century", "Dnepropetrovsk: Rocket City on the Dnieper and City of Potemkin", "Donetsk: Twentieth-Century Urbicides", "Czernowitz: City upon a Hill", and "Lviv: Capital of Provincial Europe". When describing each of the selected historical and industrial centers, the author recalls the consequences of the German occupation, being fully aware of its tragic consequences. He actively deciphers the textures of Ukrainian cities, commenting on events and rejecting the position of an outside observer.

Professor Schlögel has studied Ukraine's press, literature, and Internet, has traveled to Ukraine and walked around the streets of various places for decades. In 2013–2014 he visited the revolutionary Maidan and was shocked by the so-called "Russian Spring" in Donetsk, purposefully induced by Russia. He has communicated with people and fills his book with important contextual information, weaving it into the history of Ukraine. We thus perceive him as a person very close to us. The author is not tempted to write about what he wished he would see. He tries to be honest with himself, taking into account all available facts to represent the cities he has selected — geographically, politically, and economically. Ukraine emerges from historical evidence through breaches in imperial discourses, primarily those of Austria-Hungary and Russia/the Soviet Union, manifesting itself in its self-value and the courage to be different.

Here historical myths overlap with network technologies. Indeed, what else can explain the readiness of Ukrainians, without any central management, to unanimously undertake mass protests, build the Maidan-Sich, resolve important matters through a thoroughly medieval *Viche* (Kyiv street council) to feed, arrange medical treatment for, and arm their Maidan, fighting back against the attackers, while waking up to the bells of St. Michael's Golden-Domed Monastery? The victory of the EuroMaidan did not leave anyone on their own. This was only the beginning of a great struggle for global change. It was no longer about Yanukovych's regime or even a confrontation with the revived evil empire represented by Putin. It was about the fact that the European Union could no longer heedlessly exist next to the tectonic events taking place in Ukraine.

The chapter "The Shock: Thinking the Worst-Case Scenario" describes the emotions of the residents of Old Europe. Who, prosperous and pacified after World War II, achieved long-term peace and success. Here, the traces of war have been smoothed out and militancy has faded; shopping centers have emerged in place of churches, and new historical dates and anniversaries are now celebrated instead of dates of battles and disasters. Today's Europe, as if an illustration of Francis Fukuyama's famous thesis about the end of history, did not know how to respond to the Revolution of Dignity, Russia's attack on Ukraine, the annexation of Crimea, and a new war on the continent. Something went wrong, upsetting the expectations and plans of Europeans.

"Yet now, all of a sudden, history was back with a big bang, rending the temporal continuum; the time of an individual life and historical time stood in abrupt and stark contrast. Which image captures it best? Had we fallen into a hole, had the rug been pulled out from under our feet? What was certain was that we have reason to be deeply anxious. Something had resurfaced that an earlier age had called 'sinister'", writes Karl Schlögel.

Thus, the opening of a new European country for Karl Schlögel is not only about you and me. The Ukrainian challenge is important for the development of a critical attitude to the current world, deeper intra-European understanding, the revival of global leadership, and new breath for Old Europe.

Norman Davies on the Objective and Subjective Historian[153]

On April 30, I had the great pleasure of having lunch with the famous British historian Norman Davies in La Trobe University (Melbourne, Australia). I met a real living classic, but I also talked with an extremely polite and friendly person who listens to other people with great attention. When expressing his opinion, Norman Davies never claimed his judgements as "ultimate truths". The conversation promoted thoughtful reflections on the everlasting question of the correlation between objectivity and subjectivity in historical research.

In my opinion, the author of the book *Europe: A History*, is less interested in theoretical attitudes than in intellectual play, where, if one is so inclined, various theoretical concepts can be found. He was careful about using academic terms in conversation, probably fearing that he would fall under their "spell" as a kind of label. Undoubtedly, this kind of game is in harmony with the principle of meaningful discourse. However, Professor Davies disagrees with the idea that a historian communicates with other historians through his or her writings. Rather, and first of all, according to him, a historian keeps his readers in mind and strives to be comprehensible to them.

Norman Davies does not believe in objective history because a historian cannot achieve results of this kind. After sharing ironic comments on the dubious nature of the "methodology of historical research" approach, he said that he was trying to "study different sorts of experience" instead. I refrained from asking him a speculative question about the affinity that this strategy might have with the principles of my favored philosophical hermeneutics. That's why I will now venture to suggest that his understanding of experience is in general close to the concept of discourse: individual experience includes its own style, originality, and completion,

---

[153] May 9, 2012.

elements that define an individual style, marking the historian's resultant research.

From this point of view, experience does not really signify the "power of discourse", but rather the presence of certain subjective statements belonging to living people who have their own preferences, emotions, and who, among other things, may be wrong. Most probably, this concept of experience is not only linked to life considered as an intellectual project, but rather to actual living, the Heideggerian living of a person whose experience generates sprouts of meaningful statements.

That is, such experience can be extrapolated to both a particular person and an entire tradition. At the same time, there immediately arise threats of various speculations: what kind of experience are we talking about? Who can systematize it, how and under what conditions? And so on.

So, it is worth giving some examples of Norman Davies' subjectivism, on the one hand, and his objectivism, on the other. Davies does not conceal his wife's role in shaping his own research interests and sometimes jokingly redirects questions to her as she is "better informed". Critical thinking is also evidence of subjectivism, as it is always individual and personally responsible. In this sense, it fundamentally denies relativism. Critical thinking enables inner conviction to agree or, on the contrary, disagree with a certain statement.

If we accept that the above may confirm the subjectivist component of Professor Davies' strategy, his statement about the different "emotional" attitudes of the Western public to the Holocaust, on the one hand (something definitely frightening and evil, associated with Nazism, a core enemy of the West), and the Holodomor and GULAG, on the other (something much easier to grasp due to the effects of the long-term propaganda about Stalin being a "great anti-fascist" and ally of the West), indicates the historian's desire to find a kind of "middle justice", and, therefore, a certain objectivism.

Thus, one can broadly call Norman Davies' approach ethical — in terms of showing respect for the experiences and judgments of others. As a next step, the historian's purpose will be to find an appropriate balance between these judgments, one based on critical thinking and common sense. Such a balance would be consistent with the idea of justice, which is synonymous with truth. However, historical research will acquire meaning and importance only when it is subjective, interesting, and the outcome of an adequate comprehension of the experiences studied; that is, when it is associated with the author's unique individuality and style.

Yaroslav Dashkevych and Subjectivity in Historical Scholarship[154]

A review of Yaroslav Dashkevych's collection of historical essays "...*Teach How to Tell the Truth with Lips That do not Lie*" (1989–2008), published in 2011 by Kyiv's *Tempora* publishing house (827 pp.), represents a special project for me. This is not a "debt" to Yaroslav Dashkevych, but the carrying on of a conversation with him. Moreover, this is a conversation that was never interrupted. Dashkevych's historical works can be considered not only as scholarly, but also as essayistic, with a tint of something artistic. In this case, to better understand them, we ought to have a notion of the author's personality — a tall lanky man with long gray hair, unforgettable humor, and a noble posture.

Everything innately serious and academic becomes simple, human, and interesting in his presence. Dashkevych's smile, his persuasiveness and ironic manner create a special atmosphere of personal immersion in a problem, demanding an interlocutor's personal responses and responsible decisions.

The first thing that captures one's attention in this book are the photographs. They are startling. Why? Because of their amateur character! Usually, if a publishing house asks an author to send information about themselves along with the best personal photos, the author responds immediately. Authors seem to be waiting for such an offer, having on hand a selection of flattering photos. Dashkevych seems not to have prepared such a selection of photographs. Those that did make it into the book are mainly plain and informal photos, accidentally preserved after having been taken. This appears to be a very important feature of a scholar who cared about major things all his life. That is, about truthful things. Not about a truth resulting from academic research, but about the truth-telling of an intellectual who dwells in his own territory of truth and tries to change the outer world accordingly. When an essay appears, the

---

154 22 June 2011.

need to know the biography of the author arises simultaneously. For this reason, below, I cite my "Oxford Standard" publication from 1998, which gives a fair idea of who we are dealing with.

The introductory article by Ihor Hyrych about the unbreakable links between scholarship and sociopolitical life in the legacy of Dashkevych is, first of all, responsible. It stresses that it is impossible to separate academic research and the development of national historiography from the processes taking place in a respective society, nation, and state. Therefore, a historian does not work in a completely isolated way. A historian responds to questions raised by life. At least, this is a demand that appears on the agenda of Ukrainian historiography, if it seeks to stay within the limits of academic adequacy and deny various (post-)colonial attempts to distort the history of Ukraine. Dashkevych questions the attempts by Russian and Polish chauvinists, the consequence of certain "politically correct expediencies", the uncritical reception of Western theories by domestic scholars, and the sense of inferiority present in some Ukrainian historians, which leads them to a rejection of their own history, or, on the contrary, to its hyperbolization.

At this point a reference arises to Edward Said's *Orientalism*, which exposed the West's perceptions of the East, without asking the East about what it thinks of itself and what it really is. So, according to Dashkevych, Ukrainian historiography should get rid of the rather contrived and factually false concepts of Ukraine, accumulated over the centuries of the silent lost time of our statelessness.

He addresses the problems of the origin of the Ukrainian people, the separateness and distinctiveness of its own history and its geopolitical context, the people's historical memory, and the right of Ukrainians to a national liberation struggle. Post-Soviet/post-colonial/post-totalitarian Ukrainian historiography often produces very strange (in particular, politicized) views, which have nothing to do with academic debates. One sometimes has to question even the mental health of some authors. With his polemical discourse, Dashkevych attempts to straighten out twisted ideas and present a holistic picture of Ukraine's factual history.

It should be noted that he does not seem at all "objective" in his passionate polemical texts. To understand the limits of the academic, subjective, and truthful, we need to take into consideration the genre of the works presented in the book, i.e. "historical essay writing". Not only did Yaroslav Romanovych and I discuss many of the articles published, we also reached a shared understanding of the role of essay writing and postmodernism. The idea of an essayistic scholarly viewpoint was particularly appealing to Dashkevych. An essay does not deny one's academic nature; indeed, it polemically sharpens an author's position. This genre is in no way monologic. It relies on dialogue, with which it overlaps. Encountering a properly presented variant position (with authorial conviction, a theoretical basis, scholarly argumentation, and the ability to listen to and hear others), an essay does not resist, but is enriched by a different understanding, forming a holistic polyphonic discourse. The voice of a discourse is true to the extent that it directs us to proper thinking and compliance with known facts. Such a strategy is thoroughly consistent with the foundations of philosophical hermeneutics.

The personal involvement of the interpreter in the search for truth is also important. Discussing with me and Oleh Bahan about the language editing of the publication of Dmytro Dontsov's writings (Geopolitical and ideological works.—Lviv: Kalvariya, 2001), Yaroslav Dashkevych said: "I was familiar with Dontsov, so I have a personal responsibility to him for the quality of this book". By the way, thanks to the involvement and authority of Professor Dashkevych, Oleh Bahan later implemented an extremely important publishing project, becoming its compiler, the author of the preface and comments: Dontsov D. Selected works: In 10 volumes.— Drohobych—Lviv: "Revival" Publishing House, 2011-2016.

Dashkevych's negative assessment of postmodernism deserves special attention. When confronting representatives of the recent generation of Ukrainian social realists, hastily remodeled as postmodernists in the 1990s, he does not accept the idea of the relativity of historical truth, or the impossibility of finding it. That is, he rejects the phenomenon termed "post-socialist realism" by Viacheslav Medvid, wherein the fervor of Komsomol intolerance is intensified with new and, therefore, little-known and improperly understood "isms". Still, no debate takes place between, for instance, Dashkevych and Foucault, who undoubtedly showed signs of genius, but, rather, with the latter's superficial intermediaries and "relativist" interpreters. Dashkevych does employ some of Foucault's statements, which were disseminated in various media writings in Ukraine in the 1990s, but pays no attention to such incredibly productive concepts as "self-care". Foucault's "archeology of knowledge" refers to the history of thinking and attitudes, according to Dashkevych, rather than to the "factual history" so urgently needed by modern Ukraine. In contrast, Dashkevych's brilliant concepts of "Postmodernism-I" (in twentieth-century totalitarian regimes) and "Postmodernism-II" (spread after World War II) help to reveal the totalitarian foundations of an ideological strategy built on this intellectual product. Actually, many experts also link the double standards of the current globalized world to the ideas of postmodernism.

Having attended the Lviv and Kyiv presentations of Dashkevych's historical essays, I was very pleased to observe how warmly people in Kyiv welcomed the renowned professor who had never separated himself from his important and honest work. Also, I would like to express my sincere gratitude to the *Tempora* publishing house and Ms. Yulia Oliynyk personally for this unforgettable book, especially for their high professionalism and true support.

Oxford Standard[155]

The prominent Ukrainian historian Yaroslav Dashkevych derives from an old aristocratic family, well-known not only for its emblems and traditions, but above all for the glorious deeds of each new generation. Actually, Yaroslav, patronymic Romanovych, has a double surname: Korybut-Dashkevych. The first part of his surname indicates its ancient Lithuanian origin, and the second can presumably be attributed to Ostafiy, a famous sixteenth-century defender of Ukraine, the *starosta* ("elder") of the cities of Cherkasy

---

155 Shliakh Peremohy [The way to victory], August 26, 1998.

and Kaniv. The family tree can be traced in documents going back 3–4 centuries. Dashkevych's noble origin was confirmed in the Austrian period.

Yaroslav Dashkevych's father, Roman Dashkevych, was a Lieutenant-General in the Ukrainian People's Army and one of the leaders of the nationalist movement. His mother, Olena Stepaniv, in addition to being a woman of great beauty, gained fame as a soldier, scholar, and folk heroine commemorated in songs. Yaroslav Dashkevych was born in Lviv, and in his childhood all questions raised by life were responded to within the family circle. Ancestral dignity, nobility, responsibility, and determination became characteristic of his personality, and the basis for his tireless and heroic activity.

At first, Dashkevych received a regular gymnasium (high-school) education, which enabled him to develop his knowledge of foreign languages. From 1944 to 1949 Dashkevych studied at the philological faculty of Lviv University—in a time when good "old-fashioned" professors taught students to distinguish good from evil. He was arrested for his support of the Ukrainian underground movement and the OUN, and from 1949 to 1956, without the benefit of trial, was incarcerated in prisons in Lviv, Zolochiv, Kyiv, Kharkiv, Petropavlovsk in Kazakhstan, Karabakh, and later in Kazakhstani concentration camps. Dashkevych does not complain about those hard years, only commenting that such experience was unnecessary. He calls it lost and stolen time.

After returning to his native Lviv, Dashkevych could not find full-time employment. Without any explanation, he was dismissed from the Institute of Social Sciences and later from the Museum of Ethnography and Artistic Crafts. While unemployed, he received a scholarship and significant moral support from the Armenian Academy of Sciences. He even received an offer to move to Yerevan as a Corresponding Member of the Academy of Sciences of Soviet Armenia. However, after a phone call from the Central Committee of Ukraine's Communist Party, that proposal was retracted.

At the time, Dashkevych conducted research in libraries and archives in Yerevan, Moscow, and Leningrad. All his works were exclusively published abroad. Recalling those times, he mentions the friendly reception he felt from Russian, Armenian, and Central Asian intelligentsias who were close to the dissidents. The worst atmosphere he felt was in Ukraine. Dashkevych could officially visit the Institute of History of the USSR Academy of Sciences in Moscow, but he was not permitted to conduct research at the Institute of History of the Ukrainian SSR Academy of Sciences in Kyiv. His unemployed status came to an end in the midst of *Perestroika* (a mid-1980s attempt at a Soviet state overhaul). In 1989, Dashkevych headed the Lviv branch of the Institute of Ukrainian Archeography and Source Studies of the National Academy of Sciences of Ukraine. Professor Yaroslav Dashkevych took this position virtually "off the street". He never made a special effort to establish an academic career, defending his doctoral thesis in Kyiv in 1995, under external pressure.

Despite extremely difficult living conditions, the historian was able to achieve much. The more difficult the circumstances were, the stronger were his personal resistance and persistence. The scholarly and bibliographic collection *Mappa Mundy* (Lviv—Kyiv—New York: M. P. Kots Publishing House, 1996; 912 pp.), published in honor Dashkevych on his seventieth birthday, includes 487 bibliographic items, the number significantly increasing since then. Yaroslav Dashkevych, a Ukrainian historian, orientalist, bibliographer, political scientist, essayist, publicist, and public figure, was engaged in diplomacy, metrology, paleography, historical cartography, the history of geography, heraldry, and filigranology.

Dashkevych claims that history is no easier than modern chemistry or physics. In our time, history is facing an influx of dilettantes with hypertrophied patriotic feelings, although Ukrainians are well able to encounter their true history, rich in grand and heroic moments, with no need for embellishment. In the days when Mykhailo Hrushevsky's historical school dominated, historical myth was not pursued. A raw story was enough for the fight for independence. Now that we have obtained independence, along with an abundance of pseudo-heroic mythology, it is as if the latter were a certain compensation for mental complexes of dissatisfaction with reality. In fact, this is an escape from reality, from responsibility, and from real action.

We also see a fashion for postmodernist methodology, when research works by 3-4-5 authors studying a certain period, epoch, or phenomenon are taken as the basis for study, it then becoming clear that each of them investigates the issue in their own way. As a result, it is concluded that objective history is impossible or even unnecessary and that every historian has the right to their own subjective vision. Yaroslav Dashkevych considers such a point of view a sort of self-deception, as, in this case, no one even asks which of the authors considered comes closer to the truth. As a result, the possibility of grasping the truth is immediately eliminated. This also makes one forget that the truth of history is primarily obtained not from the works of previous historians, but through the appropriate interpretation of the sources. Postmodernism moves a single aspect of a problem to the center of interpretation, not taking into account any of the other aspects. The concepts of true and interesting history should not contradict, but rather complement each other.

However, the worst situation occurs when historical works are written in response to a financially backed request. Unfortunately, the stream of paid publications still exists. Dashkevych gives examples of "false" researchers in France and the United States. In such cases we have deliberate falsification. A distortion of truth can occur due to a researcher's subjective belief. A third direction will never lose its relevance—factual history, when scholars try to preserve a traditional path, but support their conclusions with documents, methodologies, and a certain way of thinking; this is when truth-seeking takes place. This is how so-called universal history is written. And, incidentally, we still have no complete positivist (in this context, also factual) history of Ukraine, a history Hrushevsky had worked on.

The Ukrainian historical school revolving around the vector of Mykola Kostomarov—Volodymyr Antonovych—Mykhailo Drahomanov—Mykhailo Hrushevskyi holds an important place in the development of not only Ukrainian and Russian, but also European historical scholarship. According to Yaroslav Dashkevych, today we need a kind of Oxford standard, without which the history of Ukraine will be seen in a deformed way. The creation of such a standard will enable various avenues of bold research, prevent mere hypotheses and science fiction from dressing themselves as theory, and shape the system of national historiography. Thus, archeology cannot replace an analysis of written sources, since it is a history of material culture, an auxiliary historical discipline. What often happens in our scholarship is that archeologists, departing from the tasks of their own area of research, allow themselves to "adjust" written sources.

The power of talent and professional ethics must replace the awareness of corruption. The standard is based on a chronicle, that is, a list of facts that actually took place. The next step is to interpret these facts. A dilettantish approach and exaggerated subjectivism should not be confused with the essayistic style of thinking, which generalizes broad experience. Essay writing, particularly the historical variety, is an essential need because it influences the intellectual segment of society, cultivates freshness of thought, produces unexpected views, and does not in the least contradict research activity. Essay writing is not based on fantasy; it targets the acquisition of truth.

Having chosen his path, the Ukrainian nationalist Yaroslav Dashkevych has never strayed from it, no matter the cost or obligations imposed. His high credibility and authority, sense of nobility, and place among the Ukrainian elite are based on the Ukrainian Cossack tradition — when only a cross, saber, and honest work provided grounds for speaking in favor and on behalf of the people.

About the Author

Serhiy Kvit, an expert and commentator on educational and media issues, is currently the president of the National University of Kyiv-Mohyla Academy and a professor at Kyiv-Mohyla School of Journalism. He was a literary critic and a scholar of the history of Ukrainian literature and journalism.

From 2002 to 2007, Serhiy Kvit was Dean of the Faculty of Social Studies Faculty at the National University of Kyiv-Mohyla Academy. He founded the Kyiv-Mohyla School of Journalism in 2001 and became the president of the Media Reform Center, set up to allow open debate, and promote more transparent media and government. In 2005–2010, he was Chairman of the Consortium of University Autonomy. He was rector (president) of the National University of Kyiv-Mohyla Academy from 2007 to 2014.

Serhiy Kvit occupied the position of Minister of Education and Science of Ukraine in 2014–2016 when the progressive Laws "On Higher Education" (2014) and "On Scientific and Scientific Technical Activity" (On Science and Research, 2015) were adopted. In 2015, Serhiy Kvit signed an agreement that allowed Ukrainian scientists and businesses to fully participate in Horizon 2020 (H2020), the European Union's flagship research program. He headed the National Agency for Higher Education Quality Assurance of Ukraine in 2019–2022.

Dr. Kvit's research focuses on educational and media reforms, mass communications, and philosophical hermeneutics; he has published several books and numerous articles. He has a Ph.D. from the Ukrainian Free University (Germany) and a doctorate in philology. He held a Fulbright scholarship at Ohio University and Stanford University, a Kennan Institute scholarship at the Woodrow Wilson International Center in Washington, DC, and a DAAD (German Academic Exchange Service) scholarship at the University of Cologne.

UKRAINIAN VOICES

Collected by Andreas Umland

1   *Mychailo Wynnyckyj*
    Ukraine's Maidan, Russia's War
    A Chronicle and Analysis of the Revolution of Dignity
    With a foreword by Serhii Plokhy
    ISBN 978-3-8382-1327-9

2   *Olexander Hryb*
    Understanding Contemporary Ukrainian and Russian Nationalism
    The Post-Soviet Cossack Revival and Ukraine's National Security
    With a foreword by Vitali Vitaliev
    ISBN 978-3-8382-1377-4

3   *Marko Bojcun*
    Towards a Political Economy of Ukraine
    Selected Essays 1990–2015
    With a foreword by John-Paul Himka
    ISBN 978-3-8382-1368-2

4   *Volodymyr Yermolenko (ed.)*
    Ukraine in Histories and Stories
    Essays by Ukrainian Intellectuals
    With a preface by Peter Pomerantsev
    ISBN 978-3-8382-1456-6

5   *Mykola Riabchuk*
    At the Fence of Metternich's Garden
    Essays on Europe, Ukraine, and Europeanization
    ISBN 978-3-8382-1484-9

6   *Marta Dyczok*
    Ukraine Calling
    A Kaleidoscope from Hromadske Radio 2016–2019
    With a foreword by Andriy Kulykov
    ISBN 978-3-8382-1472-6

7   *Olexander Scherba*
    Ukraine vs. Darkness
    Undiplomatic Thoughts
    With a foreword by Adrian Karatnycky
    ISBN 978-3-8382-1501-3

8   *Olesya Yaremchuk*
    Our Others
    Stories of Ukrainian Diversity
    With a foreword by Ostap Slyvynsky
    Translated from the Ukrainian by Zenia Tompkins and Hanna Leliv
    ISBN 978-3-8382-1475-7

9   *Nataliya Gumenyuk*
    Die verlorene Insel
    Geschichten von der besetzten Krim
    Mit einem Vorwort von Alice Bota
    Aus dem Ukrainischen übersetzt von Johann Zajaczkowski
    ISBN 978-3-8382-1499-3

10 *Olena Stiazhkina*
    Zero Point Ukraine
    Four Essays on World War II
    Translated from the Ukrainian by Svitlana Kulinska
    ISBN 978-3-8382-1550-1

11 *Oleksii Sinchenko, Dmytro Stus, Leonid Finberg (compilers)*
    Ukrainian Dissidents
    An Anthology of Texts
    ISBN 978-3-8382-1551-8

12 *John-Paul Himka*
    Ukrainian Nationalists and the Holocaust
    OUN and UPA's Participation in the Destruction of Ukrainian Jewry, 1941–1944
    ISBN 978-3-8382-1548-8

13 *Andrey Demartino*
    False Mirrors
    The Weaponization of Social Media in Russia's Operation to Annex Crimea
    With a foreword by Oleksiy Danilov
    ISBN 978-3-8382-1533-4

14 *Svitlana Biedarieva (ed.)*
Contemporary Ukrainian and Baltic Art
Political and Social Perspectives, 1991–2021
ISBN 978-3-8382-1526-6

15 *Olesya Khromeychuk*
A Loss
The Story of a Dead Soldier Told by His Sister
With a foreword by Andrey Kurkov
ISBN 978-3-8382-1570-9

16 *Marieluise Beck (Hg.)*
Ukraine verstehen
Auf den Spuren von Terror und Gewalt
Mit einem Vorwort von Dmytro Kuleba
ISBN 978-3-8382-1653-9

17 *Stanislav Aseyev*
Heller Weg
Geschichte eines Konzentrationslagers im Donbass 2017–2019
Aus dem Russischen übersetzt von
Martina Steis und Charis Haska
ISBN 978-3-8382-1620-1

18 *Mykola Davydiuk*
Wie funktioniert Putins Propaganda?
Anmerkungen zum Informationskrieg des Kremls
Aus dem Ukrainischen übersetzt von Christian Weise
ISBN 978-3-8382-1628-7

19 *Olesya Yaremchuk*
Unsere Anderen
Geschichten ukrainischer Vielfalt
Aus dem Ukrainischen übersetzt von Christian Weise
ISBN 978-3-8382-1635-5

20 *Oleksandr Mykhed*
„Dein Blut wird die Kohle tränken"
Über die Ostukraine
Aus dem Ukrainischen übersetzt von Simon Muschick
und Dario Planert
ISBN 978-3-8382-1648-5

21   *Vakhtang Kipiani (Hg.)*
     Der Zweite Weltkrieg in der Ukraine
     Geschichte und Lebensgeschichten
     Aus dem Ukrainischen übersetzt von Margarita Grinko
     ISBN 978-3-8382-1622-5

22   *Vakhtang Kipiani (ed.)*
     World War II, Uncontrived and Unredacted
     Testimonies from Ukraine
     Translated from the Ukrainian by Zenia Tompkins and Daisy Gibbons
     ISBN 978-3-8382-1621-8

23   *Dmytro Stus*
     Vasyl Stus
     Life in Creativity
     Translated from the Ukrainian by Ludmila Bachurina
     ISBN 978-3-8382-1631-7

24   *Vitalii Ogiienko (ed.)*
     The Holodomor and the Origins of the Soviet Man
     Reading the Testimony of Anastasia Lysyvets
     With forewords by Natalka Bilotserkivets and Serhy Yekelchyk
     Translated from the Ukrainian by Alla Parkhomenko and
     Alexander J. Motyl
     ISBN 978-3-8382-1616-4

25   *Vladislav Davidzon*
     Jewish-Ukrainian Relations and the Birth of a Political Nation
     Selected Writings 2013-2021
     With a foreword by Bernard-Henri Lévy
     ISBN 978-3-8382-1509-9

26   *Serhy Yekelchyk*
     Writing the Nation
     The Ukrainian Historical Profession in Independent Ukraine and
     the Diaspora
     ISBN 978-3-8382-1695-9

27   *Ildi Eperjesi, Oleksandr Kachura*
     Shreds of War
     Fates from the Donbas Frontline 2014-2019
     With a foreword by Olexiy Haran
     ISBN 978-3-8382-1680-5

28 *Oleksandr Melnyk*
    World War II as an Identity Project
    Historicism, Legitimacy Contests, and the (Re-)Construction of Political Communities in Ukraine, 1939–1946
    With a foreword by David R. Marples
    ISBN 978-3-8382-1704-8

29 *Olesya Khromeychuk*
    Ein Verlust
    Die Geschichte eines gefallenen ukrainischen Soldaten, erzählt von seiner Schwester
    Mit einem Vorwort von Andrej Kurkow
    Aus dem Englischen übersetzt von Lily Sophie
    ISBN 978-3-8382-1770-3

30 *Tamara Martsenyuk, Tetiana Kostiuchenko (eds.)*
    Russia's War in Ukraine 2022
    Personal Experiences of Ukrainian Scholars
    ISBN 978-3-8382-1757-4

31 *Ildikó Eperjesi, Oleksandr Kachura*
    Shreds of War. Vol. 2
    Fates from Crimea 2015–2022
    With a foreword by Anton Shekhovtsov and an interview of Oleh Sentsov
    ISBN 978-3-8382-1780-2

32 *Yuriy Lukanov, Tetiana Pechonchik (eds.)*
    The Press: How Russia destroyed Media Freedom in Crimea
    With a foreword by Taras Kuzio
    ISBN 978-3-8382-1784-0

33 *Megan Buskey*
    Ukraine Is Not Dead Yet
    A Family Story of Exile and Return
    ISBN 978-3-8382-1691-1

34 *Vira Ageyeva*
    Behind the Scenes of the Empire
    Essays on Cultural Relationships between Ukraine and Russia
    With a foreword by Oksana Zabuzhko
    ISBN 978-3-8382-1748-2

35 *Marieluise Beck (ed.)*
Understanding Ukraine
Tracing the Roots of Terror and Violence
With a foreword by Dmytro Kuleba
ISBN 978-3-8382-1773-4

36 *Olesya Khromeychuk*
A Loss
The Story of a Dead Soldier Told by His Sister, 2nd edn.
With a foreword by Philippe Sands
With a preface by Andrii Kurkov
ISBN 978-3-8382-1870-0

37 *Taras Kuzio, Stefan Jajecznyk-Kelman*
Fascism and Genocide
Russia's War Against Ukrainians
ISBN 978-3-8382-1791-8

38 *Alina Nychyk*
Ukraine Vis-à-Vis Russia and the EU
Misperceptions of Foreign Challenges in Times of War, 2014–2015
With a foreword by Paul D'Anieri
ISBN 978-3-8382-1767-3

39 *Sasha Dovzhyk (ed.)*
Ukraine Lab
Global Security, Environment, Disinformation Through the Prism of Ukraine
With a foreword by Rory Finnin
ISBN 978-3-8382-1805-2

40 *Serhiy Kvit*
Media, History, and Education
Three Ways to Ukrainian Independence
With a preface by Diane Francis
ISBN 978-3-8382-1807-6

41 *Anna Romandash*
Women of Ukraine
Reportages from the War and Beyond
ISBN 978-3-8382-1819-9

42 *Dominika Rank*
Matzewe in meinem Garten
Abenteuer eines jüdischen Heritage-Touristen in der Ukraine
ISBN 978-3-8382-1810-6

43 *Myroslaw Marynowytsch*
    Das Universum hinter dem Stacheldraht
    Memoiren eines sowjet-ukrainischen Dissidenten
    Mit einem Vorwort von Timothy Snyder und einem Nachwort
    von Max Hartmann
    ISBN 978-3-8382-1806-9

44 *Konstantin Sigow*
    Für Deine und meine Freiheit
    Europäische Revolutions- und Kriegserfahrungen im heutigen
    Kyjiw
    Mit einem Vorwort von Karl Schlögel
    Herausgegeben von Regula M. Zwahlen
    ISBN 978-3-8382-1755-0

45 *Kateryna Pylypchuk*
    The War that Changed Us
    Ukrainian Novellas, Poems, and Essays from 2022
    With a foreword by Victor Yushchenko
    ISBN 978-3-8382-1859-5

Book series "Ukrainian Voices"

Collector
Andreas Umland, National University of Kyiv-Mohyla Academy

Editorial Board
Lesia Bidochko, National University of Kyiv-Mohyla Academy
Svitlana Biedarieva, George Washington University, DC, USA
Ivan Gomza, Kyiv School of Economics, Ukraine
Natalie Jaresko, Aspen Institute, Kyiv/Washington
Olena Lennon, University of New Haven, West Haven, USA
Kateryna Yushchenko, First Lady of Ukraine 2005-2010, Kyiv
Oleksandr Zabirko, University of Regensburg, Germany

Advisory Board
Iuliia Bentia, National Academy of Arts of Ukraine, Kyiv
Natalya Belitser, Pylyp Orlyk Institute for Democracy, Kyiv
Oleksandra Bienert, Humboldt University of Berlin, Germany
Sergiy Bilenky, Canadian Institute of Ukrainian Studies, Toronto
Tymofii Brik, Kyiv School of Economics, Ukraine
Olga Brusylovska, Mechnikov National University, Odesa
Mariana Budjeryn, Harvard University, Cambridge, USA
Volodymyr Bugrov, Shevchenko National University, Kyiv
Olga Burlyuk, University of Amsterdam, The Netherlands
Yevhen Bystrytsky, NAS Institute of Philosophy, Kyiv
Andrii Danylenko, Pace University, New York, USA
Vladislav Davidzon, Atlantic Council, Washington/Paris
Mykola Davydiuk, Think Tank "Polityka," Kyiv
Andrii Demartino, National Security and Defense Council, Kyiv
Vadym Denisenko, Ukrainian Institute for the Future, Kyiv
Oleksandr Donii, Center for Political Values Studies, Kyiv
Volodymyr Dubovyk, Mechnikov National University, Odesa
Volodymyr Dubrovskiy, CASE Ukraine, Kyiv
Diana Dutsyk, National University of Kyiv-Mohyla Academy
Marta Dyczok, Western University, Ontario, Canada
Yevhen Fedchenko, National University of Kyiv-Mohyla Academy
Sofiya Filonenko, State Pedagogical University of Berdyansk
Oleksandr Fisun, Karazin National University, Kharkiv
Oksana Forostyna, Webjournal "Ukraina Moderna," Kyiv
Roman Goncharenko, Broadcaster "Deutsche Welle," Bonn
George Grabowicz, Harvard University, Cambridge, USA
Gelinada Grinchenko, Karazin National University, Kharkiv
Kateryna Härtel, Federal Union of European Nationalities, Brussels
Nataliia Hendel, University of Geneva, Switzerland
Anton Herashchenko, Kyiv School of Public Administration
John-Paul Himka, University of Alberta, Edmonton
Ola Hnatiuk, National University of Kyiv-Mohyla Academy
Oleksandr Holubov, Broadcaster "Deutsche Welle," Bonn
Yaroslav Hrytsak, Ukrainian Catholic University, Lviv
Oleksandra Humenna, National University of Kyiv-Mohyla Academy
Tamara Hundorova, NAS Institute of Literature, Kyiv
Oksana Huss, University of Bologna, Italy
Oleksandra Iwaniuk, University of Warsaw, Poland
Mykola Kapitonenko, Shevchenko National University, Kyiv
Georgiy Kasianov, Marie Curie-Skłodowska University, Lublin
Vakhtang Kebuladze, Shevchenko National University, Kyiv
Natalia Khanenko-Friesen, University of Alberta, Edmonton
Victoria Khiterer, Millersville University of Pennsylvania, USA
Oksana Kis, NAS Institute of Ethnology, Lviv
Pavlo Klimkin, Center for National Resilience and Development, Kyiv
Oleksandra Kolomiiets, Center for Economic Strategy, Kyiv

Sergiy Korsunsky, Kobe Gakuin University, Japan
Nadiia Koval, Kyiv School of Economics, Ukraine
Volodymyr Kravchenko, University of Alberta, Edmonton
Oleksiy Kresin, NAS Koretskiy Institute of State and Law, Kyiv
Anatoliy Kruglashov, Fedkovych National University, Chernivtsi
Andrey Kurkov, PEN Ukraine, Kyiv
Ostap Kushnir, Lazarski University, Warsaw
Taras Kuzio, National University of Kyiv-Mohyla Academy
Serhii Kvit, National University of Kyiv-Mohyla Academy
Yuliya Ladygina, The Pennsylvania State University, USA
Yevhen Mahda, Institute of World Policy, Kyiv
Victoria Malko, California State University, Fresno, USA
Yulia Marushevska, Security and Defense Center (SAND), Kyiv
Myroslav Marynovych, Ukrainian Catholic University, Lviv
Oleksandra Matviichuk, Center for Civil Liberties, Kyiv
Mykhailo Minakov, Kennan Institute, Washington, USA
Anton Moiseienko, The Australian National University, Canberra
Alexander Motyl, Rutgers University-Newark, USA
Vlad Mykhnenko, University of Oxford, United Kingdom
Vitalii Ogiienko, Ukrainian Institute of National Remembrance, Kyiv
Olga Onuch, University of Manchester, United Kingdom
Olesya Ostrovska, Museum "Mystetskyi Arsenal," Kyiv
Anna Osypchuk, National University of Kyiv-Mohyla Academy
Oleksandr Pankieiev, University of Alberta, Edmonton
Oleksiy Panych, Publishing House "Dukh i Litera," Kyiv
Valerii Pekar, Kyiv-Mohyla Business School, Ukraine
Yohanan Petrovsky-Shtern, Northwestern University, Chicago
Serhii Plokhy, Harvard University, Cambridge, USA
Andrii Portnov, Viadrina University, Frankfurt-Oder, Germany
Maryna Rabinovych, Kyiv School of Economics, Ukraine
Valentyna Romanova, Institute of Developing Economies, Tokyo
Natalya Ryabinska, Collegium Civitas, Warsaw, Poland
Darya Tsymbalyk, University of Oxford, United Kingdom
Vsevolod Samokhvalov, University of Liege, Belgium
Orest Semotiuk, Franko National University, Lviv
Viktoriya Sereda, NAS Institute of Ethnology, Lviv
Anton Shekhovtsov, University of Vienna, Austria
Andriy Shevchenko, Media Center Ukraine, Kyiv
Oxana Shevel, Tufts University, Medford, USA
Pavlo Shopin, National Pedagogical Dragomanov University, Kyiv
Karina Shyrokykh, Stockholm University, Sweden
Nadja Simon, freelance interpreter, Cologne, Germany
Olena Snigova, NAS Institute for Economics and Forecasting, Kyiv
Ilona Solohub, Analytical Platform "VoxUkraine," Kyiv
Iryna Solonenko, LibMod - Center for Liberal Modernity, Berlin
Galyna Solovei, National University of Kyiv-Mohyla Academy
Sergiy Stelmakh, NAS Institute of World History, Kyiv
Olena Stiazhkina, NAS Institute of the History of Ukraine, Kyiv
Dmitri Stratievski, Osteuropa Zentrum (OEZB), Berlin
Dmytro Stus, National Taras Shevchenko Museum, Kyiv
Frank Sysyn, University of Toronto, Canada
Olha Tokariuk, Center for European Policy Analysis, Washington
Olena Tregub, Independent Anti-Corruption Commission, Kyiv
Hlib Vyshlinsky, Centre for Economic Strategy, Kyiv
Mychailo Wynnyckyj, National University of Kyiv-Mohyla Academy
Yelyzaveta Yasko, NGO "Yellow Blue Strategy," Kyiv
Serhy Yekelchyk, University of Victoria, Canada
Victor Yushchenko, President of Ukraine 2005-2010, Kyiv
Oleksandr Zaitsev, Ukrainian Catholic University, Lviv
Kateryna Zarembo, National University of Kyiv-Mohyla Academy
Yaroslav Zhalilo, National Institute for Strategic Studies, Kyiv
Sergei Zhuk, Ball State University at Muncie, USA
Alina Zubkovych, Nordic Ukraine Forum, Stockholm
Liudmyla Zubrytska, National University of Kyiv-Mohyla Academy

Friends of the Series

Ana Maria Abulescu, University of Bucharest, Romania
Łukasz Adamski, Centrum Mieroszewskiego, Warsaw
Marieluise Beck, LibMod—Center for Liberal Modernity, Berlin
Marc Berensen, King's College London, United Kingdom
Johannes Bohnen, BOHNEN Public Affairs, Berlin
Karsten Brüggemann, University of Tallinn, Estonia
Ulf Brunnbauer, Leibniz Institute (IOS), Regensburg
Martin Dietze, German-Ukrainian Culture Society, Hamburg
Gergana Dimova, Florida State University, Tallahassee/London
Caroline von Gall, Goethe University, Frankfurt-Main
Zaur Gasimov, Rhenish Friedrich Wilhelm University, Bonn
Armand Gosu, University of Bucharest, Romania
Thomas Grant, University of Cambridge, United Kingdom
Gustav Gressel, European Council on Foreign Relations, Berlin
Rebecca Harms, European Centre for Press & Media Freedom, Leipzig
André Härtel, Stiftung Wissenschaft und Politik, Berlin/Brussels
Marcel Van Herpen, The Cicero Foundation, Maastricht
Richard Herzinger, freelance analyst, Berlin
Mieste Hotopp-Riecke, ICATAT, Magdeburg
Nico Lange, Munich Security Conference, Berlin
Martin Malek, freelance analyst, Vienna
Ingo Mannteufel, Broadcaster "Deutsche Welle," Bonn
Carlo Masala, Bundeswehr University, Munich
Wolfgang Mueller, University of Vienna, Austria
Dietmar Neutatz, Albert Ludwigs University, Freiburg
Torsten Oppelland, Friedrich Schiller University, Jena
Niccolò Pianciola, University of Padua, Italy
Gerald Praschl, German-Ukrainian Forum (DUF), Berlin
Felix Riefer, Think Tank Ideenagentur-Ost, Düsseldorf
Stefan Rohdewald, University of Leipzig, Germany
Sebastian Schäffer, Institute for the Danube Region (IDM), Vienna
Felix Schimansky-Geier, Friedrich Schiller University, Jena
Ulrich Schneckener, University of Osnabrück, Germany
Winfried Schneider-Deters, freelance analyst, Heidelberg/Kyiv
Gerhard Simon, University of Cologne, Germany
Kai Struve, Martin Luther University, Halle/Wittenberg
David Stulik, European Values Center for Security Policy, Prague
Andrzej Szeptycki, University of Warsaw, Poland
Philipp Ther, University of Vienna, Austria
Stefan Troebst, University of Leipzig, Germany

[Please send address requests for changes, corrections, and additions to this list to andreas.umland@stanforalumni.org.]

ibidem.eu